Leadership Principles and Purpose

This book provides a fresh perspective on leadership and the steps required to achieve high performance. It explores how we create purpose by moving from vision and values through principles to action. Effective leaders do not only support and develop people. They also develop systems (anchored in principles and procedures) that support future-focused capability. We all benefit from understanding the elements that contribute to exceptional leadership. Increasingly, we also need to appreciate the building blocks that link to Sound Third Generation Corporate Governance. Hence, the focus on *Environmental, Social Governance* (ESG) criteria. The book explains how principles shape competencies and build motivation and commitment. The insights also reveal the importance of *confirmed competence.* This enhances self-belief and increases personal confidence when faced with challenging situations. It adds to resilience. Building on principles helps clarify how energy is best directed to achieve high performance. This also ensures consistency of approach. Values need to be made explicit through principles, which support the design of systems and help shape the culture of the workplace. Principles have relevance for managers, team leaders and professionals who want to gain insight into how we enhance motivation and commitment at work. However, the information contained in this book goes further as it also raises self-awareness and encourages reflection on the broader issue of how people find meaning and purpose.

Leadership Principles and Purpose

Developing Leadership Effectiveness and Future-Focused Capability

David Sharpley

Principal Business Psychologist

Routledge
Taylor & Francis Group

A PRODUCTIVITY PRESS BOOK

First published 2024
by Routledge
605 Third Avenue, New York, NY 10158

and by Routledge
4 Park Square, Milton Park, Abingdon, Oxon, OX14 4RN

Routledge is an imprint of the Taylor & Francis Group, an informa business

ISBN: 978-1-032-57507-0 (hbk)
ISBN: 978-1-032-57506-3 (pbk)
ISBN: 978-1-003-43970-7 (ebk)

DOI: 10.4324/9781003439707

Typeset in Garamond
by SPi Technologies India Pvt Ltd (Straive)

Thanks to ChatGPT for reviewing research and checking references.

The book builds on insights from significant areas of research. Notably, **Self Determination Theory** reveals that everyone has an innate need for positive, trust-based *Relationships*. We also seek to develop the *Competence* that fuels meaningful activity and builds motivation. *Autonomy* adds to self-direction, responsibility and purpose. Underlying needs are also reflected in **Superordinate Principles** *(Super-Ps)* that support social cohesion and stability. These higher-order principles include our desire for justice, equality, compassion and accountability. Principles are closely aligned with ethical values, but expressed in the form of rules, protocols and norms. They serve to shape culture.

***

Mastery, I learned, was not something genetic, or for a lucky few. It is something we can all attain if we get rid of some misconceptions and gain clarity as to the required path.

Robert Greene – Author of *Mastery*
Interview with *Forbes* (2012)

Contents

Preface: Future-Focused Leadership

Leadership must be viewed in context. Organisations deliver a product or service, whilst larger institutions may serve to maintain order, stability and social cohesion. Effective leaders work to enhance current performance, but they also create the conditions for future success. Contrast this mindset with that of administrators or specialists who operate within existing systems. They struggle to develop capability, especially the motivation and commitment that enables people to embrace change. There is talk of *Vision, Values and Mission*, but much less on *Principles* and *Competencies* central to excellence. Leaders need to ensure the transparency, capability, accountability and trust that helps build healthy organisations. This book explores essential steps.

In the past, the purpose of business corporations was quite simple. The focus was on maximising returns to shareholders and typically doing the minimum necessary to comply with legal requirements. This is *raw capitalism*, emphasising short-term returns, but also neglecting future capability. It helped fuel 'boom and bust' economics and still mesmerises those who fail to appreciate interdependencies. Financial performance is only one measure of success and always 'historical'. It reflects previous performance. However, current financial returns are no guarantee of future success. This prompted Kaplan and Norton to develop the *Balanced Scorecard* (1992), which reviews both *internal* and *external* performance criteria. The external focus asks: *How do customers see us?* (customer perspective) and *how do we look to shareholders?* (financial perspective). The internal focus asks: *What must we excel at?* (systems and operations) and *can we continue to improve and create value?* (innovation and learning perspective).

ESG takes this thinking to the next level. The external perspective now focuses on stakeholders (not just shareholders), and there is increased emphasis on creating 'enabling conditions' that support capability. Alan Jope, CEO of Unilever, stated in 2021: '*Without healthy societies we don't have a healthy business*'. In effect, ESG represents *Third-Generation Corporate Governance* and requires a real grasp of interdependencies. ESG places increased emphasis on *how goals are achieved*. Leaders develop the capability and alignment that supports future progress. They build on vision and values, but also define the principles that guide actions. Principles provide a point of reference that supports purpose. They create consistency when responding to inevitable questions of *why? what?* and *how?* Explicit standards are important as they help safeguard values. They ensure effectiveness over time, encouraging transparency and accountability. In contrast, a task-focused and expedient mindset limits appreciation of issues, narrows our perspective and reduces consistency. In November 2021, UNESCO set out recommendations on the *Ethics of Artificial Intelligence*; it notes (p. 18, item 10), …*principles unpack the values underlying them more concretely so that the values can be more easily operationalized in policy statements and actions.*[1]

Exceptional performance requires self-discipline, conviction and consistency of approach. Principles support continuity by defining professional standards. As the context changes, leaders must adapt, but also maintain focus on overall purpose. Most importantly, leaders also actively assimilate feedback to improve systems, enhance people's motivation and take action to ensure well-being. However, there is an underlying problem, which is linked to human nature. Our responsiveness to feedback tends to decline over time. Success undermines humility. Politicians, for example, can start to believe they are special people.

Context is always changing, but principles guide actions and serve to overcome resistance. We might, for example, note the rapid pace of technological change during the 19th century. In England, this prompted the 1870 *Elementary Education Act*, which was immediately opposed by traditionalists who warned of the dangers of a better educated labouring class, and libertarians who feared indoctrination by *The State*. The Church was worried by a perceived loss of influence. A lesson for aspiring leaders is that change prompts resistance and disagreement. Whilst some see opportunities, others perceive threats. We need time to adjust to change and some require more time than others. This can trigger polarisation. People move at different speeds, which causes an emotional reaction. The *First Rule* states: *As complexity increases, the process of engaging others becomes more challenging*.

Introducing new 'points of reference' contributes to disturbance. Many people want to stay secure on an old 'three-legged stool' that offers stability.

Human personality has changed little in 2,000 years. As a result, outdated assumptions and rigid thinking are ever present. The context changes, but mindset persists. Some who opposed the 1870 Education Act would also have lamented the end of public executions and the clear deterrence of being 'hung, drawn and quartered'. The penal reforms occurred around the same time as the hesitant advances in education. History serves to remind us that, to some extent, we are all held captive by *patterns of thinking* that restrict our ability to see things clearly. Many leaders struggle to anticipate requirements or foresee the consequences of expedient action. This is not an inevitable process, but it is far more likely when *future-focused leadership* is lacking. ESG represents a force that drives transparency, consistency and high performance.

Ingrained patterns of thinking run deep. Economists and 'Political Scientists' [*sic*] still refer to *Bounded Rationality* in a misguided attempt to explain why people make sub-optimal decisions. It's argued that these 'errors' are caused by complexity, time pressure or a lack of cognitive ability. Note that this concept is applied to both individuals and groups. However, the model neglects psychological processes that shape people's perceptions, motivation and expectations. The value of outcomes is influenced by shared purpose, not simply self-interest. Contrast the dysfunctional outcomes associated with mediocre leaders and the results achieved by those who *develop enabling condition, maintain focus* and *create purpose*. Effective leaders apply principles, anticipate problems and enhance motivation linked to overall goals.

Building on the *Balanced Scorecard*, ESG helps us develop a broader perspective by clarifying both 'what' and 'how'. The focus involves recognising internal and external considerations, which can be broadly grouped in terms of 'task' and 'people'. Making progress may well involve overcoming old assumptions and restricted thinking.

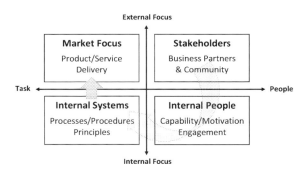

The concept of *Bounded Rationality* is linked to *Legacy Thinking*. It's part of a reductionist mindset that sidesteps unfamiliar concepts. In reality, people are not simply motivated by self-interest. However, outdated concepts are attractive, offering simplistic validity, and they have a long history. *Phrenology*, for example, was widely accepted by professionals as a scientific process. Similarly, before we appreciated the role of viruses and bacteria in causing disease, *miasma* (bad air) was blamed for epidemics. Unfortunately, inadequate theory undermines insight. This results in outdated thinking, not least in our understanding of motivation, commitment and elements that contribute to innovation. Leaders who lack insight and overlook guiding principles are then left vulnerable to error.

Effective leaders work to ensure alignment of activities, the best use of resources and clarity on how to achieve excellence. This involves building relationships, developing capability and providing support. Leaders build trust through consistency, integrity and management of interdependencies. They create shared purpose. However, a shift of context can expose shortfalls. Politicians, for example, may pursue an ideology of *laissez-faire individualism*, but struggle to find solutions to 21st century challenges. Executives strive to balance short-term priorities with wider stakeholder expectations. These include issues relating to environment and sustainability.

The new standards, e.g. '*the polluter pays*', now shape corporate governance and require leaders to understand and manage the interdependencies that are critical to future outcomes. In 2022, the UK Financial Reporting Council (FRC) stated: *Companies should disclose the effects of their policies and procedures by highlighting the outcomes and impacts of their initiatives/ actions and explaining how these relate to company purpose, strategy and values.*[2] In 2023, a *Business Green* article noted: '*dozens of companies and financial institutions have been singled out by the Science Based Targets initiative (SBTi) for failing to submit promised emissions targets for independent accreditation*'.[3] Also in 2023, the UK government announced that those that pollute the environment will face unlimited penalties.

To ensure consistency of approach, values are best expressed through operational principles. This means that standards must be explicit, not least because the culture of the organisation is shaped by a shared understanding of what is expected. Principles define what we do and how it gets done. *Without leadership, people will 'continue to do what they do'.* This means, for example, that bureaucrats will create ever more 'red tape'. We hear of theatres issuing ill-considered 'trigger warnings', e.g. 'the play "Macbeth" depicts violence'. This type of behaviour is irritating, not least because it conflicts with our core need for autonomy, i.e., self-direction, which supports healthy functioning. Rote-learned actions can threaten self-determination and prompt accusations of 'woke excess'. Leaders need to create appropriate terms of reference that safeguard purpose, respect core needs and eliminate problems created by bureaucratic diktat (or well-intentioned gestures that compromise professional impartiality and reputation).

Essential insights for leaders come from *Self-Determination Theory*. Meaningful activity, positive relationships and personal responsibility enhance our core need for relatedness, competence and autonomy. However, it's important to note that whilst good leaders appreciate individual strengths, they also prioritise alignment. Higher-order *Superordinate Principles (Super-Ps)* add legitimacy to leadership action. Principles create the foundation for transparency, accountability and agreement. Principles also help prevent development of a dysfunctional work culture. Without guiding principles we should expect naivety, impulse and reaction.

Expressing values through principles and *explicit standards* serves to protect intangible assets, e.g. a positive corporate culture, and also enhance *Business Intelligence Systems* that safeguard the health of the organisation. In the context of ESG, sound metrics provide the foundation for feedback and development. Advanced team-focused surveys, for example, highlight variations across groups and departments. They help identify *cohesive factors*, not isolated questions. Note that active monitoring is particularly important for '*values focused*' and Third Sector organisations. Values should be clarified by leaders and not left vulnerable to the opinion of individuals. Unfortunately, if left unchecked, some people seek to elevate their self-regard by criticising others and pursuing *virtue signalling*. This then undermines efforts to develop an inclusive, enabling culture. We also find that some leaders, notably from technical backgrounds, struggle with empathy and abstraction. They can gain significant benefit from clearly stated guiding principles. This helps create a healthy workplace with strong ethical foundations. Neuro-diverse team leaders, for example, may need additional training to meet role requirements.

The responsibilities of management and team leadership roles include developing positive, trust-based relationships and ensuring constructive engagement with colleagues. Operational leadership builds on trust and responsiveness to a shifting context. This requires awareness of TEAM health, which builds on *Trust, Energy, Action and Motivation*. Our studies suggest that important 'inputs' include *Leadership Style, Positive Team Ethos, Support for Personal Development, Role Clarity, Progress and Purpose.* The inputs or '*drivers*' affect outcomes, notably Motivation and Commitment. These are described by Human Resource (HR) managers, sometimes rather vaguely, in terms of '*Employee Engagement*'.

The key drivers enhance engagement and help organisations retain talented people. This becomes increasingly important in high-skill work environments. A leading consultancy firm (McKinsey) has stated that organisations must focus on '*a holistic employee experience that puts equal emphasis on growth, engagement, and well-being*' (Money Can't Buy Employee's Loyalty: March 28, 2022). Effective leaders consciously create the conditions that link to future success. They understand, for example, that the principle of *Equality* can be operationalised through action that supports *Diversity* and *Inclusion*. Note that these elements, and also initiatives to promote *Equity*, follow on from the higher-order principle of *Equality*.

We may find that well-intentioned, but confusing, HR references to 'DEI' may not grasp that the primary element is the *Superordinate Principle* (Equality). In the UK, this is anchored in the Equality Act (2010). It's an important distinction, not least because research suggests that people apply *Super-Ps* in their reasoning.[4] *Superordinate Principles* prompt strong emotion when threatened by subjective opinion or actions that undermine what is regarded as 'fair and reasonable'. *Super-Ps* are also closely aligned with *Overarching Principles* (OPs) that take account of context. For example, under English law, *Sentencing Council Guidelines* define specific conditions, so the *Super-P* (e.g. Social Justice) is linked to the OP of '*Proportionality*'. This requires the judge to consider *the seriousness of the offense and the culpability of the offender.* More broadly, OPs are perhaps more accurately described as 'Intermediate Principles' best viewed as the expression of *Super-Ps*.

Initiatives intended to promote '*Equity*' should be anchored in the *Super-P (Equality)*. Equality is a non-negotiable precondition; equity is a desirable outcome that requires a binding foundation. Everyone gains from insights that support personal development, professionalism, shared purpose and well-being. Intermediate Principles have operational relevance when they enhance consistency, fairness and development of talent. When done correctly, *Equality, Diversity and Inclusion* (EDI) helps improve an organisation's performance and future capability.

In the US, academics, sociologists and politicians have, in many instances, focused on 'equity' rather than 'equality'. However, it's evident that strategy and ESG should build on *Super-Ps*, which start with equality, accountability and sustainability. We note that EDI (as defined in this book) helps build trust and reputation, shapes competencies and contributes to commitment. Positive initiatives help support exceptional outcomes. Leaders develop capability and create enabling conditions. In the UK, the FRC guide, *Creating Positive Culture* (2022), discusses issues relating to EDI[5] (the letter 'E' refers to 'Equality'). Further consultation by the FRC in 2023 suggests: '...*companies should, when reporting on their governance activity, focus on activities and outcomes to demonstrate the impact of governance practices*'.[6] The FRC also note that '*reporting has been lacking in this respect*'.

Super-Ps help politicians deal with contentious issues, including development and implementation of immigration policy. People expect fairness, balancing the *Competing Virtues* of Justice and Compassion (Mercy). Explicit standards should reflect guiding principles, expressed through effective operational systems. Competency in *delivery of outcomes* contributes to collective purpose and supports social cohesion. This is central to leadership and enhances decision-making. The context changes, but principles continue. The *Super-Ps* relating to Freedom and Self-Determination, for example when applied to the Ukraine War, could be evaluated in the context of *Cultural Genocide*. This would have influenced the US decision in 2023 to supply Ukraine with Cluster Munitions. Although this goes against the UN Convention that prohibits the production or use of the weapon, the OP of *Proportionality* served to justify the decision, given that (1) the US, Ukraine and Russia were not signatories to the UN agreement, (2) the context is defensive, specific and within Ukraine's territory, and (3) the threat, to Ukraine's survival as a nation (and ability to maintain its own language and laws), was viewed as 'severe'.

To see things clearly, it's important to let go of old ideas. Traditional philosophy, for example, is riddled with inconsistences arising from a failure to appreciate *Self-Determination Theory* and the critical role of *Super-Ps* in shaping social identity, collective interest and shared purpose. Between the individual and the state is the community, with social norms and expectations backed by guiding principles. People are naturally 'purpose seekers', capable of self-direction – and well-adjusted individuals will pursue meaningful activity that satisfies their core need for relatedness, competence and autonomy. Nineteenth-century philosophy has no grasp of modern psychology and insights from neuroscience. The need for power, for example, is not a primary factor. It's an acquired secondary need, shaped by environment, and largely directed through socially acceptable, constructive activity. Effective leaders may have '*sheepdog genes*', i.e., they 'round-up' people and set direction, but those biting ankles are likely to be replaced. That said, Australian cattle dogs have a more forceful approach, but operate in a different context!

Leadership theory has evolved in the 21st century, but outdated assumptions still linger. To take one small example, many workplace surveys still refer to the concept of *Job Satisfaction*. However, this is not a good indicator of engagement, which builds on *Motivation* (discretionary effort) and *Commitment* (identification).[7] We are reminded that we need robust models to help make sense of complex problems. At the same time, investors and stakeholders are now more aware of intangible assets, including the impact of corporate culture, the value of positive ESG metrics and standards linked to ISO accreditation. The International Organisation for Standardisation (ISO) is an independent, non-governmental international organisation. It encourages shared standards in a complex, interdependent world. This perspective can be contrasted with the rhetoric of volatile, transient politicians who rely on emotive calls for 'freedom' but fail to grasp interdependencies and standards that protect people's well-being (and the quality of outcomes). Increasingly, leadership requires an understanding of core principles, and the insight that helps deliver exceptional results. There is also an urgent need to apply guiding principles to the development and operation of AI.

Future-Focused AI: Critical Principles

> Failing to operationalize data and AI ethics leads to wasted resources, inefficiencies in product development and deployment, and even an inability to use data to train AI models at all. For example, Amazon engineers reportedly spent years working on AI hiring software, but eventually scrapped the program because they couldn't figure out how to create a model that doesn't systematically discriminate against women.
>
> **– A Practical Guide to Building Ethical AI**
> ***Harvard Business Review*, 15 October 2020**

This book identifies important elements that impact on leadership effectiveness and the issues that affect outcomes. Part II links to the Pario Leadership Course, with the option to complete the online work preference questionnaire. Details are available at Pario360.com. Part III of the book summarises ChatGPT insights. This is a conversation you may wish to continue.

About the Author

With a professional background in Organisational Psychology, **David Sharpley** specialises in leadership development and how leaders create enabling conditions that support motivation, well-being and high performance. He has worked with many large companies, charities and the health sector in the UK and run competency and leadership training events in the Middle East and Southeast Asia. He has also worked as a visiting lecturer at Warwick University, focusing on *Organizations, People and Performance*. His wider experience includes facilitating impact investment in Ghana, most notably the Blue Skies venture (1997). This provided the start point for the development of a multinational group.

David has completed research relating to leadership assessment methods,[8] the impact of assessment methods,[9] and the significance of higher-order principles that enhance meaning and purpose.[10] He has highlighted how *Superordinate Principles* help resolve complex problems and contribute to solution-focused interventions. David has also developed the Pario online resources, used by organisations to support training and development. The tools include the TEAM Index (employee engagement survey) and tailored 360-degree feedback. The work-preference report features in the case study in Part II.

Qualifications & Accreditation

Chartered Organisational Psychologist (UK Registered)
AFBPS (Associate Fellow of the British Psychological Society)
MSc Organisational Psychology (Manchester Business School)
Certified Principal Business Psychologist - Association for Business
   Psychology (UK)

Introduction

Stories about *Great Leaders* go back centuries but are often blurred by myth and legend. Move forward to the present and we face complex interdependencies, uncertainty and the need to create shared purpose. Leaders also need to overcome *legacy thinking* that contributes to outdated assumptions and a restricted mindset. The disruptive '*tripwires*' are barely visible, but it becomes vital to recognise them. In wider society, there are also new expectations relating to integrity, authenticity and corporate governance. These serve to raise the standards expected of leaders, but also wider considerations relating to professional behaviour.

Potential *tripwires* that could reduce your effectiveness include the following:

- Assuming that others share your viewpoint
- Lacking conviction when faced with challenges
- Moving to action before fully exploring options
- Neglecting the consultation that helps engage others
- Failing to anticipate people's expectations and response

Failure to understand other people and show empathy contributes to executive derailment. This has its roots in relationship problems. *When relationships are strong, people will forgive mistakes. But when relationships erode, tolerance disappears, and mistakes will get a manager fired.*[11] To achieve positive change, you need insight into how your analysis, mindset and approach affects other people's motivation, performance and well-being. There are also underlying principles, the *Super-Ps*, that serve to translate a leader's vision and values into operational standards. They underpin the new thinking. Principles help clarify the competencies that describe *how* activities are conducted. They help us to achieve superior outcomes.

Leaders ensure that the *Rules of the Game* are clearly understood. When principles are poorly defined, communication is weakened and problems emerge, most notably in a dysfunctional work culture.

In organisations, principles help define how vision and values are expressed. They support *cascaded leadership* by ensuring consistency of approach. The themes are also articulated in the competencies linked to roles and responsibilities. Clear principles help ensure transparency and accountability. They shape the culture, and should also underpin the initial assessment of people seeking to join an organisation. In a broader context, the themes linked to *Super-Ps* are also seen in the 'triple bottom line' (TBL) criteria that underpin impact investment. They influence *Environmental, Social Governance* (ESG) and shape expectations of fairness and sustainability. Positive outcomes often require collaboration with stakeholders. Principles are also expressed through legislation designed to safeguard employees, the wider community and the environment. *Super-Ps* protect reputation and help secure the investment that supports future development.

Important themes for those in leadership positions include the following:

- Creating Purpose (e.g. through vision, role clarity and meaningful activity)
- Developing Systems that ensure fairness and consistency, and that mitigate risk
- Pursuing Actions that support integrity, safeguard values and enhance alignment
- Building Trust (e.g. positive relationships, honesty and integrity)
- Enhancing Motivation (e.g. through *autonomy supportive leadership*)
- Developing Capability (e.g. coaching and resources to meet challenging goals)
- Ensuring Responsiveness (to people and a changing context)
- Authenticity (e.g. identification and personal conviction: *why, what and how*)

Effective leaders are both reflective and 'action orientated'. They are proactive in their approach and aware of wider issues, including themes of dignity, compassion, well-being and how best to manage change. Future-focused leadership requires an appreciation of the elements that deliver results, including the systems that ensure consistency, transparency and accountability. Effective leaders also help others develop awareness and insight, clarifying issues relating to role and context. They provide the support and development opportunities that increase engagement.

Insight requires feedback that clarifies issues affecting motivation and commitment. People experience disaffection when relationships become transactional, and there is a loss of purpose. Ongoing feedback helps reveal problems and enables team leaders to self-manage. The insights will confirm, for example, that team members value opportunities for self-directed activity and personal development. The expectations go beyond old notions of '*Reward and Recognition*'.

Most importantly, we all need to develop *confirmed competence* that contributes to our self-belief and resilience. Effective leaders support the process by building confidence and capability. They also build personal networks and positive relationships that offer important sources of support. Meta-analysis of research evidence shows that four external elements, *organisational climate, organisational justice, leader–member exchange and authentic leadership*, contribute to people's Psychological Capital *(PsyCap)*.[12] The term *PsyCap* refers to the inner resources, developed over time, which increase resilience when we experience problems and setbacks.

With complexity, leaders must understand interdependencies and how these affect outcomes, but the challenge is to appreciate all the steps in the process. *Horizon Scanning* that focuses only on technological change does not equate to foresight. We need awareness of our own thinking and insight relating to wider issues. Elements that complicate outcomes include inadequate systems, conflicting goals, confusing role demands and other people's (misplaced) expectations. Attributes contributing to exceptional performance include clear analysis, positive influence and positive purpose. However, we also need the resilience required to deliver results. Leaders display these qualities, but they also help develop capability in other people. And it's never sufficient to simply focus on the task, i.e., specific goals and objectives. Leaders also consider *how* activities are undertaken. The broad vision and underlying values are expressed through *core principles* that define how things get done. These insights also help define competencies.

Note that the term '*Competence*' defines the skills and knowledge needed to perform a task. However, *Competencies* involve personal attributes and an approach that leads to effective or exceptional performance. Competencies relate to '*characteristics that are causally related to effective and/or superior performance*'.[13] Unlike personality traits, which are largely fixed, competencies can be developed through awareness and insight. A shift of mindset, for example, can enhance conviction and contribute to a new pattern of behaviour. The script has changed.

Elements of Exceptional Performance

Organisations seek to align activities, ensure effective use of resources and create a culture that contributes to high performance. The process is supported by *Super-Ps* that enable leaders to develop a strategic perspective that links vision and values through principles and competencies. The principles serve to shape an organisation's culture and help create an 'enabling environment'. They make values explicit, so they are linked to operational standards and provide the foundation for future success. However, when guiding principles are neglected, organisations start to lose focus, values are compromised and reputation is damaged. Problems frequently emerge when leaders lack the insight needed to respond to a changing context. Traditional thinking tends to be reactive and overlooks important interdependencies and expectations. We can miss changes that shape the *Rules of the Game*. Higher-order principles always underpin effective, sustainable action.

Insight builds on sound theory coupled with practical experience, but there's also a willingness to question traditional thinking. My own experience includes senior management development initiatives in large organisations, including BT, the NHS, UK banks and the Third Sector. We find that some leaders suffer an *excess of democracy*, e.g. endless meetings and discussion, but fail to show personal conviction, define constraints or create effective systems. There is no 'compelling vision'. In contrast, others are too directive, close down options and do little to encourage initiative and innovation. A good balance supports sound analysis and helps build trust. Unfortunately, we still find managers locked into 20th century thinking. In commercial organisations, too many repeat the old mantra '*our only responsibility is to shareholders*'. There is little reflection on the critical distinction between short-term profit and long-term success. Elsewhere we find careless complacency and a failure of conviction. Some may occupy a leadership role but fail to appreciate guiding principles or manage people's expectations. They neglect the 'action steps' that facilitate shared purpose and help build future effectiveness.

Leadership differs from management in its scope. It inevitably requires *Future-Focus* and insight relating to interdependencies and the ability to achieve positive change. This creates an emotional dimension that addresses the well-being, motivation and performance of others. However, the role will also place psychological demands on the leader. They arise from the personal responsibility that comes with the role – and the self-belief required to handle setbacks and adversity. There will be situations when resources are inadequate and support is lacking. As Harry S. Truman said, 'the buck stops here'. There is an *existential dimension*, so leaders need to develop the *PsyCap* to handle setbacks, disappointment and lack of support. Effective leaders also take steps to develop other people's resilience, which starts with trust and meaningful involvement in purposeful activity. However, if we look more closely at *Situational Judgement*, we find that many aspiring leaders fail to grasp key priorities and may not appreciate the implications of actions. Their thinking is restricted. Guiding principles help establish a wider frame of reference that confirms how activities are conducted. They also serve to remind us of the need for transparency and fairness – and the leader's responsibility to overcome the dysfunctional behaviour that undermines high performance.

There are consequences when leaders lack insight and neglect *Super-Ps*. Clear standards are particularly important when organisations carry political, religious or legal responsibilities. In the UK, for example, we might note that in June 2021 an independent panel reported on the 1987 murder of Daniel Morgan in Sydenham, London, and the role of the Metropolitan Police. The Chair of the Independent Panel concluded: '*…concealing or denying failings, for the sake of the organisation's public image, is dishonesty on the part of the organisation for reputational benefit and constitutes a form of institutional corruption*'. This is a deep-rooted problem in many organisations. We need to shift traditional culture, so new standards are both explicit and backed by robust systems. Effective selection processes also help block entry by dysfunctional people, and robust 360-degree feedback encourages accountability.

In a challenging world, issues relating to *mindset, principles* and *professional competencies* become central to exceptional performance. Organisations create a *vision* based on values and direction, which can be expressed in *principles* linked to the *mission statement*. Toyota's global corporate principles include the following: '*Dedicate ourselves to providing clean and safe products and to enhancing the quality of life everywhere through all our activities*'. We might note that *Super-Ps* guide *Superordinate Goals*. They establish boundaries that contribute to strategic alignment, but also support integrity and authentic leadership.

In the 2020s, expectations of *corporate governance* are changing. Look at Unilever, a global business that is aware of principles guiding the business.[14] These are shaped by values, set boundaries and clarify how activities are conducted. By 2030, the company will require all suppliers to pay a living wage above the legal minimum wage. Alan Jope (CEO) stated:

…Unilever is well-recognised for the work we've done over the years on sustainability, and (in 2020) we took a number of important steps to regenerate and improve the health of the planet… so things like climate action, regenerating nature, working on waste and plastic waste… and today we're sharing our plans to be a positive force in the world, in tackling this persistent and worsening issue of social inequality. Without healthy societies we don't have a healthy business.

(BBC Radio 4 'Today'-21 January 2021)

Jope stated that *customers want to buy products with good credentials, and that this desire has only increased during the (Covid) pandemic*. The BBC noted that the next consumer battlegrounds might not be *price, convenience or range of product*, but *environmental and social considerations*. They say: *Unilever wants to get ahead of that trend and plans to do well, by doing good*.[15] Other companies, such as Netflix, may play down the significance of 'rules', but it then becomes even more important to ensure that the culture is guided by principles. *They ensure the standards and consistency that protects the Brand*.

Systems are required to safeguard employee safety and well-being, and also to prevent potential problems. These issues include 'banter' (aggressive humour) and sexual harassment. Senior-level leaders should anticipate worse-case scenarios and ensure that systems are designed and updated to counter the threat. There are already legal obligations concerning data privacy, financial reporting and responsiveness to stakeholder interests. They require a future-focused mindset. Leaders at all levels need to understand the *Rules of the Game* expressed through the principles that guide effective action. The philosopher John Rawls introduced a thought experiment, *The Original Position*, also called the *Veil of Ignorance*. This asks us to assume that we do not know our gender, status, race or position in society. In this situation, what principles should be established to ensure solidarity? What would you expect? In an organisation, leaders must identify the *Super-Ps* that shape the culture and contribute to an *Enabling Environment*.

Warren Buffett once said, '*You never know who's swimming naked until the tide goes out*'. Think of this in terms of leadership and we see the need for principles, resourcefulness and resilience. It also becomes apparent that old 20th century ideas relating to *Charisma* and a *Compelling Vision* were never enough to make a leader. Significant qualities include the ability to anticipate problems, overcome setbacks and create shared purpose. Faced with challenging *Job Demands*, we need the *Resources* to maintain focus and support our well-being. Effective leaders create trust, encourage initiative, build motivation and support personal development. In contrast, inadequate leaders drain people's energy, create pressure and contribute to disaffection.

Rapid change and unpredictable events demand *Agile Leaders*. Organisations need people who explore options, improve systems and find innovative solutions. These are the leaders who create enabling conditions with a supportive, purpose-focused culture. Flexibility of response is also linked to commitment to high professional and ethical standards. Actions are more often guided by *Super-Ps*. The wider focus matches the TBL criteria of '*people, profit (prosperity) and planet*'. The rules involve social responsibility and sustainability as well as sound judgement relating to financial performance and business criteria. ESG is at the heart of the new thinking. KPMG make the point: *Businesses not taking ESG seriously are beginning to lose customers, employees and financing; eventually they will become unviable* (ESG Introductory Guide – 2020/08).

The new perspective emphasises a stakeholder model, rather than one based purely on the interests of shareholders. We are reminded that 'lag indicators', such as financial results, are the consequence of *what has gone before*. They do not guarantee future success. We also know that dysfunctional leadership and poor decision-making can quickly lead to corporate failure. Remember Enron, Lehman Brothers and RBS? There's also the damaging legacy of neoliberal economic theorists who failed to deliver a sustainable future. It becomes increasingly important to understand the qualities that contribute to long-term success. These include an understanding not only of *Superordinate Goals* but also of the *Super-Ps* that guide actions.

Awareness requires the ability to see things clearly and recognise options and possibilities. This also helps improve self-management. Future-focused leaders develop competencies in three broad areas. These include (i) analysing requirements and setting clear direction, (ii) enhancing people's capability, building working relationships and going beyond the immediate team, and (iii) having the drive, initiative and resilience to resolve problems and maintain focus. *Competencies* describe the *insights, approach and personal strengths* of superior, '*Star Performers*'. The attributes go beyond basic skills (competence) and qualifications – of *what is required* to be 'acceptable'. We can therefore differentiate *Competence* (threshold standards) and *Competencies* that describe *how* people achieve superior performance in a particular role.

We find that *Star Performers* are more responsive to *shifts of context* and adapt more readily to unexpected demands. Over time, effective leaders develop an *internalised gyroscope* anchored in values and principles that shape action, mission and purpose. These *guiding principles* go beyond self-interest and self-referenced thinking. They are now the new currency shaping the *Rules of the Game*. Unfortunately, previous ventures, including the UK *Management Charter Initiative* (1988) have conflated *competence* and *competency*. The confusion arises when we apply *Functional Reductionism*, which breaks things down into pieces, but overlooks *how* we go about the process, e.g. shaping culture, and achieving integrity, authenticity and trust.[16]

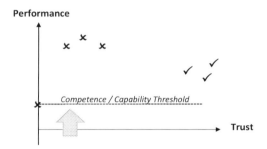

> *A high level of trust is viewed as more important than a leader's techni-*
> *cal capability and (skills) …*
> *Performance needs to be backed by attributes that support integrity,*
> *authenticity… and trust.*

Trust-based relationships shape the culture. Explicit standards create boundaries for action and help protect reputation. When this insight is lacking, problems follow. For example, in July 2023, Alison Rose (then CEO of NatWest bank) had to resign '*after leaking information to the BBC about ex-UKIP leader Nigel Farage*'. This outcome was inevitable after the government raised 'significant concerns'.[17] To put this in context, the government had to rescue RBS/NatWest after the 2008 crash and still owned 38.6% of the bank (July 2023). The episode raised wider questions about the right of banks to close accounts because the Board disagreed with a client's (legally held) political views. The events may well represent the final chapter in the RBS saga. The incident also illustrates why we need explicit principles that inform behaviour.

Issues linked to operational effectiveness, and how we achieve positive outcomes, are discussed further in *7 Principles for Exceptional Performance*. These are summarised as follows:

The First Principle: Direct the Compass

The first principle involves fundamental questions of *why, what* and *how*. It requires reflection on purpose, values and future direction. This clarity enhances personal conviction, integrity and authenticity. It helps build trust. This type of 'First Principle' thinking is the starting point for shared purpose and exceptional performance. Effective leaders will question assumptions, define boundaries and take action to shape the culture.

The Second Principle: Be Positive and Proactive

The second principle focuses on adopting a positive mindset and a proactive approach. This involves taking the initiative and also recognising issues that affect progress. Understanding the context opens up possibilities to increase effectiveness, but we must also take care to avoid the danger of hubris and self-deception.

The Third Principle: Find Passion and Purpose

Leaders understand the elements that shape motivation – and the steps required to achieve positive outcomes. Overcoming limitations in thinking helps clarify priorities. We can take steps to strengthen our sense of purpose, finding opportunities that contribute to a sense of engagement in meaningful activity.

The Fourth Principle: Take Effective Action

The fourth principle involves awareness of context and application of the competencies, backed by underlying strengths, that contribute to superior performance. Competencies describe important aspects of mindset, values, behaviour and responsiveness to demands. Building on *Purposeful Conversations* and feedback contributes to insight, helps achieve positive change and supports personal development.

The Fifth Principle: Resolve Issues

The fifth principle involves action to *fix problems* linked to dysfunctional behaviour. It's not enough to be positive. Leaders need to ensure clarity and accountability. Some people lack self-awareness and clear *professional focus*. Self-referenced thinking undermines team performance and hinders future progress.

The Sixth Principle: Develop Resilience

Resilience is needed to deal with work demands, setbacks and disappointments. We need to create the personal resources, the *PsyCap* linked to *hope, efficacy (self-belief), resourcefulness and optimism* (HERO) and *Purpose, Optimism, Will-power, Emotional Stability, and Resourcefulness* (POWER).

The Seventh Principle: Create Enabling Conditions

The seventh principle relates to *enabling conditions* that enhance well-being and high performance. Successful organisations develop an environment that enhances future growth. Contrast this with negative conditions that damage people's health and stifle innovation.

The *7 Principles* offer insight into various themes affecting mindset, response and effectiveness. They also help contrast a reductionist approach with a future-focused perspective. Principles provide the foundation for integrity and authenticity. The themes also resonate with the findings of the GLOBE leadership study (of over 17,000 managers in 62 countries). This found that effective leaders pursue high-performance outcomes and also work to inspire and motivate others. The operational principles relate to a team-orientated, participative, supportive style. Research also shows that *autonomy supportive leadership* increases people's motivation and contributes to long-term success.

  The insights suggest that impact investing might well add '*Purpose*' to the 3P model of *People, Profit and Planet*. It becomes clear that *purpose, progress and support* encourage *discretionary effort*, initiative and problem-solving. The GLOBE study confirms that performance is improved by leaders adopting a supportive, consultative style (backed by consistently high standards) and a clear focus on achieving results. We need professionalism and purpose to achieve significant progress. Future-focused leaders ensure that the activities of individuals and teams are aligned with overall objectives. *Shared Purpose* and collective interest (directed towards significant outcomes) provide the basis for building motivation and encouraging initiative. Acquiring greater insight helps leaders develop important competencies, both in themselves and in other people.

Back in the 20th century, theories of leadership focused on the personality traits of the leader. Aspects of outgoing, positive behaviour are clearly important, but leadership needs to be viewed in context. Faced with the increasing complexity of the 21st century, leaders need to do more than '*overcome people's self-interest*' or seek to '*energise*' *(passive)* '*followers*'. These are old, outdated ideas. Leaders now need to grasp context, understand *Super-Ps* and create enabling conditions.

Context can sometimes be viewed as a continuum. This moves from clearly defined activities (and a situation of consensus) to one of uncertainty and discord. In many situations, leaders also need to be aware of both the immediate task and wider *Superordinate Goals*. Alignment involves ensuring that team activities resonate with wider objectives. However, leaders are also responsible for establishing the *Super-Ps* that shape the work climate and culture. In business, politics and everyday life, it is not sufficient for leaders to simply focus on goals; they must also create an expectation relating to how things are done. This means that values must be expressed through principles that are anchored in explicit standards that serve to regulate behaviour.

Feedback systems ensure transparency and contribute to a culture of accountability. Research shows that '*people are better at selecting and coding information than they are at integrating it… the evidence shows that rules and principles can improve decision-making*'.[18] The line of sight that runs from *Vision and Values* to *Principles and Competencies* should be clear. However, it is easily obscured when there is little appreciation of issues affecting people's underlying needs and expectations. At work, guiding principles provide the link to the systems and the competencies required for exceptional performance. These start with our underlying need for *Relatedness, Competence and Autonomy*. This means that people are motivated to seek (i) trust-based, supportive relationships, (ii) the competence to make a meaningful contribution, which is then coupled with (iii) the opportunity for self-directed activity and responsibility. The underlying sequence helps build *confirmed competence*. Over time, the process contributes to development of self-belief and personal resilience.

Super-Ps reflect core needs and underlying values. Faith leaders, for example, refer to the *dignity of the individual*. There are also professional and legal obligations that create a *duty of care*. From a leadership perspective, it's important to understand the links between principles, obligations and goals. *Strategic Alignment* builds on this insight, with guiding principles helping confirm the rationale for action. Effective leaders consider context, resources and constraints, and how these influence priorities and objectives.

The process becomes more difficult when people are faced with challenging scenarios. We need to remove old assumptions and shift mindset. Leaders strive to grasp context, assess demands and review options. The professional obligation is to pursue standards of excellence, not to engage in cover-up or attempt 'protect our own' (dysfunctional staff), which has been a problem in public-facing organisations.

Super-Ps clarify standards, interdependencies and overall purpose. Maintaining effectiveness when faced with demanding and unfamiliar situations always requires cognitive flexibility. Our thinking and assumptions must adapt quickly to the next inevitable shift of context. With this in mind, Part I of the book focuses on *Leadership Insights* and how we might learn to *see* things more clearly. This goes beyond 'self-awareness' and requires real insight. Part II then builds on development modules. These also offer individually tailored content, linked to completion of the Pario work preference questionnaire. This helps clarify elements that can affect competencies. Part III focuses on insights from ChatGPT, with summaries of several important concepts. The following examples, also from ChatGPT, suggest ways we can link principles and competencies:

1. **Enhancing Diversity and Inclusion**
   - **Superordinate Principle**: Equality and Respect for Diversity
   - **Intermediate Principles**: Developing a diverse and inclusive workplace, providing equal opportunities for all, addressing any barriers that may prevent inclusion
   - **Competencies**: Cultural competency, understanding of implicit bias and how to address it, effective communication skills

   By adopting *Super-Ps* of equality and respect for diversity, organisations can develop Intermediate Principles that promote diversity and inclusion, such as developing diverse hiring practices, providing equal opportunities for all and addressing any barriers that may prevent inclusion. Developing competencies such as cultural competency, understanding of implicit bias and effective communication skills can help employees to implement these principles effectively and create a more inclusive workplace.

2. **Sustainable Practices**
   - **Superordinate Principle**: Responsibility towards the environment
   - **Intermediate Principles**: Reducing carbon footprint, using sustainable materials, promoting environmental conservation, developing sustainable business practices

- **Competencies**: Environmental management, knowledge of sustainable practices and technologies, project management skills

By adopting *Super-Ps* of responsibility towards the environment, organisations can develop Intermediate Principles that promote sustainable practices, such as reducing carbon footprint, using sustainable materials, promoting environmental conservation and developing sustainable business practices. Developing competencies such as environmental management, knowledge of sustainable practices and technologies, and project management skills can help organisations to implement these principles effectively and create a more sustainable future.

3. **Ethical Decision-making**
   - **Superordinate Principle**: Justice and Fairness
   - **Intermediate Principles**: Developing ethical guidelines and policies, addressing conflicts of interest, promoting transparency and accountability
   - **Competencies**: Ethical decision-making, conflict resolution skills, data analysis skills

By adopting *Super-Ps* of justice and fairness, organisations can develop Intermediate Principles that promote ethical decision-making, such as developing ethical guidelines and policies, addressing conflicts of interest, and promoting transparency and accountability. Developing competencies such as ethical decision-making, conflict resolution skills and data analysis skills can help organisations to implement these principles effectively and make ethical decisions that align with their values and goals.

Overall, by applying *Super-Ps*, Intermediate Principles, and competencies, organisations can enhance their future capability and create a more ethical, sustainable and inclusive future. These principles and competencies can help organisations to navigate complex ethical issues, improve stakeholder trust and achieve long-term success.

Identifying *Superordinate Principles*

Hippocrates is attributed with establishing the higher-order principle, *'first, do no harm'*. Principles guide what we do and *how* we complete things. Understanding the specific behaviour and approach that leads to superior performance is at the heart of competency-based assessment. *Super-Ps* provide the foundation for transparency and accountability. They help maintain reputation and brand. This point applies to both individuals and organisations. Leaders articulate the principles that translate values into action.

Performance

+ Superordinate Principles
Positive Values / ESG

- - - - → **Superordinate Goals**

Work Culture
Team Metrics

− Superordinate Principles
Expedient / Not Binding

Those who operate on the basis of expediency, or simply from ignorance, may well be surprised by the reaction of others when *Super-Ps* are compromised. Some leaders twist values, distort facts, conceal information and cover up difficult issues. Non-disclosure agreements also hide incompetence and malpractice in dysfunctional organisations. However, expedient action tends to undermine longer-term success. A lack of transparency also fuels social media conspiracy theories and increases the risk that objectivity and accuracy will be weakened. As complexity increases, integrity and authenticity become more significant. Principles ensure professional accountability and consistent standards, whereas a lack of clarity fuels rumour and speculation.

Super-Ps can help change people's mindset, but the vocabulary is important. The default is to seek explanation if targets are not achieved. There is reliance on *fault-finding logic*, which is designed for technical problems, but neglects context or how to achieve real insight. To develop people's capability, leaders develop rapport and purpose, which enhances motivation *and* commitment. However, many appraisal systems fail to explore interdependencies, or relate activities to wider goals and expectations. An effective process supports dialogue and requires *Purposeful Conversations* that add to motivation. These are 'focused conversations' that help raise

Awareness, increase *Insight*, encourage *Meaningful action* and also ensure that people have access to appropriate *Support*. Effective leaders maintain standards and build on *Awareness, Insight, Meaning and Support* (AIMS).

Over time, the *Rules of the Game* start to change, but *Super-Ps* also become more evident. Following the 2020 US election, large tech firms (gradually) started to remove posts with extremist views. With changing expectations, leaders face increased scrutiny. New agencies emerge. The *Systemic Risk Council* is an independent voice for reforms that are necessary to protect the public from financial instability. The UK *Digital Markets Unit* is a regulator (set up in 2021) '*to help make sure tech giants such as Facebook and Google cannot exploit their market dominance*'.[19] It gradually becomes more difficult for financially dominant corporations to 'buy or bury' competition, stifle innovation and ignore the interests of wider society.

Margaret Thatcher, British prime minister, 1979–1990, was controversial. However, she acted on principle and noted: *The first duty of Government is to uphold the law. If it tries to bob and weave and duck around that duty when its inconvenient, if government does that, then so will the governed, and then nothing is safe – not home, not liberty, not life itself* (Conservative Party Conference, 1975). Move forward to the 21st century and *Super-Ps* can be viewed alongside *Artificial Intelligence* (AI) algorithms. There is a realisation that the objective of maximising profit, regardless of the consequences, can destroy social cohesion. The technology becomes dysfunctional when leaders lack the insight or 'moral compass' required to take appropriate, corrective action. When this happens, stakeholders have to decide how best to safeguard people's well-being, social cohesion and our underlying need for justice and accountability.

There is a blurring of work, social context and identity. Working from home (WFH) increases the need for action that enhances identity, social connection and purpose. In a complex, uncertain world, principles help create the context and rationale for action. In this new scenario, personal development is made easier when we understand both the *what* and the *how*, which serve to establish the basis for effective action. The process supports development of an internalised script that builds on confirmed competencies and purpose. We might also note the 2021 BBC Reith Lectures (Part II) that focused on the advance of AI. Professor Stuart Russell commented on people's need for purpose, which will increasingly build on interpersonal skills. He noted: '*We will need to become good at being human*'. Leaders need to understand how the changing context creates new demands and the principles that support positive outcomes. Context impacts on our sense of *confirmed competence* that helps build self-belief and resilience. Personal networks, positive relationships (and coaching by team leaders) all contribute to the development of *PsyCap*. This provides the foundation for enhancing resilience at work. More broadly, *Super-Ps* support the reputation of leaders and shape the culture of organisations.

Leadership principles can be viewed as a set of obligations. They represent the organisation's desired values, aligned with actions that support integrity, authenticity and trust. There is a hierarchy that confirms the importance of specific, higher-order principles. Lord Coe (as president of World Athletics) commented in 2022, '*If you pushed me and you said, if you had to make a choice between fairness or inclusion, I will always head towards fairness because that's what sports has to be based on*'. We might also note that 'fairness' links to values, but the principle of 'equality' is expressed through explicit standards, rules and laws. Diversity and inclusion are reflected in processes and actions that support equality and enhance the future capability of an organisation. Principles are made explicit through rules, standards and competencies. They also need to be protected, monitored and developed through well-designed feedback processes.

In organisations, team leader profiling and work climate surveys offer insight into key factors affecting people's motivation, commitment and resilience. *Post-modernist thinking* suggests that everything is relative and there are no binding principles. Psychological research suggests otherwise, as underlying core needs prompt values and principles. The work of Karen Stenner[20] also shows that many will turn to authoritarian solutions when core values and principles are threatened. This is a dynamic response to a perceived external threat. We have an innate need for meaning and purpose, shaped by values and principles. *Nihilism* is not a path to well-being. Bearing this in mind, *the Second Rule states that decisions must be in accord with Super-Ps that safeguard core values.*

Future-focused leaders ensure actions are aligned with principles. Building on principles creates a foundation for explicit standards. ESG, for example, builds on metrics relating to climate change, environmental impact and the principle of *Social Responsibility*. Control of greenhouse gas (GHG) emissions is currently centre stage, but there are also principles relating to the supply chain, diversity, human rights and community relations. There are higher-order principles linked to integrity and social justice that go to the heart of corporate governance. *Super-Ps* are central to ESG. The UK 2010 Equality Act, for example, lists *Protected Categories* to prevent discrimination. Leaders of large corporates might also reflect on the UN 2030 Agenda (a plan of action for people, planet and prosperity). It sets out 17 sustainable development goals. Unilever's stance on the living wage offers an example of action aligned to UN principles. Appropriate action anchored in guiding principles helps enhance your brand.

Corporate governance now comes into the spotlight. This raises questions on how organisations operate – and issues of transparency, accountability and remuneration. The rights of shareholders and other interest groups figure more strongly. Improved metrics can assess the *enabling conditions* required for future success. Over the longer term, gender balance and diversity in Board membership can enhance decision-making. However, people also require the experience, competencies, insight and commitment that drive excellence. Unfortunately, it's easy to conflate values, principles and competencies, which can undermine high performance. For example, the UK '*Seven Principles of Public* Life' lists '*Leadership*' as a principle, with various disjointed, disparate indicators. In contrast, organisational psychologists view leadership as a multifaceted competency. We are reminded that the validity of a process starts with good design. This is a prerequisite for reliable assessment, objective monitoring and effective feedback.

We asked ChatGPT to consider how we build on SDT and *Super-Ps*:

➤ *What insights emerge for leaders from evidence relating to self-determination theory (SDT) and Superordinate Principles, e.g. equality, accountability and sustainability?*

SDT and wider *Super-Ps* suggest several insights for leaders:

1. **Promote autonomy**: Leaders should promote autonomy by providing followers with opportunities for self-direction and decision-making. This can help followers feel a sense of control and ownership over their work and decisions, which is consistent with the principles of accountability.
2. **Emphasise competence**: Leaders should emphasise competence by providing followers with opportunities for skill-building and growth. This can help followers feel a sense of mastery and accomplishment, which is consistent with the principles of sustainability.
3. **Foster relatedness**: Leaders should foster relatedness by creating a supportive environment that fosters positive relationships and social connections among followers. This can help followers feel a sense of belonging and inclusion, which is consistent with the principles of equality.

4. **Align values**: Leaders should align their personal values and the values of their organisation with the principles of equality, accountability, and sustainability. This can help establish a shared sense of purpose and values that can increase motivation and commitment among followers.

5. **Prioritise sustainability**: Leaders should prioritise sustainability by integrating sustainability practices into their organisational culture and operations. This can help create a sense of responsibility and commitment among followers towards the long-term well-being of the organisation and the planet.

In summary, the evidence relating to SDT and wider *Super-Ps* suggests that leaders should promote autonomy, emphasise competence, foster relatedness, align values and prioritise sustainability. By doing so, leaders can motivate and engage their followers towards shared goals that are consistent with the principles of equality, accountability and sustainability.

Notes

1 UNESCO AI Guidelines. Available at: https://unesdoc.unesco.org/ark:/48223/pf0000381137/PDF/381137eng.pdf.multi

2 *Review of Corporate Governance Reporting* (November 2022) – UK Financial Reporting Council. Available at: Review of Corporate Governance Reporting_2022 (frc.org.uk)

3 Business Green article. *'Commitment removed': Over 60 firms singled out by SBTi for failing to submit climate goals.* Available at: https://www.businessgreen.com/type/news

4 Manktelow, K. I., & Fairley, N. (2000). Superordinate principles in reasoning with causal and deontic conditionals. *Thinking & Reasoning*, 6(1), 41–65.

5 Financial Reporting Council (FRC) Report. (2021). Available at: https://www.frc.org.uk/getattachment/9fc6c466-dbd2-4326-b864-c2a1fc8dc8b6/FRC-Creating-Positive-Culture-Report_December-2021.pdf

6 FRC Consultation (Summarised by Stephenson Harwood). Available at: https://www.shcapitalmarkets.com/insight/frc-publishes-consultation-uk-corporate-governance-code

7 Christiansen, N. D., & Fleenor, J. W. (2019). Employee engagement: The job satisfaction myth. *Journal of Leadership and Management*, 1(1), 18–34.

8 Robertson, I. T., Gratton, L., & Sharpley, D. (1987). The psychometric properties and design of managerial assessment centres: Dimensions into exercises won't go. *Journal of Occupational Psychology*, 60, 187–196.

9 Robertson, I. T., Iles, P. A., Gratton, L., & Sharpley, D. (1991). The impact of personnel selection and assessment methods on candidates. *Human Relations*, 44(9), 963–981.

10 Sharpley, D. (2021). Applying superordinate principles to resolve complex problems and support solution-focused interventions. *Transpersonal Psychology Review*, 23(2), 10–15.

11 Management derailment – Personality assessment and mitigation, Hogan. *Book of Industrial & Organizational Psychology, 2010 Vol 3 (Published by the American Psychological Association)*.

12 Kong, F., Tsai, C., Tsai, F., Huang, W., & De la Cruz, S. (2018). Psychological capital research: A meta-analysis and implications for management sustainability. *Sustainability*, 10, 3457.

13 Boyatzis, R. E. (1982). *The Competent Manager* (p. 23). Wiley.

14 See Appendix – *Superordinate Principles*.

15 BBC Report. *Marmite maker Unilever to insist suppliers pay 'living wage'*. Available at: www.bbc.co.uk/news/business-55735108

16 Jong, Bart A. De, Kurt T. Dirks, & Gillespie, Nicole. (2016). Trust and team performance: A meta-analysis of main effects, moderators, and covariates. *Journal of Applied Psychology*, 101(8), 1134–1150

17 BBC Report. (July 26, 2023). Available at: https://www.bbc.co.uk/news/live/business-66296935

18 Zamzow, J. L. (February 2015). Rules and principles in moral decision making: An empirical objection to moral particularism. *Ethical Theory and Moral Practice*, 18(1), 123-134

19 UK Digital Markets Unit. Available at: www.gov.uk/government/news/new-watchdog-to-boost-online-competition-launches--3

20 Stenner, K. (2005). *The Authoritarian Dynamic*. Cambridge University Press.

GAINING INSIGHT

Chapter 1

Leadership Essentials

Effective leaders clarify goals and priorities. However, this implies a *clear vision* and sense of shared purpose. Leaders set direction, provide meaning, encourage initiative and generate commitment. The core themes help set us on the path to exceptional performance. Important elements come together to support positive change, but it's not an easy process. It's also clear that leadership becomes critical as soon as we move from a situation of stability and consensus to one of uncertainty, doubt and disagreement. There is then a need to focus energy and build motivation. Successful leaders create the momentum to 'make things happen'. There is transition from uncertainty to a situation characterised by purpose and progress.

Something else also features strongly in this process. Positive leadership involves developing people's capability, resilience and willingness to overcome challenges. Most importantly, leaders also require the *agility* to anticipate requirements and proactively manage change. They minimise disruption, loss of motivation and the risk of disaffection. Over time, they have the opportunity to develop the insight required to handle dynamic, unpredictable events. In the 21st century, organisations increasingly need agile, cascaded leadership. This offers increased responsiveness to unexpected demands, but some fail to see things clearly. In August 2023, *The Economist* published an article: '*Why China's economy won't be fixed*'. The article highlighted various factors, including '*Mr Xi's centralisation of power and his replacement of technocrats with loyalists in top jobs*'.

In a VUCA World[1] characterised by *Volatility, Uncertainty, Complexity and Ambiguity*, there is growing emphasis on flexibility. New challenges disrupt established procedures, fixed plans and centralised control.

DOI: 10.4324/9781003439707-2

The harsh reality is that many organisations are slow to adapt, particularly to new technology that threatens their longer-term survival. As an example, remember that Kodak invented the first digital camera in 1975, but the Board failed to see the potential. In January 2012, Kodak filed for Chapter 12 bankruptcy protection. Move forward again, this time to 2020. The global reality of uncertainty and risk is now made explicit. COVID-19 accelerated economic disruption and longer-term changes in how we work.

Understanding a VUCA World

The threats to performance, linked to the elements in the VUCA model, and how best to respond have been summarised as follows[2]:

Volatility: Relatively unstable change; information is available and the situation is understandable, but change is frequent and sometimes unpredictable.

Response: Agility is key to coping with volatility. Resources should be aggressively directed towards building slack and creating the potential for future flexibility.

Uncertainty: A lack of knowledge as to whether an event will have meaningful ramifications; cause and effect are understood, but it is unknown if an event will create significant change.

Response: Information is critical to reducing uncertainty. Firms should move beyond existing information sources to both gather new data and consider it from new perspectives.

Complexity: Many interconnected parts forming an elaborate network of information and procedures; often multiform and convoluted, but not necessarily involving change.

Response: Restructuring internal company operations to match the external complexity is the most effective and efficient way to address it. Firms should attempt to 'match' their own operations and processes to mirror environmental complexities.

Ambiguity: A lack of knowledge as to the basic *Rules of the Game*; cause and effect are not understood, and there is no precedent for making predictions as to what to expect.

Response: Experimentation is necessary for reducing ambiguity. Only through intelligent experimentation can firm leaders determine what strategies are and are not beneficial in situations where the former rules of business no longer apply.

The pace of change now requires people to go beyond the skills and knowledge that underpin traditional ideas of *competence*. Qualifications are simply a ticket that enables someone to join a professional group. However, when faced with significant challenges, it becomes increasingly important to understand wider *competencies*. These define *how* effectively people direct energy and attention: How do you respond to unexpected problems? Competencies involve more than the conventional notion of *competence* because they encompass the approach, mindset and professional behaviour that differentiate *exceptional performance*. Two consultants, for example, may have similar levels of specialist knowledge and technical skill. However, one may be far more effective at *active listening* and *enquiry*, resulting in much greater responsiveness and awareness of underlying issues. This improves problem-solving and team leadership. Understanding *context* and *competencies* enables people to develop the attributes needed to excel.

So, what are the qualities required to be an effective leader? It's a tricky question to answer, not least because leadership is a broad concept and applicable across a range of situations. However, there are consistent elements that link to successful outcomes. For example, a leader requires skills and experience that are relevant to the task. That said, they do not need to be a specialist or a technical expert. What's important is that they *understand how the pieces fit together*. I remember an experienced engineering manager at Ford saying, with reference to specialist sub-contractors, *you learn to ask the right questions*. These are the managers and team leaders who are able to make sense of what is happening, identify interdependencies and see things in context. It reminds us of the need to be aware of the bigger picture.

This wider perspective becomes more important when leadership involves working with a range of people – including associates and stakeholders. These individuals are rarely passive followers. They need to be persuaded to support a course of action. The challenge is made greater because everyone has an opinion, which is then 'verified' by social media repetition. In 2009, a US conservative writer (Selwyn Duke) said, *'The further a society drifts from the truth, the more they will hate those that speak it'*. This was attributed (incorrectly) to George Orwell, and has been widely repeated by people on social media, who failed to check the source of the quote. It sounds like Orwell, but the real point of interest involves the underlying assumption that 'truth' is some type of binary construct. Is it something you switch 'on' or 'off'? Unfortunately, this conflates numerous emotive themes within a single word and is used to secure some pristine 'moral high ground'. Look more closely, and we find that 'truth' is actually tied up with *Superordinate Principles (Super-Ps)* that help maintain integrity, consistency and social cohesion. They provide the foundation that underpins deep-rooted rules, shared standards and future expectations.

Words like 'truth' are emotive, easily manipulated and potentially divisive, so they offer leverage for populist politicians. And focusing on a single emotive word also serves another purpose. As Orwell astutely observed, when vocabulary is restricted, thinking is narrowed. When complexity increases, but concepts are missing, we struggle to understand the issues. Inevitably, we then fall back on gut feeling. I have worked with (too many) managers in big organisations, helping clarify selection criteria. Their start point has often been subjective, with talk of 'gut feeling', which is not a good base for reliability (consistency) and validity (accuracy). A leader clearly requires specific competencies, e.g. *persuasion and persistence*, to overcome problems, but this also draws on a *meaningful rationale* that confirms the reason for proposed action. This is backed by principles. Over time, we come to recognise that big concepts like 'truth' need to be unpacked and put in context. It's only then that we can begin to see the real issues.

The tough reality is that technological and social change cannot be reversed; but it can be managed and controlled. People are particularly wary of change that threatens principles, causes disruption and creates excessive demands. In a leadership role, it's wise to assume that most people will not initially share your perspective. They may argue for an alternative approach, or simply express genuine concerns about the proposed course of action. However, this creates an opportunity to engage others in discussion on how best to move forward. The issue is not about some absolute 'truth'. It's more about how we engage people in conversation that builds on principles and helps gain agreement on the best approach.

Effective leaders also know that it's not sufficient to simply focus on the immediate task. They have an awareness of wider considerations and longer-term objectives. However, this means that some people will struggle with leadership responsibility. They fail to explore issues beyond what is immediate and obvious. The problem is that what is currently 'evident' is also 'historical' and only forms part of the picture. Data highlighted in business reports, for example, comes from yesterday, not tomorrow. It typically focuses on what is easily measured and may neglect other factors that offer insight into future capability. Important, often neglected questions include the following: *Are we creating conditions for discretionary effort and inno-vation? Is there a trust-based foundation that supports motivation and com-mitment?* Faced with complexity and change, leaders require a mindset that assesses context, trends and future possibilities. This helps create a vision of what is possible. The vision may not be compelling, but the reasoning should support a leader's personal conviction about longer-term objectives. A meaningful rationale is needed to support dialogue and create direction. This helps clarify what action is required and how best to make progress.

An effective leader builds on a vision of the future. This creates direction, defines priorities and clarifies responsibilities within a team. Perhaps you remember the old 20th century descriptions of leadership that emphasised the importance of 'charisma' and a 'compelling vision'? These qualities were said to '*overcome the problem of individual self-interest*'. However, the real problem is not 'self-interest'. In many situations, the main challenge comes from conflicting perspectives on how to proceed, or a reluctance to contrib-ute! There are always issues linked to varying levels of motivation and commitment. One challenge for leaders is to ensure that energy and resources are focused on the overall goal. The activities of individuals must be aligned with the work of other people and focused on the primary objective. It is not enough to simply align tasks and different areas of activ-ity. The motivation of individuals needs to be maintained over time to encourage initiative with alignment. However, there is a tension. Not all views are valid and personal preferences and 'passions' (such as some speculative project) can undermine high performance.

It becomes apparent that there is often an *optimum path* for leaders, which helps deliver positive outcomes. This can be contrasted with the *critical path* that underpins project management, which may require that step 'C' follows 'B', which in turn relies on the initial work 'A'. However, for a team leader the scenario is more often related to an issue, the 'problem' (P), which creates a task (T), with activity to fix the problem. There is a pressure to move quickly from P to T, but the optimum path may involve a detour. This can be time-demanding, but it's usually worthwhile. Managers come to recognise that results improve when they ask questions (Q), reflect on responses (R), check the situation (S) and take account of context. Effective leaders think about possible outcomes and consequences. They invest time to develop the best approach, and this builds on the sequence: P-Q-R-S-T. Proposed action must be matched to context.

Vision and goal-setting is one part of the equation leading to high per-formance, but this needs to be balanced with awareness. People want to make progress in meaningful activity. Creating a sense of purpose also contributes to well-being and personal resilience. The research evidence reveals that everyone has an underlying desire to develop competence (capability and skills) and have a sense of control and discretion over activities. Motivation is therefore strengthened by an enabling work culture linked to positive work relationships and support from colleagues. It also means that leaders can benefit from a better understanding of people's need for professional identity and clear purpose. We can easily overlook important questions. These include the following: *Does this organisation have a good reputation? Does it make a positive contribution? Is it a good place to work?* And finally: *Does it add to my sense of (positive) identity?*

Our sense of identity is shaped by *points of reference* that support self-validation. These encompass a range of factors, which include work activities, professional relationships and standards of excellence. The various elements create expectations that shape goals and influence how we respond to situations. Our work, and connection to the organisation, contributes to our identity. However, this can change over time. Leaders create purpose and support progress through meaningful activity. They help people gain insight, develop new skills, and acquire the capability and self-confidence that enhances well-being and resilience. This leads on to a central theme associated with leadership. Solving complex tasks requires collaboration. Over time, team members develop the capability and mindset to resolve problems and deal with setbacks. The team leader manages these relationships and seeks to create a sense of shared purpose. Performance is improved if team leaders help people move forward, build competence and achieve results. With increasing complexity, it becomes evident that leaders are required at all levels. These are the people who understand the immediate context, appreciate wider issues and identify options for progress. They are willing to take responsibility for creating clear direction and meaningful activity. They also make the time to develop competencies (in others) that help unlock people's energy, enthusiasm and initiative.

In the 21st century, we need in-depth capability far more than clichéd ideas about *charismatic leaders* and *passive followers*. Very often, the skills and expertise required to resolve complex problems lie within the team. The leader's role is to build on this latent potential and align individual and team activities with overall goals and values. The steps include clarifying context and priorities, identifying options and deciding on action. We need to be wary of ill-defined labels that focus on aspects of personality, e.g. 'courage', or some vague sense of 'doing what is right'. For example, the concept of

Compassionate Leadership has gained popularity in some sectors, but this needs to be supported by a coherent underlying model. It's essential to understand how leaders resolve complex problems, overcome resistance and enhance people's motivation. Attractive words do not resolve the challenge of creating alignment, of matching individual activities with wider goals, or deciding how best to enhance well-being and achieve exceptional performance.

To achieve progress, it's important to view activities as part of an ongoing, iterative process. You can only go so far with theory and abstract concepts. New initiatives require testing and evaluation; so feedback, review and adaption then become the norm.

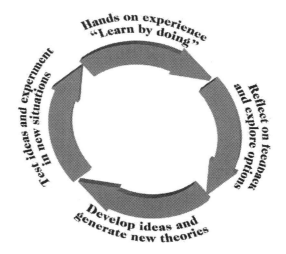

For a leader, it's important to have a sense of overall goals, immediate priorities and how best to proceed. Linking issues (relating to *what* and *how*) improves self-awareness and enhances self-management. Gaining feedback helps us adapt more easily to changing demands and a shifting context. However, there is a risk that some phrases and ideas become so commonplace that they start to lose meaning. We may find that some words appear familiar, and can trigger impressions and associations. This makes it difficult to see things clearly. Words like 'leadership' have a familiarity that fuels assumptions and misconceptions. Imagine meeting a distant acquaintance, someone you knew many years ago. By chance you meet, but then realise that your memory doesn't match current reality. Bearing this in mind, when we hear talks about leadership, we need to be particularly careful. Our impressions are distorted by myths and folk tales. We inherit vague notions of 'great leaders' and the emotion carried in the soundtrack of epic movies. It's difficult to identify essential qualities, understand the context or appreciate why in the real world things start to go wrong. The bottom line is that we need to let go of old ideas and develop a fresh perspective.

It's important to recognise that 'leadership' is a broad term and applied across many situations. We may, for example, imagine a 'wise leader' with the experience that supports a strategic perspective. This is a *reflective style* and looks to the future. The focus might be on what is required in six or seven years. Contrast this *strategic perspective* with that of *operational leaders*, working under time pressure, who need to quickly decide how best to allocate resources and achieve goals. We also see that some situations are well defined, offering clear, tangible objectives, but others are complex and involve far greater uncertainty. There may be a range of options and conflicting views on how best to move forward. In this context, skills of influence and persuasion become increasingly important.

Equally significant is the need to establish systems that are appropriate to the challenge. It's important to remember that a series of steps (processes) come together to create an integrated system. This needs to support people in demanding roles with significant responsibilities. Weak links stem from shortcomings in structure, systems, culture and people. To take one example, the UK National Health Service (NHS) has the potential to be a great institution. However, the Department of Health and Social Care (DHSC) is the government department that defines targets and seeks to 'protect the brand'. However, concern about 'reputation' and 'brand' can undermine the need for transparency, feedback and accountability. These are essential for excellence. So what happens when the pressure directed towards senior managers in the NHS undermines guiding principles? When things go badly wrong, who's really responsible? The problem may start with the culture of the DHSC. As elsewhere, this is an element in the leadership equation, and bureaucracy can damage integrity of purpose. There are some senior managers in the NHS who resist feedback and fail to assimilate anomalies in data. These systemic faults increase the risk of negligence, malpractice and error. Tension and antagonism develop when feelings override leadership objectivity.

Leaders at all levels have responsibility for ensuring that effective systems and appropriate resources are in place. They enable people to make progress in their work. When this input is lacking, energy and momentum start to decline and 'things fall apart'. A clear sign, both in the public sector and in commercial organisations, is when people shrug their shoulders and say '*it's not my problem*'. A failure to take responsibility is often an indication of a more serious, underlying issue. If an organisation suffers from the ubiqui-tous *Shrug Culture*, the mindset is: '*I don't know… it's not my problem*'. For a leader, this means that urgent action is needed to achieve change. Passive, reactive thinking undermines future success. *The Shrug* (*Shouganai* in Japan) is indicative of passive acceptance and a lack of motivation and commitment.

To understand leadership, we need to understand people's thinking and motivation. We also need to appreciate the diverse elements that shape the context. There are *internal* and *external* factors which can be broadly related to *task* and *people*. The external task for organisations relates to the product or service that is being delivered – a process supported by internal systems. However, effectiveness also depends on the skills and motivation of the people. Effective leaders help develop people's current skills and future capability. They also respond and manage the expectations of exter-nal stakeholders, including business partners, government agencies and other groups. There is a need to consider the complexity of the task, the culture of the organisation, and the interdependencies and expectations of other people. These elements help define important leadership *competen-cies* that enable senior professionals deal with complex, challenging situa-tions. We can, for example, contrast traditional ideas of management, which builds on logical analysis and decision-making, with the dynamic aspects of leadership that energise other people.

Developing High Performance

The various factors come together in four elements, which clarify the focus for action in a particular situation. This model can also help clarify the competencies that link to exceptional outcomes.

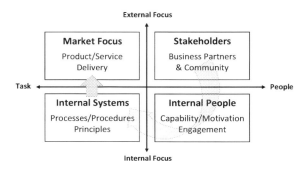

The essential elements can be explored by asking straightforward questions. These prompt reflection and help clarify the action needed to achieve objectives. They also encourage a shift from a *self-referenced* perspective, to a mindset that takes account of other people's position and their initial 'start-point'.

Three *prompt questions* that might start the process of review can be summed up as follows:

■ Where are people 'coming from' in terms of practical issues and context? You might reflect on the roles, sense of direction, the location, resources and constraints. In new and unfamiliar situations, it is important to avoid making assumptions based on your own mindset and expectations.

■ Where are people 'coming from' in terms of their mindset and motivation? How are they likely to respond to the task? Remember that professional effectiveness is increased by understanding what will help or hinder other people's response.

■ Has there been sufficient active listening and dialogue to clarify points 1 and 2 and to gain clear agreement on action?

It's important to be mindful of potential issues that affect outcomes. In a broader context, organisations require decision-making that is responsive to complexity and fast-changing demands. The context can suddenly change, and this presents new challenges. It also means that overall effectiveness requires cascaded leadership, backed by robust systems and resources. Complexity creates turbulence, increased by the rapid pace of technological change, market uncertainties and the threat of global pandemics. Over time, AI will have a role in identifying changing patterns, emerging trends and anomalies. Active leadership is also required at all levels to support the overall system. This insight may prompt us to start asking the question: *Is the success of an organisation really anchored in the vision of one individual?* The evidence suggests otherwise. Old myths of exceptional leaders could increase the risk of abrupt failure. Remember that the senior executives at Enron were called '*the smartest guys in the room*'. And auditors failed to probe and question their actions. In contrast to these celebrity CEOs, effective leaders value feedback and develop transparent systems that ensure accountability. In a complex, fast-changing environment, *humility* becomes a quality that helps reduce error. The structure of the organisation is also important. Hierarchical structure and bureaucracy slow down decision-making, create functional 'silos' and hinder communication.

Increasingly, the need is for 'matrix', project-focused solutions that integrate resources from different specialities. This approach is more responsive to the demands of complex projects and assignments. However, it also means that first-line operational leaders, who may be relatively young, need to understand the elements that affect outcomes. We need to understand the *Rules of the Game*. It's then possible to create a script that supports exceptional performance. The challenge is to identify guiding principles that shape the key steps. And to develop the script, it's important to be aware of role requirements. These include grasp of data, anticipation of future demands, clarity of purpose, e.g. in communicating objectives, and awareness of how best to engage other people. Personal conviction is important, but leaders need to operate within boundaries, appreciate feedback (from data and people) and take account of expectations. Guiding principles include accountability, and this also involves the development of positive, trust-based relationships. These require transparency and discussion focused on factors that are critical to future success.

Trust starts with consistency, anchored in shared principles and underlying values. Empathy and rapport develop from responsiveness to other people's concerns, ideas and suggestions. Being aware of significant elements provides a foundation for focusing personal strengths through competencies linked to exceptional outcomes. However, there is also a need to confront dysfunctional behaviour. Analysis of employee surveys, for example, shows that team members expect prompt, fair and consistent action, which supports high performance. Effective leaders require clarity of purpose, but also benefit from understanding issues that affect motivation. People are also more likely to flourish when they have the opportunity to input ideas, help resolve problems and develop new skills, enhanced by involvement in meaningful work. Trust and rapport are increased with consistent standards, clear purpose and support for personal development. The elements contribute to a professional approach that builds on progress, not frustration.

Professional people want to feel involved, understand the rationale for action and have some discretion and control over their work activities. They expect leaders to be competent, and although it may be unspoken, it's expected that *Super-Ps* take priority over other considerations. They prompt questions that help clarify values, purpose and vision. *Why* are we doing this? *What* action is needed? *How* do we achieve results? Values are expressed through *Super-Ps*, which then translate into action. Core values, such as 'fair treatment', create expectations, which can be expressed through systems. We need clarity concerning *why?* (purpose), *what?* (objectives) and *how?* (competencies) that shape the culture.

Steps to Increased Effectiveness

To be effective, leaders must be forward-looking. They help ensure that people's energy and attention is directed towards positive outcomes. Essential 'core competencies' therefore include the following:

- Showing conviction and vision; clarifying current objectives and future purpose
- Building relationships and managing expectations, both 'within and without', so beyond the team or department
- Improving processes and systems, applying the *guiding principles* required to achieve outstanding results
- Developing people's capability, skills and motivation to make progress and respond to future challenges

Role demands create operational challenges. To achieve superior performance, leaders require competencies across three areas. These clusters of activity include the following: (i) effective analysis and reflective, 'broad based' thinking; (ii) interpersonal skills, relating to teamwork, developing capability and commitment; and (iii) adaptability, resilience and perseverance to maintain focus and overcome obstacles. Effective leadership requires an appreciation of the optimum path that leads to exceptional outcomes. This involves recognition of restraints, obligations and interdependencies. It goes beyond analysis focused on task completion.

Leadership starts with *why*, but we also need to consider *what* and *how*. This contrasts with traditional thinking, which can neglect the links between an enabling culture and high performance. In many scenarios, not least in healthcare, we find a clear process that delivers the best results. Effective solutions build on an evidence-based approach. Objective analysis requires data, not subjective opinion or ideology, and reveals the need for a coherent strategy, sound infrastructure and awareness of interdependencies. Maintaining high performance also requires the application of *Super-Ps*. The siren song of 'free choice' is illusory when it increases cost and leads to sub-optimum outcomes. This is the triumph of ideology over design, of hubris over operational excellence. Future-focused leaders strive to appreciate the bigger picture, engage people in dialogue and clarify the rationale. Organisational culture is important, and managers should be held to account. The goal is excellence, but we don't enhance productivity with 'performance related pay' (PRP) that not only pursues short-term goals but also damages intrinsic motivation and shared purpose.

As noted earlier, positive outcomes are supported by competencies that can be clustered into three broad categories. For example, 'interpersonal effectiveness' requires influencing skills. They help persuade people about the best course of action. In practice, leaders require a range of skills, and also the ability to 'flex' their style. As the context changes, the operational demands shift. It becomes important to have the ability to engage team members, energise colleagues and help ensure focus. Conviction and clarity of purpose help maintain people's attention on important objectives. We find that references to *agile leadership* include mention of *delighting customers, descaling work, enterprise-wide agility* and a *nurturing culture.*[3]

One emerging theme, supported by research studies, is the need for *Autonomy Supportive Leadership.* It helps develop individual initiative, energy and enthusiasm. Positive, discretionary activity is encouraged by building enabling conditions. A leader must be clear about the overall requirements, but then actively engage and support people in developing solutions and pursuing the best course of action. There are also wider considerations, so it's not sufficient to work from old clichés, such as *'delegate tasks', 'think differently'* or *'challenge the status quo'.* Leaders must understand context. In the UK, this includes the Equality Act (2010) that identifies ten 'protected categories' and helps prevent discrimination. It's worth noting that actions to improve diversity and inclusion start with steps to ensure equality. This encourages an inclusive, positive work culture that can enhance performance and productivity. In the specific context of AI design and operational practice, e.g. staff selection, a failure to build on *Super-Ps* becomes costly. *Super-Ps* are fundamental to sound business, and in many countries are backed by law.

It takes time to achieve significant change. Education shapes mindset, but it can also create deficits, and perhaps complacency. We need to build on *awareness*, e.g. by understanding alternative viewpoints, which leads on to *insight*. This involves appreciating context, seizing feedback, recognising new developments and managing interdependencies. Analysis and reflection contribute to *meaningful action*, backed by the *support* and resources to make progress. The four steps create AIMS and contribute to positive change. It's worth noting that to remain motivated over time, people need to feel that progress is being achieved. There is also a need to develop the skills, capability and confidence that encourage self-directed activity. Not everyone can list all the issues affecting motivation. However, if core needs are neglected, high performance becomes elusive. Effective leaders start by appreciating that consistency and fairness are important elements, and they help create a heathy work climate.

People want leaders to articulate a vision that clarifies why we should commit to action. They also need to be engaged through dialogue, ideally with opportunities to review problems and contribute to solutions. We want purpose and progress that build on *Super-Ps*. We also need to consider how these fit with new technology. Self-learning AI, for example, does not share our interest in people-focused principles. Advanced AI has the capability to make a totally dispassionate assessment on how best to achieve its goals. Over time, this could make it extremely difficult to safeguard how objectives are achieved. There are also problems if tech-focused companies, which espouse innovation and *First Principles*, neglect the role of *Super-Ps* in shaping culture and creating shared values. Voracious monopolies could represent an existential threat. In Part III, ChatGPT contrasts *First Principles* and *Super-Ps*.

Notes

1 VUCA Model: *Volatility, Uncertainty, Complexity, Ambiguity*. Wikipedia.
2 Bennett, N., & Lemoine, G. J. (2014). What a difference a word makes: Understanding threats to performance in a VUCA World (Science Direct).
3 Forbes. (October 15, 2017). What is agile? The four essential elements. https://www.forbes.com/sites/stevedenning/2017/10/15/what-is-agile-the-four-essential-elements/

Chapter 2

Invisible Tripwires

Why do leaders fail when faced with new challenges? A primary reason is because they do not see things clearly. We may, for example, assume that requirements are understood and other people share our viewpoint. As a result, problems are not scoped out and issues are overlooked. Lack of clarity also leads to confusion about people's roles and responsibilities. However, it's not simply a deficit, as a potential strength can also contribute to problems. Some managers, for example, place significant emphasis on consulting others. However, there may be a lack of personal conviction in defining the constraints that limit what is possible. A team leader may seek people's involvement, but fail to define the boundaries or clarify key issues. Constraints need to be made explicit and objectives should be stated with conviction. If the terms of reference are not clear, it can easily result in disagreement and can waste time and undermine motivation.

These problems are often linked to mindset rather than underlying personality traits. Clarity of purpose requires *conviction* rather than the more typical references to 'courage'. People are more likely to struggle if they lack insight into their strengths and limitations. *High performance competencies require a script that we develop over time.* This shapes assumptions, thinking and behaviour that affect work relationships. A team leader may have a great relationship with people in their group, but fail to meet the expectations of colleagues. There may be varying feedback on competencies relating to *'building relationships'* or *'developing capability'*. The variation often increases when the context extends beyond the immediate team. Without effective feedback, we may follow a faulty script, and this

DOI: 10.4324/9781003439707-3

creates potential tripwires. There are things that we just don't see. We need feedback to clarify the important elements that affect outcomes.

In practical terms, our blind spots undermine effectiveness in three broad areas: (i) the ability to analyse requirements and set clear direction; (ii) skills linked to building relationships, developing capability and team motivation; and (iii) personal resilience under pressure, e.g. in maintaining focus and the perseverance required to deliver results. Adopting the wrong tactics makes it more difficult to gain *leverage of strengths* and the ability to respond appropriately to challenging demands. Greater awareness and self-management help you achieve exceptional results. Our mindset influences thinking, interaction with others and how we respond to events.

Underlying problems that affect analysis, decisions, relationships and outcomes can include the following:

- Emphasis on quick decisions and speedy action (closing down analysis) – *being impulsive*
- Decisions based on 'gut feel' and first impressions (the 'primacy effect') and *reacting to events, rather than responding* – this also links to *'Salience Bias'*, which relies on automatic, default thinking
- Being unduly positive on some points, but highly critical on others ('halo-horns' effect), so *easily swayed by initial impressions* (and this may also be linked to a 'judging' mindset)
- Categorising people, but with little information or awareness of context (the trap of binary thinking) – often associated with *stereotyping and unconscious bias*
- Linking problems or the actions of others to a trait or weakness, but with little analysis of context or intention – *the error of attribution*
- Making a general criticism because of excessive concern about a specific issue, causing an over-reaction to a specific incident or event – *the red flag mindset* (also reinforced by legacy thinking)
- Failing to clarify context or operational/role demands (and failing to maintain direction and consistent standards) – *being indecisive and lacking conviction*

Everyone is susceptible to mindset traps, which can also contribute to implicit/unconscious bias. Assumptions and *reaction* need to be balanced by the professional objectivity that leads to a measured *response*. The likelihood of negative outcomes is reduced through self-awareness, professional standards and clear operational procedures. To make progress, it's important (i) to make standards explicit and (ii) support these with clear reasoning. Building on a meaningful rationale is also an essential step in conveying personal conviction – and starting to change other people's thinking.

Self-management improves significantly when there are feedback processes that enhance transparency and accountability. Police body-cams are an obvious example. In organisations, there is a scope to improve performance through the use of 360-degree feedback, team-referenced review ('team indexing') and well-designed employee surveys. These form part of a process to develop and enhance 'enabling conditions'. The tools contribute to the responsiveness required for long-term success. Senior leadership responsibility also involves introducing systems that protect against human error. These expectations require leaders to develop the awareness and insight that enhances self-management. When faced with a dynamic, shifting context, we need to flex our style in response to different people and situations. This involves anticipating inevitable, but unexpected *Critical Incidents*.[1] There is a need to develop skills that lead to a better appreciation of issues. It's not a cliché for organisations to talk about developing a 'learning culture'. A healthy organisation builds on feedback and develops systems that encourage continuous improvement.

Research suggests that effective leaders do share certain attributes, but these need to be considered in context rather than viewed as 'essential' or 'innate' personality traits. For example, leadership is often associated with *achievement motivation*, but this clearly needs to be seen in context. We might, for example, consider the motivation of a leader in a not-for-profit organisation with that of someone working in a demanding commercial environment. Points of similarity include the need for personal conviction and clarity in defining goals and priorities for action. We also find that people's motivation increases with consistent standards, equitable reward, steady progress (in meaningful activity) and shared purpose. The challenge is to get a clear view of what it takes to be an effective leader.

We are presented with a series of images, ranging from politicians, once labelled as *great leaders*, to short-lived celebrity CEOs. We have stories from the military, sport and history. People also have their own personal notion of what it takes to be a leader. These stories often involve personality traits and the qualities that make someone 'special'. We also find old assumptions that lead to the separation of *leaders* and *followers*. Most often in these stories, the followers are passive. The Anglo-American mythology creates the impression that the leader 'energises people' through a compelling vision, charisma and exceptional personality traits. Unfortunately, this picture looks ever-more outdated. It's the clichéd leadership of old Hollywood films and romantic novels.

In a complex, challenging world, we are now focusing on a different type of leadership. Some of the traditional qualities may add to effectiveness, but the starting point has changed. In the modern world, we increasingly need 'cascaded leadership' with effective decisions being taken by people with expertise, who are close to the action. They also have the perspective and insight required to achieve *balanced processing of information*. Nor is leadership simply about analysis and energising other people; it's also about making sure that effective systems and procedures are put in place. To remain motivated and effective, people need the resources and support that help them resolve problems and achieve objectives. One effect of the COVID-19 pandemic of 2020 was to reveal the weakness of traditional 'strong leadership' and the real implications of living in a VUCA World. Unfortunately, many of our politicians are victims of legacy thinking.

Agile, authentic leaders build on feedback and develop the perception to sense changes in context. They are more able to adapt to changing demands. Awareness of *Superordinate Goals and Principles* helps guide action, which also involves separating the *urgent* and less immediate but *important* tasks. We need to remain clear about overall goals in order to maintain clarity of purpose. Effective leaders are responsive to context, but they are also consistent in their approach. They not only *Direct the Compass* by referencing principles and defining priorities, but also note how activities are completed. Leadership therefore involves not only an appreciation of what needs to be done but also awareness of how objectives should be achieved. In the context of COVID-19, it was people like Jacinda Ardern (previous PM of New Zealand) who took prompt, effective action. This was less evident in many other countries, including the UK, the US and Brazil. The skill comes from seeing things clearly and engaging effectively with others. Leadership also involves developing an awareness of what shapes the motivation and commitment of other people.

In many work scenarios, the 'followers' will be skilled and experienced professionals. The challenge is to *coordinate activities and ensure alignment, across teams and departments*. These goals must match overall objectives. Most organisations have a *Vision* that describes their purpose and values. This will be supported by a *Mission Statement* that describes broad areas of activity, and these provide a point of reference in determining activities across functions. Principles then serve to define how things get done.

Effective leaders not only have responsibility for achieving specific objectives but also need to be mindful of the wider priorities. They need to be aware of the interdependencies beyond their team and ensure positive relationships with business partners and stakeholders. There is a need to manage role relationships and demonstrate an understanding of what other people require. This means that all leaders must be responsive to feedback and develop the *cognitive flexibility* to adapt to new demands. As the context changes, the focus shifts. Traditional 'command and control' thinking reduces agility and undermines the process. The challenge is to create leadership that is close to the action, whilst maintaining alignment and shared purpose.

In the context of sustainable, productive progress, leaders are also at the forefront in shaping organisational culture. In other words, they need to be mindful of how they can build positive work relationships in teams and departments, and create the enabling conditions that support motivation and commitment. It's not always appreciated that there are strong business reasons for developing leadership anchored in authenticity, integrity and shared purpose. These elements contribute not only to people's well-being but also to improved productivity and long-term success. *Charisma* or a *compelling vision* are not enough to win the game. Success increasingly requires *autonomy supportive leadership (ASL)*. The good news is that this builds on skills that can be learned. Effective analysis, personal conviction and clear purpose, backed by *Superordinate Principles* (*Super-Ps*), help us develop a more-effective response and overcome faulty assumptions.

Albert Einstein is attributed with the following comment, apparently dating back to 1929:

> You have to learn the Rules of the Game. And then you have to play better than anyone else.

Achieving Exceptional Performance

Leadership involves developing the ability to see things clearly, prioritise activities and motivate other people. However, there are also wider issues, which can be separated into the internal/external and task/people clusters noted earlier. The broad focus involves consideration of internal issues (within the organisation) and external issues in the wider environment. In both cases, we might then separate activities involving 'People' (e.g.

managing relationships with external contacts) and 'Tasks' (such as defining markets or improving internal procedures). This is useful, as we are reminded that leadership involves looking at systems, resources and 'logistics' as well as the needs and expectations of colleagues, stakeholders, customers and business partners. The various elements in this model also contribute to the overall vision, which is periodically shaken by unpredictable events and technological change.

Many leaders start to lose effectiveness in as little as four to five years, becoming less responsive to external events. *Management derailment* is also an issue and links to problems with relationships. These are managers who lack interpersonal skills, cognitive flexibility and empathy. They fail to develop capability and struggle with complex demands. They may have technical expertise, but important competencies are frequently overlooked in the selection process. If notions of 'high potential' are accompanied by the phrase '*demanding and abrasive*', it should be viewed as a serious concern or even a 'red flag'. It undermines trust, damages people's motivation and also removes any prospect of ASL.

To understand leadership, we need to separate core activities, context and the competencies that contribute to exceptional results. What is required of a leader will vary with the situation, but this involves far more than simply switching from being 'directive' to 'supportive'. We need to understand the factors affecting people's motivation and commitment. There will always be new and unexpected demands. In some cases, there may be a need to deal with complex technical or specialist issues. However, there will always be a need to engage with people, seek their input and scope out problems. There is also a core need to clarify requirements, discuss roles and responsibilities – and create a sense of purpose. These fuel the metrics of success. In *Doughnut Economics*, Kate Raworth makes the point that '*the neoliberal narrative claimed that the market mechanism is what makes firms efficient, and so ignored what goes on inside them*' (p. 88). The reality is that effective leaders create *enabling environments* that unlock discretionary effort and commitment. This requires both insight and the competencies that lead to effective action.

In some instances, the task is clear and the objectives are well defined. However, in other situations the time horizon is extended and interdependencies mean that outcomes become less predictable. With increasing complexity, we start to see the *wicked problems* that defy traditional, reductionist logic. There may well be conflicting views and competing demands. There is then a need for dialogue, empathy and careful evaluation of possible options. Skilled leaders use *Purposeful Conversations* to establish a meaningful rationale and build commitment. This is no longer the world of heroic leaders and simplistic solutions. We move from 'self-evident truth' and the fallacy of *Bounded Rationality*, much loved by economists, to the reality of complex three-dimensional interaction. *The Economist* noted the problem in an article '*Why economics does not understand business: Dogma gets in the way*' (4 April 2023). It states:

> most of what makes for a flourishing business cannot be captured in a tight theory with a few equations. Often it is a matter of how well ideas, information and decision-making spread throughout the firm. And pay is not the only motivation. Strong businesses are shaped by shared values and common ideas about the right way to do things – by corporate culture. People take pride in their work and their workplace. These are not natural subjects for economists.

In daily life, differences of opinion and disagreements are often the norm. This means that the competencies required to deliver outstanding results become increasingly important. These define the behaviour, approach and attributes that differentiate superior performance. They build on underlying strengths that are directed through effective action. Understanding the process is important because it enables energy to be focused effectively. We should also take time to understand the difference between *competence* (skills, knowledge and qualifications) and *competencies*, i.e., the behaviour, capabilities and mindset that link to superior performance.

Skills and knowledge that support operational competence – the ability to perform a task – are simply the *threshold level* that guarantees a minimum level of capability. For example, someone may have relevant skills, but not be a team player. This makes them unsuitable for a number of roles. The classic example involved the assumption that ex-military pilots, with superb flying skills, would make good civilian pilots. Unfortunately, this ignored the importance of teamwork, collaboration and dialogue to support action on the flight deck. Civilian aircraft are more likely to crash if there are problems with ego, interpersonal relationships and poor communication. We can build on this insight when we look at leadership requirements. Many years of experience suggest that organisations require people with capability in three broad areas. The level of ability required in each of these areas will vary, depending on the context and the role demands. We can also separate key elements (specific competencies) within each cluster.

Moving beyond a focus on skills/qualifications (technical capability), i.e., *threshold competence*, many organisations have invested considerable time and effort in developing their own competency and 'strength-based' models. However, despite distinctive labels for each dimension, we find broadly similar themes, moderated by role, work culture and managers' imagination. In broad terms, what *makes a difference* and supports *superior performance* across a wide range of situations can be summarised as follows:

- The ability to evaluate trends, see the bigger picture, assess priorities and monitor activities. These attributes are associated with analysis, reflective thinking, cognitive flexibility and insight.
- Interpersonal skills, enabling effective communication, team ethos, influence and developing capability in others. The process enhances shared purpose, motivation and commitment.
- Personal conviction, initiative and resilience, maintaining focus and overcoming obstacles. There is a willingness to take responsibility, get things done and maintain the quality of outcomes.

The clusters link to the 3H Model that involves *Head* (analysis, planning and monitoring), *Heart* (influencing others and developing capability) and *Hands* (taking action and maintaining direction). The final cluster includes the drive to overcome problems and achieve results.

Barriers to Learning Agility

Learning agility requires cognitive flexibility and has been described as *knowing what to do when you don't know what to do.*[2] It requires the ability to respond to a shift of context, restructure existing knowledge and question assumptions. However, numerous issues create barriers that need to be overcome.

The first step towards positive action involves an appreciation of essential principles and the overall vision, which underpins the *Superordinate Goals*. Leaders clarify what needs to be done by setting direction, showing conviction and taking responsibility. The process starts with personal conviction, linked to translating goals into specific objectives for the team or work group. This involves clarifying priorities and discussing how activities will be completed. The process builds on *Purposeful Conversations*. Leaders communicate the rationale for action. This requires personal conviction, which may be enhanced by *charisma* and a *compelling vision*. However, clear conviction and a meaningful rationale provides the real foundation for action. The aim is to engage people in a way that ensures role clarity, encourages discretionary effort and creates purpose that builds performance. The focus is on how people go about completing activities. Differences in perception create the insight that separates *Star Performers*, including the leaders who achieve exceptional results.

With this in mind, it's important to remember that leadership skills develop over time. We should be wary of any suggestion that leadership depends on specific personality traits or innate strengths. As you gain experience and develop competence, you become better equipped to deal with setbacks and adversity. Insight requires a grasp of context. This broadens our appreciation of boundaries and possible response options. However, reactive thinking blocks useful reflection and ideology undermines a measured response. This is most evident with 'red flag' reactions, and particularly 'dog whistle' politics that cause a knee-jerk reaction. Tripwires permeate social consciousness. The word 'capitalism', for example, describes a way of raising money to do business, and responding quickly to market requirements, but it's amoral, as it's simply a process. It's not some form of unified, corporate identity. In reality, there is wide variation in corporate culture and how things get done. Guiding principles, backed by rules and regulation, are required to control how activities are conducted. It makes no sense to categorise something as a vice or a virtue when there is no fixed point of reference.

However, if greed and asset-stripping shape culture, they destroy sustainability and undermine purpose. Highly leveraged business takeovers, for example, often lead to negative outcomes for end users. Selling the freehold of UK nursing homes, for example, left organisations facing prohibitive rent increases. ChatGPT notes:

> In 2012, Four Seasons Health Care was purchased by private equity firm Terra Firma, which subsequently sold the freehold of many

of the company's properties to a separate entity called H/2 Capital Partners. This left Four Seasons with a significant rental bill, which it was unable to pay, and the company eventually entered into administration in 2019. The example illustrates the concept of asset stripping, which refers to the practice of selling off assets of a company for short-term gain, often at the expense of the company's long-term financial health.

This all occurred with UK government permission.

There is a default mindset, driven by *laissez-faire ideology*. In the UK, for example, people buy second homes in areas with beautiful countryside, escalating prices and damaging local communities. Purchasers can also list these properties as 'holiday homes', leveraging the power of the internet, further adding to property price increases, but with a devastating effect on local housing affordability and provision. Curiously, many middle-class purchasers do not see this as anti-social behaviour. They also enjoy wood burning stoves (in city homes) and somehow overlook the impact on air quality. We safeguard individual freedom, but neglect guiding principles and the consequences for communities.

Politicians who lack insight fail to recognise interdependencies. Prof Mariana Mazzucato has noted that the success of smartphone manufacturers builds on the substantial investment made by the US government in GPS, micro-chips, cellular networks, touchscreens and the internet.[3] Objective analysis of complex interdependencies challenges neoliberal mythology that innovation always comes from individuals acting independently of government. Increasingly, we see that interdependencies are critical to success. In a VUCA world, we must progress from ideology, emotion and opinion to insight, which supports meaningful change. In practical terms, effective leaders are responsive to people's concerns and strive to build robust systems. Future-focused leaders resolve problems, safeguard resources, develop systems and strive to deliver positive outcomes. However, they need essential infrastructure to be in place. They then build motivation, commitment and capability. With enabling conditions, we visualise possibilities and develop a balanced perspective. We identify what went well, define areas for improvement and strive to learn from mistakes.

In contrast, a negative outlook dwells on setbacks, fuels criticism and undermines self-belief. It is psychologically unhealthy, hinders development of competence and reduces our sense of agency. Reactive thinking also triggers emotions that block *balanced processing of information*. A primary goal of future-focused leaders is to help people develop competence and make progress in doing meaningful work. However, activities also need to be aligned with overall goals, which involves thinking about how we create a sense of shared purpose. In Part II, these themes are explored further, with specific suggestions on how to develop leadership capability. The insights also serve as an introduction to consultancy skills.

Tripwires are ever present. We find, for example, that academic psychologists, lacking wider experience, may question the value of competencies. Statistical analysis of Assessment Centre (and 360-degree feedback) shows that competency ratings vary across activities (exercises). It's then argued that this undermines the validity of competency models. However, an alternative view of effective performance is to consider context. We know that assessment ratings are task/activity focused, and link to the source of feedback. This insight is not new. It was the focus of my MSc thesis relating to Assessment/Development Centre design.[4] This revealed that competencies are expressed in different ways, dependent on task and context. Superior performance requires a *flexing of style*, so competencies, e.g. *Influencing Others*, are expressed differently in group-based and 1:1 situations. The view that competencies are anchored in context is backed by other research; most notably, we have the Bell Labs study of *Star Performers*[5] that linked specific competencies to context and results. Focused training over one year resulted in increased productivity.

The real-world limitation of the 360-degree feedback process arises when important issues are hidden under the surface. For example, in the case of Carillion,[6] a British multinational construction and facilities management services company, managers received regular feedback based on a well-designed 360 review. Positively skewed ratings were evident, and may well have reflected the belief '*we must be good because we're here*' (enjoying the C-suite), but the real problem lay elsewhere. The 360 did not focus on financial recklessness, hubris and greed. The 360-degree feedback methodology did not probe the financial systems or the (assumed) quality of the auditing. It was only after Carillion's collapse that KPMG settled a £1.3 billion lawsuit from Carillion creditors over alleged negligence. The collapse of Carillion came after annual accounts were approved by KPMG.[7] Sound corporate governance and transparent systems are critical.

Professionalism requires high standards. Sociologists may suggest that adjusting to role requirements equates to *Emotional Labour* and that ethnic minority groups may face unfair demands. However, we should not conflate issues when reviewing specific role requirements. Organisational psychologists try to look at things with objectivity. As a first step, we clarify what outcomes are required, so review role purpose. We can then ask: *'how do people achieve high performance?'* This helps clarify attributes and underlying strengths, which might include analytical ability, flexibility and compassion. Strengths are expressed through competencies that support exceptional outcomes. Spurious criteria can be challenged. Organisations can cast the net wide to attract suitable candidates from diverse backgrounds. Realistic job previews are important, as these help clarify demands, support mental rehearsal and reduce discrimination. We start with desired outcomes and then work back through the steps. It's not unreasonable to expect candidates' attributes to match role demands, and the pool of candidates can be representative of the wider population.

In a broader context, a UK report (March 2021) from the Commission on Race and Ethnic Disparities[8] concluded that a number of factors affect people's life chances. It found that family structure and social class had a bigger impact than race. Studies reveal, for example, that children of West African heritage living in the UK do well academically. This may, at least in part, link to positive expectations, well-focused, effective support, and a good understanding of systems. We need insight into how things get done and a grasp of possible options. To achieve progress, we need clear goals and an appreciation of how things work. And we all benefit from support that creates insight, enhances capability and builds motivation.

The Importance of Insight

All too often leaders are selected with little assessment of underlying attributes and suitability. Problems follow when assessors have a restricted vocabulary and lack understanding of competencies. Reliance on 'gut feeling' is no substitute for clear analysis. Board members may be swayed by previous success and fail to consider future demands. There are issues of *Corporate Governance* and how challenges will be resolved. *What is the style and approach? What principles dominate?* Lack of insight means that significant elements are not assessed. Performance criteria remain ill-defined and essential competencies are overlooked.

There are always significant risks when organisations are appointing senior-level executives. One stems from leaders with dysfunctional personality traits. They may demonstrate drive and a story of achievement. Any evidence of abrasiveness, harsh risk-taking and excess ambition are played down, or even seen as virtues. A failure to screen out these people from the C-suite (top tier) roles puts the organisation at risk. In contrast, we have 'conscientious', dependable 'time-served' individuals with technical capability and business knowledge. However, this can conceal *cognitive rigidity*, reductionist thinking and misplaced values. These are people who struggle to change mindset and reassess concepts as the context shifts. Some senior-level executives struggle to see a changing reality. Remember that Kodak invented the digital camera, but the Board neglected the new technology. There was a failure to appreciate that the game had changed.

In the UK, the failure of the Post Office to respond to evidence of weaknesses in the 'Horizon' computer software resulted in a major scandal.[9] Innocent people were prosecuted for fraud. It exposed serious shortcomings that went to the top of the organisation. This tale of cover-up and incompetence raises wider questions about the ability of those who appoint senior managers. Do they make explicit (or even understand) the *higher-order principles* that shape competencies? Is there a formal demand for decision-making that safeguards integrity of purpose? Without explicit standards, expedient leaders will conceal mistakes to protect reputation regardless of the cost. Assessment criteria should reference both *cognitive flexibility* and *integrity/authenticity*. There should be a default requirement for ethical action, driven by higher-order principles, even though this may cause short-term discomfort or damage.

When appointing someone to a leadership role, it's important to reflect on these issues. Assessors must resist the charms of the charismatic, the steadiness of the inflexible and the vagaries of those who lack conviction, vision and principles. The *mindset of superior performance* should be captured in competencies backed by guiding principles. Ignore this model and we get complacency, confusion and incompetence.[10] Reflect on your own approach. By way of introduction, *sample statements* linked to leadership competencies are shown below. These are taken from a Pario 360-degree feedback questionnaire:

Setting Direction
   …Display energy, enthusiasm and conviction about future possibilities
Working with People
   …Treat people in a way that makes working life enjoyable
Building Relationships
   …Discuss issues with a range of people to review problems and opportunities

Influencing Others
> *...Listen carefully and respond constructively to differing viewpoints*

Developing People
> *...Make sure that people understand the standards that are expected*

Gaining Commitment
> *...Understand the feelings and views of others on important issues*

Managing Performance
> *...Provide regular, timely feedback to help people improve their performance*

Achieving Results
> *...Demonstrate the drive and resilience to overcome problems*

How would colleagues assess you on each dimension? Note that the attributes include managing people's expectations, identifying interdependencies and evaluating possible outcomes. Also remember that people who gain the label '*demanding and abrasive*' always represent a serious risk. It is informative to review the 2007–2008 Global Financial Crisis and the attributes of the CEOs of Enron, Lehman Brothers and RBS. Unfortunately, far too many executives and politicians still 'default' to the DRAAB model. Their approach is described as '*Demanding*', with a style that is described as '*Robust*', '*Abrasive*', '*Aggressive*' and '*Blunt*'. The 'I' word *Integrity* is replaced by *Impulse* and *Instability*. Feedback from colleagues will also reveal other 'I' words, linked to *Impatience, Irritation and Intimidation*. Lacking insight, rogue operators, including overly ambitious politicians, are guilty of bullying and dysfunctional behaviour, often belatedly explained in terms of '*setting challenging targets*'.

At various points in the book, reference is made to the problems that arise with reductionist thinking. This mindset overlooks underlying patterns, emerging trends, interdependencies and the consequences of action. Reductionist thinking is separate from IQ[11] and creates the dominant mindset in *Finance, Economics, Law and Technology* (the classic FELT professions). It's not the only pattern of thinking in these organisations, but problems develop when it shapes culture and policy. FELT Thinking results in a *closed-loop logic* that misses the bigger picture and fails to anticipate the consequences of decisions.

It's important to note that this is not simply some academic, theoretical, psychological model. It has an impact in the real world. Not least, many in the UK have noted the decline of the London Stock Exchange, clearly evident in the early 2020s. Richard Buxton, formerly of Jupiter Asset Management, was interviewed on the BBC (Radio 4) and described the 'unholy' alliance of *'the accountant, the actuary and the regulator.'* He concluded:

> This has forced pension funds to invest in seemingly safe fixed-income investments and come away from equity investment. Risk Adjusted Returns is one of the key driving forces behind it, where risk is defined as volatility. If you are a quoted company, just because your shares are priced daily in the stock market, you are deemed to be volatile. Now for a long term investor, short-term volatility is completely irrelevant. And yet, the consulting actuaries, because they force pension schemes to consider risk-adjusted returns, have ended up going, 'oh, equities are risky, because they are volatile, whereas fixed income is deemed less risky because it is less volatile'. … It's been entirely driven by originally well-meaning, well-intended regulation, but the consequences have ended up in disaster. There is no equity-orientated saving space (in London) and there is now a recognition that we need to change. Companies are (currently) choosing to list in New York, because they do have a big, deep, liquid, equity-orientated savings culture.

(BBC Today programme, 1 September 2023: interview extract timed 06.18–06.23)

Insights from neuroscience reveal that specific areas of the brain are associated with analytical thinking, logic and language. Other areas support creativity, intuition and holistic thinking. It has been argued that reductionism has led to an over-reliance on the left hemisphere's analytical, problem-focused perspective, at the expense of the right hemisphere's more holistic view of the world.[12] Neuroscience also confirms long-standing psychological insights relating to *Salience Bias*.[13] In organisations, functional reductionism has also contributed to an inability to differentiate *competence* and *competencies*. In the case of the Confederation of British Industry (CBI), the UK's leading 'business interest' representative, the BBC reported in 2023 that the '*CBI hired "toxic" staff and failed to sack offenders*'[14]. The CBI admitted to its members that it paid '*more attention to competence than to behaviour*'. Note that 'competence' refers to technical skills, whereas 'competencies' define wider behaviour – and the approach linked to superior performance. It is worrying that a business advisory group did not appreciate that guiding principles shape competencies. Principles are also critical in developing a business culture that values transparency and accountability.

FELT Thinking reduces anticipation, intuition and lateral thinking. It can also serve to distort and manipulate communication, damaging empathy and responsiveness. Politicians, for example, may divert discussion of 'air quality' (in cities) to issues relating to 'climate change'. This is an expedient, evasive tactic, particularly favoured by individuals not directly affected by local conditions. Emissions clearly impact on health as well as climate. In the UK, for example, vote-seeking opportunists promote the 'freedom of motorists', but ignore the impact of air pollution on communities.[15] This point also highlights the problems that arise with top-heavy government, which undermines cascaded leadership, local autonomy and community-based action.

A lack of institutional memory compounds failures of governance. In March 2023, following the collapse of Silicon Valley Bank, *The Economist* posed the question: *'What went wrong at Silicon Valley Bank?'* This was followed by a wider concern: *'What's wrong with the banks?'* They noted: *'rising interest rates have left banks exposed, and it's time to fix the system (again)'. The Economist* concludes: *'Many years of low inflation and interest rates meant that few considered how the banks would suffer if the world changed and longer-term bonds fell in value'*. This is yet another example of a pattern linked to FELT Thinking.

The FELT Deficit results in systems that fail to anticipate external change. Personality factors add to the limitation, reinforcing a work culture rooted in 'Sensing' and accepting 'facts as presented'. This hinders the ability to see the bigger picture. It's coupled with decision-making anchored in 'Thinking' based on straight-line, logical analysis. There is a tendency to close down on options, applying a 'Judging' mindset to eliminate ambiguity and determine priorities for action. However, the *Sensing-Intuition* perception preferences are not binary; there is a continuum. The problems arise when balance is lacking. Leaders might well pause to reflect on the question: *How well do you assess risk and opportunity?* Whilst 'Sensing-Thinking' leaders maintain a singular focus on the task; they can neglect principles, context and constraints. Volkswagen, for example, developed software to conceal the true level of diesel engine exhaust emissions. From a technical perspective, it was a clever solution, but overlooked *Super-Ps* and the (presumably unforeseen) outcome, which was the *Dieselgate Scandal*.[16]

A contrasting *tripwire* involves passive-aggressive behaviour (PAB). This can be reflected in sarcasm, procrastination or deliberate inefficiency. It tends to be associated with not only strong opinions and entrenched personal values but also a lack of assertiveness and influencing skills.

Whilst *Feeling* (the cognitive function) can support empathy and enhance decision-making, the flip side is dysfunctional. People who score high on measures of PAB tend to have strong personal opinions and values that they are unwilling to compromise.[17] This mindset is also associated with a lack of assertiveness, which requires recognition of alternative perspectives, and inadequate influencing skills.[18] Individuals who are passive-aggressive may seek to manipulate others, not least with calls to 'values' and 'principles'. However, it's important that leaders consciously surface issues and promote dialogue. Don't be deterred by emotionally loaded tripwires. The leader must clarify context, define constraints and confirm the consequences of action.

Future-focused leaders, notably in charities, not-for-profit organisations and the public sector, must deal with the QOBO problem. This is more accurately described as QOBO-V, which relates to people who are *Quickly Offended By Others' Views/Values*. They react to a comment by 'classifying and categorising' without first seeking clarification of context or conditions. This may well reflect elements of 'Cancel Culture', but can also be linked to the PAB issue. For example, some pursue an emotive, singular form of 'social justice' or concerns about 'redress', but do so without reference to *Super-Ps*. Excessive concern about historical wrong does not support future progress. Psychologically, it's healthier to visualise possibilities and create a sense of agency. This requires solution-focused insight and action that delivers sustainable, positive progress. A narrowing of perspective, as well as emotional disturbance, increases as political mindset shifts, whether to the left or to the right. It becomes another variant of the FELT Deficit.

The 'FELT' acronym has also been linked to the phrase *Failure to Embrace Lateral Thinking*, notably with reference to the negative implications for policy and practice in health and social care.[19] The term *lateral thinking* was itself coined by Edward de Bono, who suggested six 'thinking hats' (1985) that help improve creativity. With increasing complexity and interdependence, uncertainty and ambiguity are the new (external) default settings. Leadership training needs to recognise this uncertainty. Coincidentally, *Superposition* (Feynman, 1982) is central to quantum computing. This observes that a flipped coin, in the air, has a probability of being heads or tails. Both events are possible and coexist before the final outcome.

There is scope to get better at perceiving options and consequences, but many organisations are currently ill-equipped to deal with a rapidly shifting context. Perception and response are influenced by various elements, notably *cognitive function* and *psychological type*. Cognitive function is shaped by our neural networks and disposition, but important elements are also influenced by education and culture. They affect perception and response. This is discussed further in the introduction to Part II. The FELT mindset is prevalent in banks/finance, police forces and technology/engineering, but also other groups that (i) favour order and predictability, (ii) operate and maintain inflexible systems and (iii) fail to recognise the boundaries of their expertise, and generally overlook the need to apply *Super-Ps*. In Family Law, for example, the concept of '*Parental Alienation*' has been applied without any analysis of patterns of coercive and controlling behaviour, and with undue reliance on speculative theories that lack empirical support.[20] Progressive ideology invariably restricts analysis, neglects research and easily slides into FELT Thinking.

It's not only institutions that have a restricted perspective. Professional groups, including sociologists, clinicians and academic psychologists, have little appreciation of *Organisational Psychology*. They therefore lack understanding of how systems, context, culture and *Super-Ps* affect resilience, motivation and behaviour. *Occupational Psychology* focuses on individual and group performance, motivation and employee well-being. *Organisational Psychology* takes a broader view, addressing *the functioning of organisations, leadership, culture and overall organisational dynamics*. The insights help improve performance, purpose and engagement. Real progress should build on substantive research evidence, but is more often undermined by personal opinion, misplaced assumptions and faulty judgement.

Subjective opinion can quickly slip into emotionally driven ideology, which inevitably results in bad governance. It is an ever-present risk to charities, the Third Sector and organisations that lose clarity of purpose. Not all principles have equal status or confer automatic legitimacy. Too many organisations also carry the burden of leaders who fail to recognise interdependencies, neglect customer or client expectations, and are reluctant to defend the culture. They also fail to anticipate the consequences of decisions. *Super-Ps* support the design of systems, guide actions and help maintain focus. If guiding principles are neglected, the culture of the organisation is left vulnerable. In the case of the CBI (noted previously), there was a failure to protect cultural values. We have too many leaders who operate with a restricted perspective, a 'tick box' mindset, and struggle with abstract reflection. They are slow to embrace new ideas, lack strategic awareness and often resist moves to develop greater accountability.

Viewed from a historical perspective, it seems likely that *Systemic Educational Deficits* have contributed to reductionist, functional ways of thinking. With this legacy, FELT Thinking (traditionally characterised as 'left brain' and reductionist) is the norm. Educational institutions are themselves left vulnerable when higher-order principles are neglected and insight is lacking. Insights from *Organisational Psychology* are important. Outcomes are rarely binary or captured in a few words. In England, the *Office for Standards in Education, Children's Services and Skill* (OFSTED) has for many years categorised schools with short labels, e.g. 'Outstanding' and 'Inadequate'. However, these simplistic categories neglect more nuanced evaluation based on meaningful assessment criteria. We find that reduction-ism operates with a self-referenced logic that overlooks wider consider-ations. In schools, careless categorisation undermines guiding principles and serves to increase work-related stress, and also undermines teachers' motivation.

The legacy of 19th-century thinking runs deep. Clearly there is value, in terms of efficiency and 'getting things done', of straight line, logical analysis backed by a clear focus on operational goals. The problem is that this is no longer sufficient, particularly when values, principles and ESG move centre-stage. The challenges require enhanced critical thinking with a grasp of context, causal effect and consequences. This also means that we would all benefit from a basic understanding of multivariate statistics, regression analysis, 'simple structure' (the primary factors in a model) and the insights offered by structural equation modelling. Finance professionals will need these skills to stay a few steps ahead of AI. We might also note that when vocabulary is restricted, analysis is curtailed and everyday conversation lacks essential concepts. This is one reason for culture wars, when both sides lack essential insights. We find that models with binary outcomes omit other, more important variables. The concept of 'learning style', for exam-ple, is not the 'field-independent/field-dependent' dichotomy presented on many training courses. This oversimplifies the complexity of cognitive processes.[21] Whilst it can be tough to escape outdated theory, solution-focused conversations can help change mindset and behaviour. A positive shift of culture requires insight, which can cascade through the organisa-tion. Whilst a talented CEO may shape strategy, team leaders carry direct responsibility for creating the enabling conditions that contribute to future success.

Enabling Conditions, which contribute to equity and well-being at work, are enhanced by government policy. For example, virtually all countries offer **paid** maternity leave. US policy is stated in the Family and Medical Leave Act (FMLA), which requires '*covered employers to provide at least 12 weeks of **unpaid** family leave time after the birth or adoption of a child. Multiple exceptions to this law exist*'.[22] Declining birthrates may prompt change, but in 2023 we can only contrast US policy with that of Germany, which offers 14 weeks (full salary) and the option of a further 44 weeks at 65% of income. Italy provides 21 weeks at 80% of income, and an additional (optional) 26 weeks at 30%. Policy is affected not only by national wealth but also by a grasp of longer-term social, educational and economic benefits. Economists note a 'return on investment' (ROI) linked to spending on young children and cite research, e.g. Perry Preschool Project (2010). We can look at international literacy rates[23] (and see that standards need to be improved). There is evidence that organisations *in developed countries* have to '*adapt their activities to compensate for the poor skills of their employees*'.[24] Leaders considering the implications of ESG (and equity of outcomes) might take time to review *10 Facts about Global Literacy*.[25] Note the benefits of the high levels of literacy, and potential opportunities that are evident, e.g. in Vietnam (where government policy clearly values education). Equity is not something achieved through misplaced ideology. It's best delivered by clear analysis of strategic factors that shape outcomes – and clarity on the steps leading to positive results.

Unfortunately, strategic analysis and grasp of interdependencies are lost in reductive thinking. In the UK, the BBC observed (May 2023) that '*a government preoccupied with Brexit and political turmoil may have missed the start of a carve-up of future industries between giant trading blocs coming out of the pandemic*'.[26] Ad hoc agreements with individual manufacturers do not represent an integrated strategy. Too many politicians operate within a paradigm shaped by distorted history, nationalism and outdated notions of politics, philosophy and economics. These are the people who deny evidence of *invisible tripwires*. They also fail to appreciate the role of the state in creating an 'enabling environment' that supports future success. Education and healthcare are critical. *The Times*, for example, noted in July 2023: *the UK has one of the lowest numbers of PET scanners per person in the developed world*.[27] This is not the result of chance or some *upset of nature*. Future outcomes require strategic insight, but this is blocked by the inherent limitations of traditional, reductionist thinking. Equity of outcome needs informed vision and resources.

The late Charlie Munger, vice chairman of Berkshire Hathaway (2023), commented on YouTube:

> If I had to name one factor that dominates bad decisions, it would be what I called 'denial'. If the truth is unpleasant enough, people kind of… their mind plays tricks on them and they think it isn't really happening. And of course, that causes enormous destruction of business, where people will go on throwing money into the way they used to do things, and this isn't going to work at all well.[28]

More broadly, we need to identify elements that hinder anticipation and slow effective development and contribute to denial. Leaders might benefit from a better appreciation of the *Kessler Syndrome*. The original model focused on ever-escalating collisions of space junk. However, we can also (in the workplace) envisage a series of internal issues, interdependencies and failures that have a cumulative effect. An event triggers a cascade of problems, each magnifying the consequences of others. At the very least, this will disrupt operational functioning. In many instances, it could threaten the future of the organisation.

Notes

1 Critical Incident Technique: See Wikipedia Summary.
2 *Tips for Improving Your Learning Agility* (December 2020). Center for Creative Leadership.
3 Mazzucato, M. (2013). *The Entrepreneurial State: Debunking Public vs. Private Sector Myths*. Anthem Press.
4 Robertson, I. T., Gratton, L., & Sharpley, D. (1987). The psychometric properties and design of managerial assessment centres: Dimensions into exercises won't go. *Journal of Occupational Psychology*, 60, 187–196.
5 Kelley, R., & Caplan, J. (1993). How Bell Labs Creates *Star Performers*. *Harvard Business Review*, July–August 1993 … Available at: https://hbr.org/1993/07/how-bell-labs-creates-star-performers
6 Carillion: Summary. Available on Wikipedia.
7 The Guardian. (Friday, 17 February 2023). Available at: https://www.theguardian.com/business/2023/feb/17/kpmg-pays-13bn-to-settle-negligent-auditing-claim-by-carillion-creditors
8 Commission on Race & Ethnic Disparities Report. Available at: https://www.gov.uk/government/publications/the-report-of-the-commission-on-race-and-ethnic-disparities

9 The Horizon Scandal. Available at: https://www.bbc.co.uk/news/business-56718036

10 BBC Report (August 2023). Councils failing to tackle anti-social behaviour. Available at: https://www.bbc.co.uk/news/uk-politics-66512729

11 Stanovich, K. E. (2009). *What intelligence tests miss: The psychology of rational thought*. Yale University Press.

12 McGilchrist. (2021). *The Matter with Things: Our Brains, Our Delusions, and the Unmaking of the World*. Perspectiva Press.

13 Salience (Neuroscience) – Wikipedia Summary (includes reference to Salience Bias).

14 BBC Report. Available at: https://www.bbc.co.uk/news/business-65375311

15 BBC Article. Available at: https://www.bbc.co.uk/news/uk-politics-66351785

16 Wikipedia: Volkswagen emissions scandal.

17 Klotz, A. C., Hirsch, R. D., & Gower, A. L. (2015). The role of passive-aggressive personality traits in negotiation: Relationships among personality, behavior, and outcomes. *Journal of Personality Assessment*, 97(3), 309–318.

18 Frodi, A., Macaulay, J., & Thome, P. R. (1977). Are passive-aggressive personalities maladjusted? *Journal of Consulting and Clinical Psychology*, 45(6), 1206–1215.

19 Martin, L. E., Cook, G., & Hatzidimitriadou, E. (2016). The failure to embrace lateral thinking: Implications for policy and practice in health and social care. *Health & Social Care in the Community*, 24(2), 135–144.

20 BBC Report. (September 2023). Family Courts. Available at: https://www.bbc.co.uk/news/uk-66531409

21 Sternberg, R. J., & Zhang, L. F. (2001). *Perspectives on thinking, learning, and cognitive styles*. Routledge.

22 World Population Review: Summary data. Available at: https://worldpopulationreview.com/country-rankings/maternity-leave-by-country

23 Wikipedia. *List of countries by literacy rates*.

24 Mallows & Litster. (2016). Literacy as supply and demand. Zeitschrift für Weiterbildungsforschung – Report. *Journal for Research on Adult Education*, 39(2), 171–182.

25 Literacy Review. Available at: https://lukukeskus.fi/en/10-facts-about-global-literacy/

26 BBC News. *Is the UK too late to beat the US in the global trade war?* 14 May 2023.

27 'Step change' for Alzheimer's treatment as new drug lecanemab is licensed in US. The Times, 7 July 2023.

28 YouTube: *Charlie Munger Roasting Active Investors and Fund Managers*.

Chapter 3

Motivation and Commitment

Effective leaders need to understand issues that affect motivation and impact on performance. It's a mistake to assume that motivation is simply driven by money and reward. An effective model should explain (i) what influences people's thinking and (ii) how important elements interact. To gain insight, we must understand people's expectations, sense of identification and the value of outcomes. This means that people are unlikely to commit effort if they (1) think the task is beyond their capability, (2) the outcome is not worth the time and effort, or (3) the activity goes against social norms and guiding principles. There is also a point when perception and mindset may shift. We may, for example, invest time and effort repairing something or attempting to rebuild a relationship, but at some point simply decide that it's no longer viable.

Important insights are obscured by inadequate models, not least those developed by economists with little understanding of human psychology. They refer to Adam Smith, but neglect his *Theory of Moral Sentiments* and the emphasis on social responsibility. Unfortunately, *FELT Thinking* has for many years influenced politicians and policy. One example of this hubris can be found in *Agency Theory*, developed in the 1970s, notably a paper by Jensen and Meckling (1976). This suggests that conflicts of interest may arise between agents (managers) and principals (shareholders) due to divergent interests, leading to 'agency costs'. It's argued that these costs can include inefficient decision-making and 'moral hazard' (e.g. excessive risk-taking without personal responsibility). It assumes that the prime element of motivation is self-interest and that financial rewards (e.g. share options) are needed to secure alignment.[1] In reality, the argument simply reveals a lack

DOI: 10.4324/9781003439707-4

of psychological insight. Motivation is complex, and the underlying dynamics of the process generally contradict the speculative theories of economists. The hubris flowing from the 1970s has contributed to the development of toxic cultures and dysfunctional organisations.

Research indicates that financial incentives can actually undermine intrinsic motivation.[2,3] We also know that to develop trust, we require a sound foundation, not least a reasonable level of economic security. This is not enhanced by excessive pay ratios of CEOs relative to workers. The *Institute for Policy Studies* noted that in the US, CEO–worker pay ratios averaged 830 to 1 in 2020.[4] This lowers employee morale, reduces productivity and increases disaffection. It runs counter to essential *Superordinate Principles* (*Super-Ps*) and damages social cohesion. Commenting on the excessive pay of top executives, Warren Buffet made the observation: '*the system has evolved in such a way that many of them take huge sums, and I think that's obscene, but I can tell you, there isn't much you can do about it. The system feeds on itself… it's not anything that's going to go away… the people who have their hands on the switch are the beneficiaries of the system*'. Charlie Munger added, '*at the very top, corporate salaries in America are too high. That is not a good thing for a civilization, when the leaders are not regarded as dealing fairly with the institutions*'.[5]

Effective leaders develop enabling conditions and aim to encourage discretionary effort. Reflect on the question: *Why do we sometimes choose to commit extra effort, or persist with a problem until we find a solution?* This is not simply because of differences in personality (or pay). Very often there are issues relating to leadership, work culture and the quality of work relationships. Motivation increases with *shared purpose* and when the value of our work is recognised. Positive relationships also contribute to trust, identification and engagement. Identification creates commitment and contributes to purpose, effort and resilience. It binds people to action and helps maintain motivation during tough times. However, motivation is reduced by setbacks, lack of progress and the unwelcome and unresolved issues that fuel a toxic culture.

There are of course differences in personality, which means that individuals vary in their level of achievement motivation. However, personality traits do not explain wide variations within similar professional groups. In many cases, people complete psychometric tests and structured interviews as part of a selection process. Test publishers and psychometricians proclaim the 'significance' of the assessments. However, validity is limited. *Conscientiousness* (a Big Five trait) is often mentioned because it is the

most predictive, but in reality achieves modest correlations with job satisfaction and performance,[6] explaining less than 5% of the variance.[7] To understand motivation, we need to look beyond personality traits.

In an organisational context, differences in motivation may well result
from the team leader's behaviour. Whilst some teams are highly motivated,
others dream of escaping a dysfunctional boss. Disaffection escalates when
people don't feel valued, support is inadequate and trust is squandered.
The problem is made worse by (i) a lack of prompt action to address performance issues and (ii) the perception that some receive preferential
treatment. This damages professionalism and the need for fairness, equity
and 'social justice'. Effective leaders work to confirm purpose and ensure
progress. This helps build identification and commitment, usually expressed
as 'employee engagement'. *Identification, shared purpose, development and
support help enhance motivation.* Exceptional performance is not simply a
result of personality traits or people's innate qualities. It requires effective
leadership that serves to unlock underlying potential.

For anyone aspiring to a leadership role, or to enhance effectiveness, it's
essential to understand motivation. This insight can be increased with
appropriate tools. A prime function of an employee survey should be to
inform team leaders of the *action steps* needed to improve engagement. It
can offer insight into the drivers of motivation and commitment.
Unfortunately, this insight is often lacking. The situation is not helped by
the outdated motivation theory presented on training courses, including
Maslow's *Hierarchy of Needs*. To take effective action, it's important to clarify
the elements that affect behaviour. You can start the process by reflecting
on your own experiences. For example, can you recall the following?

1. An activity you found positive and energising
2. An activity that encouraged initiative and enthusiasm
3. An incident or setback that reduced your motivation

Think about the skills required, the support available, the rate of progress
and the value of the outcome. Finally, also think about other (tedious)
activities that *have to be completed*, such as doing a tax return. What does
this tell you about motivation in situations where the task is important, but
not much fun? Perhaps this is best described as '*the motivation of
obligation*'.

Motivation does not fit neatly into 'boxes' or predefined levels, but there
are *hygiene factors*, such as *reasonable work conditions* and a *reasonable*

level of economic security. What is regarded as *acceptable* is shaped by context and creates *threshold criteria*. We need food and shelter in the same way that we need clean air and water. Then, quite separately, we have things that contribute to motivation and discretionary effort. This means that if you travel 15 miles to a restaurant, it is more likely to be a special occasion motivated by *relationships* rather than the need for food. There may even be *social status* in going to a special place. We shift our perspective by applying a lens shaped by points of reference, which include our *personal anchors*. You might, for example, be reluctant to walk three miles in the rain, but would do so willingly to help a close friend. Our behaviour is not driven by instincts or 'levels' or hierarchies. What matters are (i) expectations, (ii) the type of lens filtering our view (of context, capability and principles) and (iii) the value of the outcome. This anticipation and evaluation will shape meaning, purpose and direction. We also react strongly when binding principles are compromised. For example, in the UK, people's reaction to politicians breaking Covid 'lock down' rules, which the rest of the population had to follow.

A significant leadership challenge involves situations that start with initial agreement, but also require ongoing commitment. There may be difficult conversation about objectives, timescales and approach. We need to decide priorities and how best to meet goals. Ideally, people are *intrinsically motivated*, and it is often assumed that this is sufficient for high performance. They are more likely to demonstrate discretionary effort and initiative. Whilst this is true up to a point, it neglects an important step in the process. Without dialogue and direction, there is a risk that people may direct their energy and attention in inappropriate ways. Technical specialists, for example, may get immersed in detail, whilst other professionals can lose sight of the bigger picture of future possibilities and current constraints. We start to see functional divisions and the 'silo mentality' that leads to a fragmented response. Energy and resources are not used effectively.

It's important to recognise that not all activities are intrinsically interesting. Some are significant, rather like your tax return. There are some things that have to be done to a high standard. Important tasks are easily overlooked unless systems are put in place, and everyone needs a clear understanding of interdependencies. At work, this is more easily achieved when people appreciate the value of activities and are aware of the expectations of others. In the past, *Bounded Rationality* has been used to excuse shortcomings in communication.[8] Problems arise when organisations lack

Purposeful Conversations neglect feedback and fail to appoint leaders who anticipate important issues and reflect on possible outcomes.

To understand motivation, we need to identify critical elements. These include the quality of social relationships, scope for meaningful activity and a sense of purpose. It's also important to appreciate people's underlying *core needs* for competence (developing skills and capability), autonomy (self-direction and control over activities) and 'relatedness'. The last element involves a sense of connection with others. It builds on trust, fairness and reciprocal support. Integrity and authenticity are important, particularly for younger, educated people. The elements also contribute to the process of developing capability and building intellectual capital. This *internal capability* can be measured, in part, by focused surveys. People are motivated by purpose, progress in meaningful activity and trust-based relationships. We find that well-being is enhanced through meaningful activity that enhances competence, autonomy and relatedness.

Our ability to remain motivated is increased when we can identify with our work and feel committed to the organisation. The manager or team leader plays an important part in this process. They help create the enabling conditions required for exceptional performance. Personal conviction and a clear view of objectives is supported by dialogue and a meaningful rationale. The challenge of building engagement is enhanced through the use of *Purposeful Conversations* that enhance *Awareness, Insight, Meaning and Support (AIMS)*. Motivation is underpinned by meaningful work, role clarity, opportunities to use initiative and resolve problems. However, it is also maintained and strengthened through commitment, which builds on relationships, identification and shared purpose. *We are more likely to commit effort to tasks that are not intrinsically motivating if they are important to peers/colleagues and contribute to overall outcomes.*

However, our interest in things that are not interesting or 'attention grabbing' can quickly start to decline. Our attention is boosted by regular updates, feedback and dialogue that helps us maintain focus.[9] These operational imperatives, default thinking and active, external focus are neglected in traditional theory. In the past, we find models of motivation with pyramids and speculative 'levels', but no evidence of validity. People do not move up some notional hierarchy! However, there are *core needs* (relatedness, competence and autonomy) and acquired *secondary needs*, e.g. the need for power and control, which add to the model. Insight into key factors is central to positive outcomes. Context will prompt questions for team leaders. These include the following: *What level of direction or consultation is appropriate? How demanding is the task?*

Setting Objectives and Creating Incentives

We assess *what to do* and how much effort to apply. These calculations may be quite subjective, but they affect how people respond. And it is possible to identify key elements in the process. This is important because it enables leaders to better understand how to build motivation and commitment. Some factors have little direct impact on motivation as they are threshold (hygiene) elements. However, recognition, financial security and equity are relevant. Material possessions also link to self-esteem and status (relative to some reference group). However, the links are not straightforward. Reward is best viewed in the context of what is reasonable and paid to others doing similar work. Increasingly, people also ask why large bonuses are paid to executives for simply doing their job to the target 'superior performance' standard.

At some point, the greed of top CEOs might be curbed. As people develop an expectation of fairness, the principle of *Social Equity* becomes more important. Once reward achieves a satisfactory level, energy comes from meaning and purpose. Cultural norms define the boundaries. Money and bonuses can drive short-term motivation, but may also undermine long-term commitment. See ChatGPT Insights on *Performance Related Pay* (PRP) in Part III. Research also highlights that 'relative disadvantage', i.e., income inequality, creates problems. Global happiness and well-being surveys show that higher levels of income inequality are associated with lower average happiness scores. Positive factors include social trust, access to public services and social mobility. They serve to enhance social cohesion and well-being.

People receive high salaries when businesses can offer that level of reward. Personal experience, e.g. in completing executive assessments after a takeover, confirms that high salary may not equate to talent. The financial sector creates its own brand of hubris. Reward and recognition serve to enhance people's self-esteem, but we should remember that there are two types of self-esteem. The first is classified as '*robust*' and draws on inner resources and Psychological Capital (*PsyCap*). The second is '*fragile*' and bolstered by possessions, status and recognition. Unfortunately, fragile individuals are less able to handle feedback, and are more sensitive to perceived criticism and setbacks. In extreme cases, this may reflect a narcissistic personality disorder. Problems develop in organisations that are unresponsive to external demands, lack transparency and neglect feedback. We like to note our strengths, but we need maturity (and openness) to acknowledge errors and recognise the limits of our capability. Effective leaders value feedback that helps shift *points of reference.*

Goal and role clarity are important elements of motivation. People are also more likely to engage in activities that satisfy the core needs for competence, autonomy and relatedness. Acquired secondary needs, shaped by personality traits and early experience, are also significant. Henry Murray (*Explorations in Personality,* 1938) coined the term *Environmental Press* to describe important elements, e.g. deprivation, isolation and neglect, which impact on people's desire for power, achievement or affiliation. With relevant skills, training and experience, these attributes contribute to *Personal Strengths* and support role-related competencies. We also find that when people are able to apply their strengths, e.g. through challenging, meaningful work, they can become immersed in the activity. This is described as a state of 'flow' (Csikszentmihalyi, 1990). The task or activity is immersive and pushes capability. It might involve a technical task, or resolve a difficult problem for a customer. Competencies align with the challenge. However, this also means that you should not appoint, to a customer-facing advisory role, a technician with poor interpersonal skills. Fortunately, *Artificial Intelligence* can now offer *a face with a smile*, endless patience, sympathetic enquiry and access to an ever-expanding database of knowledge. Many professionals need to develop new insights, acquire future-focused capability, and prepare for the inevitable advance of AI.

From a leader's perspective, it's important to recognise that not all activity is intrinsically motivating. Individual activities need to be aligned with wider objectives. The challenge is to maintain people's motivation over time, which is easier to achieve when there is effective teamwork, shared purpose and underlying commitment. *Extrinsic Task Motivation*, which relates to less interesting but important activities, requires energy to maintain focus. Appropriate systems will contribute to professional rigour and discipline. Regular discussions provide the opportunity to check progress, clarify requirements and review the expectations of others. The process enables the team leader to confirm and agree key points. This sets activities in the wider context, ensuring progress with full awareness of important interdependencies.

Traditionally, there has been a tendency to categorise 'ability' and 'motivation' in terms of personality traits, strengths and intelligence. However, operational experience is critical, notably in helping people develop the *Personal Resources* and *PsyCap*. This underpins resilience and the ability to deal with challenges, and also resonates with the *Job Demands and Resources* (JD-R) model. Every job creates demands and people need the personal resources to deal with them. We also know that less experienced people (and anyone faced with new challenges) can benefit from dialogue and support. An effective leader seeks to understand people's ability, assess *confirmed competence* and gauge their breadth of experience, viewed in the context of work demands.

Management Standards and the *Motivational Pathway*

In the UK, the Health and Safety Executive (HSE) have set out *Management Standards* that cover six aspects of work that, if not properly managed, via competencies, capability and involvement, are associated with poor health, lower productivity and increased absence. These standards relate to *Work Design* and are backed by extensive research. The key areas need to be well managed by developing a clear understanding of actions contributing to positive outcomes. This helps minimise the pressure people experience at work. The elements linked to the HSE 'Management Standards' can be summarised as follows:

- **Demands**: which relate to employees' workload, work patterns and the work environment
- **Control**: the discretion employees experience (with reference to control of their work activities)

- **Support**: access to appropriate resources, encouragement and constructive feedback
- **Relationships**: positive working that avoids unacceptable, dysfunctional behaviour
- **Role Clarity**: clear goals, avoiding conflicting role demands
- **Change**: effective management and communication of change

If we feel we lack the ability, experience and self-belief to deal with a problem, we may reduce discretionary effort and 'switch off'. Internalised, 'reflective questions' a team leader might consider include the following:

- *What's required to clarify priorities, or identify key steps?*
- *How can I (or the team member/s) gain insight from others?*
- *Is there value in connecting with people outside the team?*
- *How do we clarify the wider context, and/or identify opportunities for support?*

Transformational Leadership theory suggests that *individualised consideration* is important. Not least, this is because ability is affected by self-belief. People's perception of *their own ability and experience* shapes their mindset. Constructive feedback enhances competence, builds self-belief (personal conviction) and improves resilience. Remember that we can easily overlook context, which shapes competence. As noted previously, we need to learn the rules of the game. It's important to understand the 'why' the 'what' and the 'how'. This awareness builds on ability, insight and conviction. Issues relating to role and goal clarity are important if people are to focus their energy effectively.

Ability, experience and insight are a resource, but they need to be activated in an operational context. We know that people with a high need to achieve are more likely to set themselves challenging but realistic goals. *Goal Setting Theory* also shows that difficult goals encourage high performance, but people must have the underlying ability, self-belief, resources and support. Remember that motivation can be viewed in terms of (i) engaging in discretionary behaviour and (ii) maintaining effort over time. It raises questions about what we choose to do and how much energy we commit to an activity. Helping people maintain motivation is one responsibility of the leader. However, fresh leadership challenges arise with remote working, virtual teams and people operating in different locations.

Leaders need to understand the elements affecting outcomes. A clear model helps you to plan interventions and maintain focus. The first cluster in the model involves ability and self-belief. However, there is a risk that we see these issues simply in terms of personality traits, 'strengths' or intelligence. The publishers of psychometric tests may have encouraged this perspective. Other factors, such as experience, help us develop the *PsyCap* required to handle challenges. This links to the JD-R model and also supports the useful process of *Job Crafting*. (See ChatGPT Insights in Part III.) Leaders can develop people's skills, experience and confidence. They create energy by showing conviction that problems can be overcome. Insight is enhanced by ongoing feedback and solution-focused coaching that enhances people's self-belief and helps change mindset. One critical insight, a probing question or a significant, contrasting example, can totally change thinking.

Effective leaders work to ensure individual and team activities are aligned with overall objectives. *Goal Setting Theory* suggests that people respond well to challenging and demanding goals, but these need to be clearly defined. However, we also know that people move forward at different speeds. *Superordinate Goals* help avoid potential conflict, fragmentation and functional 'silo' thinking. *Super-Ps* are required to guide activities and inform *Environmental, Social Governance* (ESG). Developing Vision, Mission and Principles helps clarify critical questions of *Why, What* and *How?*

There is always a risk that groups develop separate identities and pursue divergent goals. With social media, polarisation can quickly increase, fuelled by distorted opinion. More generally, healthy democracies will require 'three-party' systems, backed by a single transferable vote (to safeguard the centre). This will encourage consensus and help overcome extremism. The 'leadership lesson' is that there is a need to identify the weakness of the system.

In the context of motivation, a model must explain how leaders create purpose, clarify roles and develop people's ability. If done well, this contributes to the energy, enthusiasm and initiative required to meet or exceed objectives. The rationale for action needs to be meaningful, and the model should identify the critical elements that affect outcomes. The *Motivational Pathway* helps map the process. *Purposeful Conversations* build on neuroscience and can help increase motivation and commitment. The practical steps are discussed further in Part II.

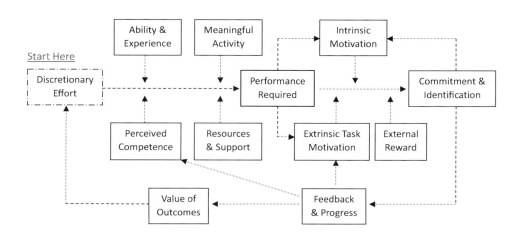

In considering *Discretionary Effort*, elements 1–4 of the *Motivational Pathway* highlight the importance of experience, competence, self-belief, meaningful activity and support. Before committing real effort, people assess the value and importance of the activity. Sometimes this will be self-evident, but leaders can help create purpose and confirm process. Points to consider in any discussion include the following: *How does this work contribute to overall outcomes? Do people feel they have the ability to meet new demands? Are there opportunities for people to develop their competence? What support will be available?*

If the 'effort-outcome' equation fails to meet expectations, people will 'switch off'. This is evident in the 'lying flat' (*tangping*) response of over-worked young people in China, and/or those faced with high rates on unemployment. The sensible response is to reject traditional ideas of 'struggle' and favour psychological health over consumerism. This later evolved into *bai lan*, which translates as 'let it rot'. It reflects a retreat from pursuit of unrealistic, unattainable goals. Psychological theory might identify elements of *learned helplessness*, which is triggered by setbacks and loss of hope. Even if conditions change, people are slow to respond. Insight on how we view and respond to situations is clarified by reference to neuroscience, which reveals that the *Salience & Emotion Network* (SEN) can prompt 'active situational processing' by engaging the *Executive Control Network* (ECN). More routinely, we use the *Default Mode Network* (DMN), which switches to familiar pathways, thinking and assumptions. This is internally referenced. The autopilot operates when patterns are established and we follow a set routine. The SEN 'scout' triggers default scripts. If nothing new engages the brain, it's more difficult to get engaged, active, logical thinking.[10]

It has been noted that 'Gen Z' (Centennial Generation) acquired the mindset of *Quiet Quitting*. This implies that you do your job, but reduce discretionary effort and the 'loyalty' associated with working long hours. Disaffection is more likely when leaders neglect the *Motivational Pathway*, and this 'disconnect' is more likely with younger people. However, getting stuck in a DMN loop can lead to a loss of energy, hinder external response and undermine purpose. Education changes awareness and raises expectations, but it can also cause tension when options don't align with higher-order principles. Unrealistic promises damage trust. Unfortunately, closed loop SEN-DMN thinking patterns do little to develop competence and self-efficacy.

The elements linked to effort-outcome perceptions shape the first part of the *Motivational Pathway*. However, leaders also need to help people maintain focus on activities that are not intrinsically motivating. Examples might include *threads of communication* with colleagues, and *active anticipation* of operational requirements. This 'diligence' requires *Extrinsic Task Motivation*, which deteriorates over time, but can be supported through dialogue. Systems and processes also need to be created to safeguard operational procedures. The enhancement may involve colleagues, possibly in other locations, getting regular updates on new developments, or clarifying changes in design, or the steps in a process, or updates to a mechanical function. *Do colleagues know, for example, what happens to the 'O' rings in cold weather?* Leaders need to identify interdependencies and safeguard less 'accountable' or indirect (but significant) activities that can affect overall outcomes. The motivation to complete mundane tasks will fade unless the rationale for action has become fully internalised in professional thinking. Operations always need to be supported by a meaningful rationale and backed by clear procedures and appropriate feedback loops.

The Pario *Motivational Pathway* draws on expectancy theory, goal-setting and elements of the *Job Characteristics Model* (Hackman & Oldham, 1976). This confirms the importance of meaningful activity, task variety, control (discretion) and role clarity. The Pario model also builds on insights from *Self-Determination Theory* (SDT), which highlights people's needs to develop *Competence, Autonomy and Relatedness*, i.e., positive relationships. SDT also clarifies how ideas become '*internally regulated*', as the rationale for action becomes part of one's own thinking. *Superordinate Goals and Principles* support the process and create 'boundaries for action'. We also need to consider the importance of commitment, which underpins longer-term motivation and builds on relationships, trust and identification.

This helps engage people and sustain them in following-through on activities. *Employee Engagement* combines professional motivation and a *psychological contract* that encourages identification with the organisation. Factors such as brand, reputation and social responsibility affect people's perceptions. Finally, the **Progress Principle** is also important in maintaining motivation. This involves incremental, positive advance, and it's significant in our day-to-day work. It's been described as the *Power of Small Wins* (Amabile & Kramer, 2010).

In this integrated model of motivation, *Autonomy Supportive Leadership* contributes to progress, backed by an awareness of people's core needs. For those in need of pyramids, the *Motivational Pathway* can also be viewed in terms of the elements that support self-directed, meaningful activity.

Elements of Motivation

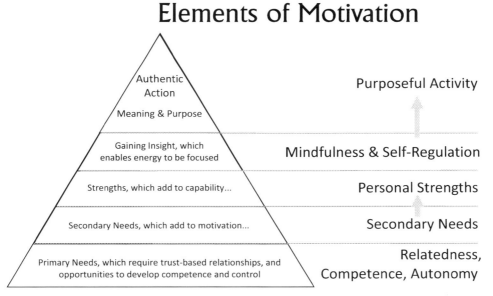

The *Elements of Motivation* build on personal strengths, help develop capability and support purposeful activity. This enhances self-directed action, authenticity, resilience and meaning.

The *Motivational Pathway* creates a new pyramid, comprising core needs, acquired secondary needs, leading to personal strengths, supported by self-regulation – and progress through purposeful activity. It's a continuous process and there is no end point.

Motivation builds on our underlying needs and perception of possibilities. Core needs (and acquired secondary needs) contribute to personal strengths. These are directed towards purpose and progress. Energy is focused through meaningful activity. Awareness and insight then support self-management. The process is ongoing and contributes to self-development. More broadly, well-being and resilience also have an impact on people's quest for meaning and purpose.

Set in a social, macro-economic context, the insights might prompt economists to develop new models. AI algorithms, for example, could reveal how total disposal income (equating to 'self-interest'?) is moderated by high-quality, *free* public services, notably those supporting education and healthcare. Variables shaping national happiness/well-being surveys might also include income distribution and relative inequality, which impact on social cohesion. Over time, the new metrics might also encourage political leaders to better balance the 'competing virtues' of justice and mercy.

ChatGPT suggests that important elements in this wider 'motivation and happiness' framework include the following:

- **Comprehensive social welfare systems**: High-quality public services include education, healthcare and social security. The aim is to ensure equal access to essential services and support for all citizens, promoting social cohesion and reducing inequality.
- **A focus on education**: This is a fundamental element of social well-being and builds on well-funded, high-quality, inclusive educational systems. These support equal opportunities, empowering individuals, fostering social mobility and gender equality.
- **Universal healthcare**: Some countries, notably in Scandinavia, have efficient, accessible healthcare systems that provide universal coverage to their citizens. Everyone has access to quality healthcare without financial barriers, enhancing health outcomes and well-being.
- **Work–life balance**: Countries that prioritise the well-being of citizens also value work–life balance. Initiatives include flexible working hours, generous parental leave and vacation time, allowing individuals to maintain a healthy balance between work and personal life.
- **Trust in institutions and social capital**: Systems are needed to achieve high levels of trust in institutions, including government, and help develop strong Social Capital. This helps create an enabling environment of cooperation and constructive decision-making.
- **Progressive taxation and redistribution**: Higher-income individuals contribute more in taxes that support social welfare and public services (and reduce income inequality). In many countries this is viewed as the cost of living in a civilised society.

Many would argue that we need to move on from old theories of motivation. Outdated ideas block insight and increase the risk of fuzzy thinking. A failure to understand real-life motivation stems in part from Maslow's theory, which is still included in many training courses. It has little value, but the image of a pyramid will persist. A sound model should recognise not only core needs, but also our concern for principles and our volatile expectations. Response is shaped by a mix of needs, 'outcome value', self-belief and social norms. *Super-Ps* reinforce themes of freedom, self-determination, justice, compassion and consistency. People also have a dislike of duplicity, the disingenuous and (unfair) double standards. Motivation theory should recognise that 'principle-violation' triggers emotions. This affects *balanced processing of information*. Over time, increased insight supports both professional objectivity and personal development.

To check the limitations of Maslow's motivation model, we asked ChatGPT to comment. This generated the following summary of potential problems:

Cultural bias: One of the primary criticisms of Maslow's theory is that it is culturally biased. Maslow based his theory on observations of middle-class Americans, and it may not apply to people from other cultures. Some researchers have found that the hierarchy of needs may not hold in non-Western cultures or in societies with different values and priorities.

Empirical evidence: Several studies have failed to find support for Maslow's hierarchy of needs. For example, a study by Wahba and Bridwell (1976) found that there was little evidence to support the idea that people must satisfy lower-level needs before they can move on to higher-level needs. Other research has found that people can be motivated by different needs at the same time, and that the hierarchy of needs is not a fixed sequence.

Lack of clarity: Another criticism of Maslow's theory is that it lacks clarity and specificity. The hierarchy of needs is described in vague terms, and it is not always clear how the different needs relate to each other. For example, some researchers have pointed out that the distinction between self-esteem needs and self-actualisation needs is not well defined.

Alternative theories: Finally, there are alternative theories of motivation that provide different perspectives on human needs. For example, self-determination theory suggests that people have three basic psychological needs: autonomy, competence and relatedness. These needs are thought to be universal and not hierarchical, and they can be satisfied in a variety of ways.

In summary, while Maslow's hierarchy of needs is still widely known, there are criticisms and alternative theories that suggest it's not a complete or accurate model.

Our comment: *We should note that Maslow's mechanical, hierarchical model dates back to 1943 and draws on elements of Murray's theory of needs,* in Explorations in Personality *(1938). We should note that America was never threatened with invasion or annihilation in World War II. We can review Maslow's model against the situation in Ukraine following invasion in 2022. People are willing to sacrifice everything to defend the Super-Ps of freedom and self-determination.*

A clear grasp of factors affecting motivation and well-being is important. If leaders are to create enabling, high performance environments, they need feedback systems that highlight emerging problems. Human nature means that dysfunctional behaviour is always a possibility, and effective systems are required to enhance motivation, control risk and safeguard reputation. To take one example, a BBC investigation in 2023 reported that *'a toxic culture of sexual assault, harassment, racism and bullying has been alleged by more than 100 current and recent UK staff at outlets of the fast-food chain McDonald's'.*[11] We are reminded that the role of leaders is to achieve alignment of individual and team activities. This requires effective systems that evaluate feedback and create transparency. Behaviour should be subject to guiding principles. Principles enable standards to be made explicit, encourage accountability and shape the work culture.

A wider observation is that, in many situations, autonomy supportive leadership is important, but this is never an easy option. It requires conviction about standards, open communication and clear 'outcome expectations'. This is backed by effective operational procedures. People also need work conditions that ensure psychological safety. Enabling conditions help people work effectively, find new solutions and develop a sense of purpose. In most work situations, outcomes are enhanced when people can take responsibility and have the confidence to display initiative.

Maintaining Balance

People's motivation is linked to expectations concerning outcomes and their value to you and others. In the longer term, meaningful activity and opportunities for self-direction are important. However, we also need to consider the balance of JD-R. Sustainable conditions that support well-being will require resources that *match or exceed* the demands.

Developing capability requires effective systems and operational resources, but dealing with work pressure also needs *PsyCap*. This builds on a positive organisational climate characterised by fairness/consistency, authentic leadership, dialogue and support. People need the self-belief to pursue possibilities and must also learn the *Rules of the Game*. Effective leaders therefore work to create an enabling environment that mitigates pressure. Dialogue is important. We get errors if decisions are based on straight-line analysis, but neglect wider issues. Leaders who lack cognitive flexibility will inevitably create turbulence. Unfortunately, old assumptions persist when awareness is restricted, new ideas are overlooked and systems are inadequate.

We are reminded that future-focused leaders demonstrate *active listening* which helps them make sense of new possibilities. It makes sense to understand alternative views before launching into your own agenda. Most importantly, if you expect other people to comply with your personal expectations, it's quite possible that your analysis is emotionally driven. This makes it more difficult to achieve a measured, well-balanced response. One solution is to develop an internalised script that acknowledges feelings, but also makes reference to guiding principles. We then move to analysis based on balanced processing of information. We can reduce the risk of entrenchment by considering context, conditions and constraints.

There are also wider considerations. Organisations must create systems that not only ensure transparency and accountability but also prevent corrupt behaviour. There is an ever-present risk that some individuals will exploit any weakness, possibly to secure a lifestyle and status that cannot be achieved within the limits of their salary. We should also remember that emotionally driven action, sometimes well intentioned, can have unforeseen consequences. Those who neglect cultural norms can appear to threaten higher-order principles, which will trigger a heated response. Careless comments and misinformed or mistimed policy can create considerable jeopardy when leaders neglect social norms. It's important to appreciate how *Super-Ps* link to context (see Appendix 1) and particularly issues of identity.[12] Cultural intelligence is important.

Effective leaders work to maintain stability, encourage shared purpose and support positive change. They seek to develop awareness, create insight, ensure meaningful action (linked to a clear vision) and ensure that people have appropriate support. Significant progress is made much easier with *Purposeful Conversations* that explore context, build on AIMS and minimise the risk of emotional entrenchment.

Notes

1 Ginis, D. (October 2020). On the origins, meaning and influence of Jensen and Meckling's definition of the firm. *Oxford Economic Papers*, 72(4), 966–984. Available at: https://academic.oup.com/oep/article/72/4/966/5899892

2 Deci, E. L., Koestner, R., & Ryan, R. M. (1999). A meta-analytic review of experiments examining the effects of extrinsic rewards on intrinsic motivation. *Psychological Bulletin*, 125(6), 627–668.

3 Gneezy, U., & Rustichini, A. (2000). Pay enough or don't pay at all. *Quarterly Journal of Economics*, 115(3), 791–810.

4 Institute for Policy Studies. Executive Excess 2020: *How the CEO-to-Worker Pay Ratio Harms Workers and Corrodes Democracy*. Available at: https://ips-dc. org/report-executive-excess-2021/

5 Available on YouTube: https://www.youtube.com/watch?v=IrtKb5kseGI (6 min 30 secs in.).

6 Barrick, M. R., & Mount, M. K. (1991). The Big Five personality dimensions and job performance: A meta-analysis. *Personnel Psychology*, 44(1), 1–26. ** Conscientiousness – job performance correlation: $r = 0.22$.

7 Judge, T. A., & Bono, J. E. (2001). Relationship of core self-evaluations traits – self-esteem, generalized self-efficacy, locus of control, and emotional stability – with job satisfaction and job performance: A meta-analysis. *Journal of Applied Psychology*, 86(1), 80–92. ** Conscientiousness – job satisfaction correlation: $r = 0.18$ (3.2% of variance).

8 Starbuck, W. H., & Farjoun, M. (2005). *Organization at the Limit: Lessons from the Columbia Disaster*. Blackwell Publishing.

9 Neuroscience reveals the significance of the ECN and frontoparietal network. Wikipedia summary at: https://en.wikipedia.org/wiki/Frontoparietal_network

10 Snipes, D. E. (2021). *DMN and the Amygdala in Neuropsychiatric Issues*. Overview available on YouTube: https://www.youtube.com/watch?v=DGVgoaeltig

11 BBC Report. (July 2023). *McDonald's workers speak out over sexual abuse claims*. Available at: https://www.bbc.co.uk/news/business-65388445

12 Baisley, E. (2015). Framing the Ghanaian LGBT rights debate: Competing decolonisation and human rights frames. *Canadian Journal of African Studies*, 49(2), 383–402. Published online: 24 Jul 2015 (Taylor & Francis).

References

Amabile, T. M., & Kramer, S. J. (2010). What really motivates workers. *Harvard Business Review*, 88(1/2), 44–45.

Hackman, J. R., & Oldham, G. R. (1976). Motivation through the design of work: Test of a theory. *Organizational Behavior & Human Performance*, 16(2), 250–279.

Jensen, M. C., & Meckling, W. H. (1976). Theory of the firm: Managerial behavior, agency costs and ownership structure. *Journal of Financial Economics*, 3(4), 305–360.

Murray, H. A. (1938). *Explorations in Personality*. New York: Oxford University Press.

Wahba, M. A., & Bridwell, L. G. (1976). Maslow reconsidered: A review of research on the need hierarchy theory. *Organizational Behavior & Human Performance*, 15(2), 212–240.

Chapter 4

Leadership Insights

Many leadership models rely on anecdotal stories of special people, characterised by 'charisma' and a vision of future possibilities. There is often little real analysis of the elements contributing to exceptional performance. Even worse, the success of those highlighted in these stories is often transient. We find the companies that were once called 'Great' can quickly decline and disappear. We also discover that chief executives, lauded as *Exceptional Leaders*, fade as quickly as images conjured up with the aid of smoke and mirrors. All too often, leaders struggle to anticipate events and adapt to a changing context. The Institute of Policy Studies found that many highly paid, top-ranking CEOs do not deliver positive results.[1]

Shareholders are particularly vulnerable if organisations fail to appoint high-calibre people. They are also potentially at greater risk if they allow the same person to occupy the role of Chair and CEO. Having one person in both roles tends to reduce accountability and transparency. It could also weaken the integrity of *Environmental, Social Governance* (ESG) and wider principles of effective leadership. It's important to remember that all organisations have a tendency to fall apart, a process that accelerates if they fail to anticipate future challenges. We find that the organisational growth and decline curve can accelerate in a VUCA World. The bottom line is that despite the mystique surrounding 'leadership', many senior-level executives fail to develop innovative solutions or create the conditions for long-term success. The 2005 Corporate Leadership Council study found that 71% of high performers had limited potential at the next level. It's not simply a matter of IQ, innate ability or lack of a dynamic personality. Issues include clarity of purpose, personal conviction and identification with overall

 DOI: 10.4324/9781003439707-5

objectives. The 'unique qualities' myth is particularly dangerous. It distorts our view of what is required for outstanding leadership, but old assumptions often go unchallenged.

So why do we ignore the evidence relating to executive failure? Part of the answer seems to be that we are drawn towards stories of charismatic, heroic leaders who appear exceptional and rise above the crowd. There are echoes of Nietzsche's (misguided) philosophy in images of powerful individuals ('Supermen') leading passive followers. There is also the financial motivation of those aspiring to join the C-suite. Do you remember Enron, referred to as 'America's Most Innovative Company' for six consecutive years? This acclaim was accompanied by an almost-reverential focus on the 'brightest guys in the room' who then presided over the subsequent bankruptcy. The documentary film should be compulsory viewing for every aspiring executive. We can place this alongside *The Big Short*, focusing on events leading to the global financial crisis of 2008 and *The Rise and Fall of Nokia Mobile*. Add the BBC documentary, *The Bank That Almost Broke Britain*, and we are able to see issues more clearly.[2] It is not sufficient to focus on attributes of short-term success. We also need to address dysfunctional thinking, which undermines sound judgement, and issues that prevent the development of enabling conditions.

There is also an additional problem. It is very easy to confuse activities that preoccupy many senior managers, e.g. business strategy, with the wider demands of leadership. It's important to remember that 'management' is a rational and logical process, but this often fails to unlock people's motivation and commitment. Leadership, in contrast, involves everything that impacts on building a sustainable and productive future for the organisation and stakeholders. This includes creating the conditions that enable and support innovation and future growth. We should remember that charisma fuels a manipulative short-term fix, but good psychometrics can help reveal the threat. Increasingly, high calibre, talented people, particularly those born since 1990, expect integrity. People's expectations of organisations are changing.

Leadership requires a combination of analysis, imagination, interpersonal skills and personal conviction. Many demanding leadership roles also require a strong *personal desire* to exercise control and set direction. The notable academic Prof David McClelland, building on the work of Henry Murray, recognised that the need for power (N-Pow) and achievement (N-Ach) is a key driver of effectiveness in leadership roles. However, energy and ability must be focused effectively. McClelland differentiated 'socialised' (productive) use of power and the pursuit of personal (corrupted) power, which can drive reckless expansion and risk-taking. We also know that when the power motive is frustrated and not expressed productively, it easily leads to dysfunctional behaviour. This sense of frustration and personal inadequacy contributes to alcohol and drug abuse, coercive control and domestic violence. The positive aspects of power and achievement motivation need to be expressed through purposeful activity. This is particularly important when organisations are faced with complexity and change. There is then a need to use this personal energy to build consensus, engage others in developing innovative solutions, and identify how best to unlock talent.

Future-focused leaders seek to develop people's capability, but it's important that underlying trust is backed by effective systems. Unfortunately, many organisations will contain individuals with a dysfunctional mindset and possibly an anti-social personality disorder. They may outwardly appear pleasant and friendly, but are actually manipulative, which may be motivated by a desire for control or 'unseen influence'. Sometimes this can be an asset. Many years ago (in the late 1980s), I completed initial personality assessments of 'second career' candidates aspiring to join Britain's MI5 intelligence service. I recall that some were outwardly insignificant, but had this inner dynamic. From a leadership perspective, it's important to ensure that trust is backed with objectivity. We must balance cognitive functions that integrate facts, possibilities, feelings (emotion) and logic. This in turn requires effective feedback systems that help maintain transparency and accountability. Anomalies can then be reviewed, which may well require an appreciation of statistical significance to identify unusual patterns. Assumptions should never take precedence over facts supported by the objectivity of logical analysis. At the time of writing, a UK nurse has been found guilty of murdering babies, and evidence suggest that hospital managers ignored warnings.[3] To achieve insight, lines of accountability should be clear – and all leaders should appreciate the significance of data.

A shift of perspective often follows the shock of a traumatic event. In the years after the 1914–1918 war, for example, the military had to recognise the importance of cognitive abilities like problem-solving, critical thinking and adaptability. These attributes gained prominence in the selection processes developed in subsequent years. However, in the 2020s, we still find shortcomings. Not least, the third sector, charities and healthcare and social services, have been slow to establish threshold standards, anchored in essential competencies. In terms of mindset, leaders must also appreciate that deviation from a normal pattern represents an anomaly, which is never ignored. If you do not understand the issues, you seek expert advice. Future-focused leaders ask the questions that help create insight. Unfortunately, if a leader lacks a grasp of *Superordinate Principles (Super-Ps)*, they are more likely to worry about 'reputation' or allow their own sense of emotional disturbance to undermine conviction. In modern organisations, leaders need to have a script that is anchored in *Super-Ps* and the competencies that drive excellence. If you are one of many who view competencies as a tedious checklist, then you don't understand their purpose. They should reflect principles, directed through the role, that support excellence and help shape the culture. Unfortunately, many HR departments have reduced competencies to check lists because they fail to appreciate their significance.

Long-term success is elusive without insight, which also contributes to the development of motivation and commitment. Effective leaders appreciate the need to create enabling conditions. However, if you don't relish the pressure and responsibility, leadership (in a demanding role) is probably not an optimum career path. It's advisable to gain insight relating to your work preferences and underlying career drivers. Becoming a CEO requires insight and a lot of motivation. You need the personal conviction that drives professional excellence and overcomes complacency, attributes that then help drive long-term success.

Vision and Effective Action

Effective leadership is always context specific. Personal conviction needs to be linked to a meaningful rationale, which contributes to momentum and the development of shared purpose. Winston Churchill, widely regarded as a 'great leader', said that *success is about going from failure to failure, without losing your enthusiasm*. However, the impact of poor decisions on others can be significant. Whilst Churchill is viewed as an effective wartime leader, he demonstrated poor judgement in his analysis and response to many situations. Not least, he returned Great Britain to the Gold Standard in 1925, worsening economic conditions and prompting Keynes to write his critical analysis: *The Economic Consequences of Mr. Churchill*. A century later, many still struggle to see things clearly. For example, people deride 'fiat currency', i.e., money not backed by gold. However, the real problem is the *fiduciary issue*, the ratio of debt to GDP, and rates of economic growth. Germany recorded a debt/GDP ratio of 69% in 2023, the US 122% and Greece 178%. A World Bank study indicates that ratios exceeding 77% for prolonged periods are associated with significant slowdowns in growth.[4] These are tough metrics for politicians, and some struggle with complex analysis and longer-term vision. Returning to Churchill, it became clear in 1945 that he had no 'compelling vision' for social and economic development. His underlying strength was his ability (in the 1930s) to see things clearly, with a strategic perspective and sound grasp of principles. Many other politicians of the time failed to appreciate the threat of fascism.

The concept of a compelling vision is a central theme in most books on leadership. However, it's important to recognise that an effective vision needs to be anchored in sound analysis and backed by clear values and principles. These take precedence over *self-referenced thinking* or 'self-interest' and expedient short-term action. This is a critical underlying requirement. It also helps clarify an important difference that separates *Charisma*, associated with populism and manipulation of others, and a *Vision* that articulates *Superordinate Goals* based on consistent values and higher-order principles. This is the element that provides the foundation for longer-term shared purpose. It is important, both for politicians and for business leaders, that the vision expresses a coherent policy backed by a meaningful rationale. The time horizon is also important. In senior-level roles, leader assess challenges and demands, ideally at least six or seven years in the future. In contrast, operational managers may only consider requirements that will emerge over a period of 6 to 12 months. The time horizon varies with the responsibilities of the role. In 2023, Toyota, one of the world's largest car manufacturers, was still assessing options for future power systems.

From a motivational perspective, other people are always evaluating the leader's vision and gauging possible outcomes. We tend to review leadership capability as events unfold. This evaluation is likely to raise questions about principles and also essential competencies. There is a desire for progress, which prompts evaluation of the process being followed. A clear vision creates the opportunity to engage others in constructive discussion concerning goals and the overall strategy. In situations characterised by complexity, leaders need to set overall direction, clarify key issues and then engage others in finding realistic solutions. As noted earlier, it's also important to differentiate equality and equity. The higher-order principle prompts action to support equality of opportunity. In contrast, pursuit of equity, i.e. 'equality as an outcome', can undermine *Super-Ps* and trigger a reaction.

It's important that EDI initiatives are aligned with primary *Super-Ps*. These in turn can be referenced against emerging challenges and anticipation of consequences.

Challenging scenarios create new insight. In the context of the COVID-19 pandemic, very few political leaders in the period 2010–2019 really understood the early warning signs offered by the SARS, MERS and Ebola outbreaks. These were the years before COVID-19. In the UK, there was a general failure to initiate a strategic, long-term plan of action. There was no coherent response, evident in limited *Personal Protective Equipment* (PPE) for front-line staff. History will also note that this was when the Conservative prime ministers (i.e., David Cameron, Theresa May and Boris Johnson) were preoccupied with Brexit. They did not take appropriate action, which required anticipation of a significant threat, which was very real, but simply lying dormant.

Rational analysis based on *facts as they currently appear* is the mindset of *FELT Thinkers*. This paradigm suggested that a pandemic was a vague possibility – a distant event that could be dealt with at a later date. It also seems likely that advance resourcing of PPE would have been viewed by British 'Euro-Sceptics' as evidence of excessive regulation, wasteful spending and bureaucracy. Germany was criticised by some for spending money on preparations. In the UK, the period after the financial crash of 2008 prompted a culture of austerity that shaped government policy. Spending money to prepare for the 'theoretical possibility' of a pandemic did not fit within the mindset of reductionists. However, when the crisis hit the UK in 2020, the lack of preparation was suddenly exposed. This was highlighted in the context of testing and contact tracing. There were also weaknesses relating to delivery of adequate PPE to the NHS and care workers.[5] There was evidence of indecisive leadership, with a delay in closing large public events. The Cheltenham Racing Festival (10–13 March 2020) with over 68,000 visitors, and possibly 250,000 points of contact, was allowed to run as normal. A failure to take decisive action often represents a lack of imagination; the essential element required to anticipate future consequences.

In evidence to the *Commons Health and Social Care* Select Committee (April 2020), Prof Costello, the chairman of global health at University College London, criticised the UK government's strategy in tackling COVID-19. He said the failure to conduct widespread testing in favour of relying solely on the lockdown would leave Britain facing wave after wave of Coronavirus until a vaccine was found. The government's response was too slow.[6] The *Sunday Times* ran an article (April 2020) headed:

Coronavirus: 38 days when Britain sleepwalked into disaster. The report describes the failure of the government to understand the problem, a woeful lack of preparation and a general sense of complacency. No effective action was taken during January or February. However, we might note that 31 January 2020 was celebrated by supporters of Brexit. It was the day that the UK, in the words of Brexit ideologues, *finally escaped the regulations and inefficiency of the EU.* There was no awareness or reference to the pending Covid disaster, and no appreciation of the interdependencies that affect economic outcomes. The country was drifting into a period of social and economic chaos.

Germany, Ireland, South Korea and New Zealand were more effective in their initial response than the UK or the US. Future reviews may be critical of the failure of the UK government to build on the capability of notable, independent labs. They could have accelerated large-scale testing. The pandemic also revealed limitations in functional structures. Public Health England, an executive agency of the Department of Health and Social Care, adopted a centralised, sequential approach. It did not involve independent labs or achieve the speed of response of the devolved approach adopted in South Korea and Germany. Evidence emerged of a chaotic procurement system. A BBC Report (20 April 2020) referred to the Department of Health and Social Care suffering from *a lack of the right skilled commercial people, a lack of risk appetite, a huge bureaucracy and a tick box culture.*[7] At the same time, independent labs were left idle. We might also note (in contrast) the innovative approach of other groups, such as the Oxford Vaccine Group, seeking to maximise faster, results-focused solutions.[8] The UK experienced the 'VUCA world' consequences of inadequate planning, a fragmented response and NHS Trusts left in the position of trying to source their own PPE. However, the roll-out of the vaccine in 2021 was enhanced by the UK's unified health service and a well-organised, decentralised delivery process.

Unfortunately, people struggle to quickly shift mindset or escape years of *FELT Thinking.* Nor can a leader 'wing it' and then deny personal responsibility when overtaken by wicked problems. Effective 21st century leadership involves creating systems and capability well in advance of any operational crisis. Bill Gates identified the risks posed by a pandemic in a Ted Talk in 2015 when Obama was president in the US and Cameron was prime minister in the UK.[9] Obama had in fact already recognised the risk in 2014 and took steps to prepare, saying *we have to put in place an infrastructure, not just here at home, but globally.* However, when President

Trump was elected, the White House '*Pandemic Office*' was disbanded. Trump stated: *Some of the people we cut, they haven't been used for many, many years. And if – if we ever need 'em, we can get 'em very quickly. And rather than spending the money – and I'm a business person – I don't like having thousands of people around when you don't need 'em.*[10] History will judge the factual accuracy and the wisdom of Trump's thinking. A formal review will also evaluate the UK government's failure to plan and take action before COVID-19 spiralled out of control.

Taking a wider view of developments, we should note that some countries did take firm, decisive action once the pandemic started its global spread early in 2020. The list did not include the US, the UK, Italy or Japan. Those that responded more effectively included Germany, South Korea and New Zealand. Jacinda Ardern, prime minister of New Zealand, emphasised the need for firm action ('*go in fast, go in hard*') to stop the spread of the virus. This was *the window of opportunity* before it really took hold. She communicated a clear message in an empathetic way, backed by sound reasoning. This helped create a meaningful rationale and a strong sense of shared purpose.[11] It reminds us that effective leadership involves clarity of assessment and the ability to set clear direction. This is required before the follow-up action that builds on agility of response and operational efficiency. These become essential once events start to unfold.

The *Sunday Times* article (19 April 2020) notes that Martin Hibberd (a professor of emerging infectious diseases at the London School of Hygiene and Tropical Medicine) visited Singapore in 2003 and 2009. He stated that *basically they copied the UK pandemic preparedness plan. But the difference is they actually implemented it.* There might therefore be a degree of sympathy for those politicians appointed to senior-level roles in 2019 or early 2020. The situation was rather like running the last stage in a relay race, only to find that those running the previous legs had dropped the baton, damaged its integrity and failed to recognise its importance. Some in senior-level roles also lacked the experience, insight and competencies that are needed in a crisis. They struggled to respond effectively. Reliance on centralised control is not the best approach in an emergency that requires cognitive flexibility and operational efficiency. Effective solutions require speed of response and devolved leadership – and the expertise of people who are able to deliver results when working under real pressure.

Leaders should also note that context is always important. A 'compelling vision' can sometimes prove to be a dangerous distraction and produce unintended consequences. Personal conviction always needs to be balanced by responsiveness to feedback, appreciation of the wider issues and tested against *Super-Ps*. As an example of intransigence, we might recall the iconic UK prime minister Margaret Thatcher, and her commitment, despite widespread opposition, to introduce a regressive 'Poll Tax'. Most recognised that this would have a disproportionate impact on poorer people. However, she ignored the criticism. Her reluctance to accept feedback, coupled with her abrasive relationship with colleagues, inevitably undermined support. The events triggered riots and contributed to a loss of confidence in her ability. She failed to overcome a leadership challenge, which resulted in her resignation in November 1990.[12] This reminds us that a compelling vision is of no value unless validated through feedback and grasp of key issues. Sound analysis rarely emerges from rigid ideology, dogmatic opinion or short-term thinking. One of the lessons of history is that hubris easily overtakes those who are driven to succeed and are reluctant to relinquish power. After seven or eight years, most leaders start to lose responsiveness to feedback and have less understanding of a changing context. Politicians should also note that their ability to win elections is made much easier when the opposition is in disarray and lacks credibility. A successful period, characterised by a series of wins, could conceal underlying weaknesses in leaders, and hide significant shortcomings within organisations.

Personality traits, 'straight-line' intelligence (IQ) and traditional 'critical reasoning' test scores offer limited insight into leadership potential. The graveyard is full of intelligent but unsuccessful people with such traits as *courage, optimism and risk-taking*.[13] Now this might simply indicate that success depends on luck! Alternatively, it could mean that we need to gain a better understanding of the elements that shape outcomes, and particularly the competencies that lead to superior performance.

Profiling Effective Leaders

Leadership models are useful in clarifying how effective leaders create focus and generate energy in others. There is a process of interaction that involves creating purpose and enhancing people's motivation. Leadership is not simply a matter of someone possessing special personality traits. Simply constructing a list of 'leadership qualities', such as *courageous, optimistic* and *charismatic*, does not have much practical value. In order for strengths to be used effectively, people in professional and leadership roles need to appreciate essential competencies, comprising the mindset, behaviour and approach that contribute to high performance. Popular descriptions of *Great Leaders* rely on *general descriptions of personality*, with little evidence of how elements interact or relate to essential competencies. Personality traits do not make leaders. The speculative ideas fail to take account of context and motivation – and how outcomes are achieved.

Back in the 1980s, significant attention was placed on elements linked to *Transformational Leadership*. The term is associated with the idea of *Transformational Change* in the culture of an organisation. This approach is also contrasted with *Transactional Leadership*, which is essentially rational and impersonal. The model proposed four dimensions linked to the transformational style, which contribute to effectiveness:

- Idealised influence: acting as a charismatic role model to followers
- Inspirational motivation: expressing a clear, inspiring vision
- Intellectual stimulation: questioning assumptions and challenging the status quo
- Individual consideration: attention and support to the needs of followers

In contrast, transactional leadership is largely an impersonal, mechanistic *Performance-Reward* perspective. The transactional style may be associated with excessive monitoring and 'micro-management' or a 'hands off' approach that offers little support or encouragement:

- Contingent reward: reward linked to effort and performance
- Management by exception-active: monitoring performance and taking corrective action
- Management by exception-passive: only making an intervention when really necessary
- Laissez-faire: avoidance of leadership responsibility

There is evidence that aspects of the transformational style contribute to greater motivation and improvement in performance. However, the essential steps in the process are not clearly explained or linked to a psychological model. It can also give the impression that 'followers' are passive recipients in their interaction with 'leaders'. The more recent concept of 'Authentic Leadership' offers greater insight, helping to clarify how the leader's 'vision' must build on a *meaningful rationale* and *clearly expressed values*. These contribute to the leader demonstrating personal conviction, rather than relying on 'charisma'. The enhanced model also explains how others come to identify with goals and principles. In practical terms, it means that conviction, shared purpose and consistent values are more effective in building motivation than reliance on a 'compelling vision'. This approach also highlights the importance of dialogue, which helps influence others, build commitment, and supports effort through identification and purpose.

Authentic leadership seeks to develop people's capability whilst also focusing on principles, performance standards and outcomes. Contemporary leadership themes place emphasis on unlocking people's strengths and building trust. Contrast this with outdated theories that suggest that transformational leaders use charisma to '*overcome people's self-interest*' and so gain commitment to goals. These words echo the mindset of economists and a legacy of reductionist thinking. We find the old notion of 'self-interest', which runs alongside '*Bounded Rationality*'. The shortcomings are comparable to the concept of 'miasma' (bad air) that was used to explain the spread of disease before John Snow's statistical analysis (and microscopes) exposed bacteria.[14] Unfortunately, inadequate theories develop when science is lacking. This prompts a *reaction*, based on assumptions, emotion and impulse. In contrast, a professional *response* requires self-management, appreciation of context and anticipation of consequences. Real effectiveness builds on experience, awareness and insight into data and possibilities – and a clear appreciation of options.

When we look at a large sample of people, we find that the '*reaction–response*' distribution is skewed. Reflective thinking and *balanced processing of information* is frequently less developed. This makes it more difficult to achieve a measured response. People accept technical data as a 'list' or 'facts as presented'. Reductionist leaders also tend to focus on specific targets, financial results and 'returns to shareholders'. Evidence suggests that some CEOs have psychopathic traits,[15] whilst others could improve empathy and awareness. A culture that encourages anticipation helps eliminate the 'law of unintended consequences'.

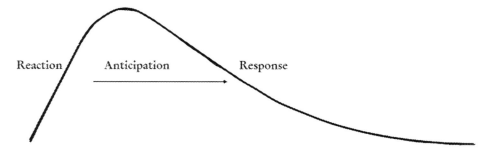

Reaction   Anticipation   Response

The challenges facing team leaders increase with remote working. This also reminds us of the dangers of a transactional style. If a leader is too concerned about control, it can easily undermine trust. The benefits of remote working build on *flexibility* and *self-direction*, but key objectives and priorities must be clear. Role clarity is a cornerstone of motivation, but it may also involve giving people choices about *where* and *when* they work. Self-directed activity raises numerous issues for leaders with a traditional mindset. However, there are clear steps. We should first clarify *outputs* and *interdependencies*, then consider the level of contact/engagement required to keep people involved and actively sharing information. Effective leaders offer support and don't allow work pressure or personal anxiety to turn into micro-management (or fuel personal criticism).

Motivation and Purpose at Work

Following the 2020 lockdown, a Pario TEAM survey revealed that a client achieved *increased* levels of employee engagement. This was linked to the business actively working to maintain team support despite social isolation, i.e., working from home. More generally, we find that effective leaders seek to anticipate problems. They also appreciate that whilst solitary, remote working can offer benefits, it must be balanced with human connection to support *relatedness* and develop relationships and commitment. There is such a thing as a free lunch, and it can result in tangible benefits by encouraging people to commute to the office. However, the real leadership 'take-away' is that effectiveness is enhanced when people have purpose and are able to see the bigger picture. No one wants to be a cog in a machine. Looking to the future, ESG will require leaders to take account of *Super-Ps*, shared purpose and the need for a meaningful rationale. This is best served through *Authentic Leadership* that builds motivation and longer-term commitment.

Modern psychometric tools offer an opportunity to gain insight into attributes that contribute to anticipation and *balanced processing of information*. This is not simply a matter of intelligence or IQ. Whilst we would expect leaders to have above-average critical reasoning ability, appropriate to the demands of the role, this is not the primary consideration. Above a certain level of intelligence, other factors become more important. These include *mindset issues* and the *cognitive flexibility* required to adjust to a rapidly changing context. Essential qualities include recognition of interdependencies, 'big-picture' reflective thinking and the ability to perceive 'how things connect'. Future-focused, authentic leaders evaluate emerging trends and engage others in developing appropriate solutions.

It's also possible to draw on insights from occupational/organisational psychology. These can help leaders identify the most appropriate ways of improving performance, well-being and commitment of people at work. There is scope to apply psychological principles in an operational context. The ideas are backed by scientific research and help clarify how best to develop purpose and build an enabling environment. The underlying rationale of work-focused applied psychology can be related to important themes that affect outcomes. The themes include the following:

Enhancing productivity and performance: This builds on selection, performance appraisal, training and development. Activities should be aligned with values, principles and role-related competencies. Effective strategies encourage higher levels of productivity and achievement. The process requires insight into systems, objective evaluation, motivation and factors affecting well-being and resilience.

Fostering employee well-being: Future success requires healthy and supportive work environments. Important factors include work–life balance, meaningful work and a sense of progress. Work pressure can also be mitigated by autonomy supportive leadership, team collaboration and resource availability. TEAM indexing can profile important factors affecting employee engagement and well-being.

Promoting fair and diverse workplaces: *Super-Ps* reflect important values, e.g. fairness, that ensure consistent standards of equality, with systems that support diversity and inclusion. Feedback processes encourage transparency and accountability, with a focus on the principles guiding actions. To be objective, impartial and consistent, values should be expressed through principles and competencies.

Enhancing organisational culture: The overall functioning and effectiveness of an organisation depends on systems that support delivery of a product or service, but also an appreciation of *how things get done*. To avoid dysfunctional behaviour, we need leaders with integrity and conviction. They set high standards, create a positive team ethos and ensure a sense of purpose and progress.

In summary, workplace outcomes can be enhanced by applying psychological insights, backed by research, to improve productivity, enhance well-being, increase organisational effectiveness and achieve better decision-making. ESG increases the focus on people, systems, culture and social responsibility. Leaders are now expected to create enabling environments that benefit employees and organisations. This is the reality of third generation corporate governance.

We asked ChatGPT to identify the factors that have most impact on motivation:

> ➤ *With reference to research evidence (2010–2023), which factors have most impact on people's motivation and sense of purpose at work?*

There is a significant body of research on factors that impact people's motivation and sense of purpose at work. Here are some key findings from research published between 2010 and 2023:

Meaningful work: Research has consistently shown that people are more motivated and engaged when they feel their work is meaningful and aligned with their values and goals.

Autonomy and control: Employees who have more control over their work and decision-making are more likely to be motivated and committed. This can include having the ability to choose how to complete tasks, and being given the autonomy to make decisions about work-related issues.

Positive relationships: Positive relationships with colleagues and managers are important for employee motivation and sense of purpose at work. Research has shown that supportive and respectful relationships with colleagues can enhance job satisfaction, reduce turnover and improve overall well-being.

Career development: Opportunities for career development and growth are important for employee motivation and engagement. Providing employees with opportunities to learn new skills, take on new challenges and advance in their careers can enhance motivation and commitment.

Recognition and rewards: Employees who feel valued and appreciated for their work are more likely to be motivated and engaged. This can include providing regular feedback and recognition, as well as offering rewards such as bonuses or promotions.

Work–life balance: A healthy work–life balance is important for employee motivation and well-being. Research has shown that employees who have more control over their work schedules and who are able to balance their work and personal lives are more likely to be motivated and engaged.

Organisational culture: A positive and supportive organisational culture can enhance employee motivation and sense of purpose. This can include a focus on employee well-being, open communication and a commitment to values such as fairness, respect and inclusivity.

In summary, research has consistently shown that meaningful work, autonomy and control, positive relationships, career development, recognition and rewards, work–life balance, and organisational culture are important factors that impact employee motivation and sense of purpose at work. Leaders who prioritise these factors are more likely to create a supportive work environment that enhances employee motivation and engagement.

Notes

1 Anderson, S., Klinger, S., Pizzigati, S. (2013). *Executive Excess 2013: Bailed Out, Booted, and Busted, Institute for Policy Studies*. Report available at: https://ips-dc.org/wp-content/uploads/2013/08/EE13-FINAL.pdf

2 In 1999, RBS implemented an excellent leadership development programme. However, the BBC documentary suggests that the Board had little real grasp of critical competencies when they appointed Fred Goodwin CEO in 2001.

3 BBC Report. (August 2023). *Hospital bosses ignored months of doctors' warnings*. Available at: https://www.bbc.co.uk/news/uk-66120934

4 Grennes, T., Caner, M., & Koehler-Geib, F. (2010). *Finding The Tipping Point – When Sovereign Debt Turns Bad*. Policy Research Working Papers, August 2010.

5 Coronavirus: Social care concerns revealed in leaked letter. BBC Report, 16 April 2020.

6 Coronavirus: UK 'probably' has 'Europe's highest death rate' because government was 'too slow' to act, expert warns. ITV News Report, 17 April 2020.

7 Coronavirus: The political mood is becoming more scratchy. BBC Report, 20 April 2020.

8 Oxford COVID-19 vaccine programme opens for clinical trial recruitment, April 2020. Available at: http://www.ovg.ox.ac.uk/w

9 Bill Gates Ted Talk. (2015). *The next outbreak: We're not ready*.

10 Obama Warned the U.S. To Prepare for A Pandemic Back In 2014 – YouTube.

11 Alistair Campbell. (2020). Jacinda Ardern's coronavirus plan is working because, unlike others, she's behaving like a true leader. *The Independent*, 12 April 2020.

12 BBC Documentary TV Series. (2019). *Thatcher: A Very British Revolution*.
13 Taleb, N. (2007). *The Black Swan: The Impact of the Highly Improbable*. Penguin.
14 Miasma Theory, Wikipedia Entry.
15 Psychopathy in the workplace – Wikipedia.

Chapter 5

Authentic Leadership

Authenticity has its roots in Greek philosophy and the principle, *to thine own self be true*. The concept has also been described as *the unobstructed operation of one's true, or core, self in one's daily enterprise*.[1] However, leaders must ensure alignment of individual interests with the activities and objectives of the organisation. Guiding principles create expectations concerning what we do and how we interact with others. Organisations need selection systems that ensure a good fit between person and role. Individuals are drawn to roles and work cultures aligned with their values, but also want to satisfy primary and secondary needs. Psychometrics can help screen out those who appear plausible, but could prove toxic. Problems will arise if a work culture allows personal interests and *self-referenced thinking* to take precedence over professional standards and overall purpose. Authenticity is therefore set in the context of an enabling environment and starts with role clarity. Effective leaders take steps to prevent dysfunctional outcomes.

There is a danger when people espouse *progressive values*, but there are also those who attempt to impose *traditional values*. Both threaten established paradigms and could run counter to *Superordinate Principles* (*Super-Ps*). There are inevitable risks when values of a minority are pushed without reference to higher-order principles, such as those associated with fairness, equality and due process. Effective decisions require a balanced evaluation of context. Authenticity, viewed in a professional context, has certain preconditions. Unfortunately, a sense of moral virtue, or a vision driven by emotion, fails to build a strong foundation for action. The problem is made worse by ideological bias, reinforced by the confirmation bias

DOI: 10.4324/9781003439707-6

created by social media. A failure to apply *Super-Ps* prevents *balanced processing of information* and fuels disagreement. The pursuit of authenticity requires awareness and insight, with appreciation of context and conditions.

Without insight, people may assume that their personal opinion justifies unprofessional behaviour. This could include personal criticism of colleagues, which hinders progress, weakens team ethos and undermines professional standards. If a leader fails to maintain consistent standards or is slow to take action, motivation and shared purpose are weakened. Problems develop when systems are inadequate. We might note Amnesty International's 2019 Staff Well-being Review that identified a 'toxic work environment'. It noted that *most efforts to support staff well-being have been ad hoc, reactive and inconsistent, and staff do not feel well equipped with regards to developing personal resilience or supporting the well-being of their colleagues.*[2]

Oxfam was also severely criticised in 2019 by the UK Charity Commission. The report noted that, *over a period of years, Oxfam's internal culture tolerated poor behaviour, and at times lost sight of the values it stands for*, and that *some of the organisation's failings amounted to mismanagement.*[3] The report notes that the most stinging criticism was reserved for the way Oxfam was seen to be placing its own reputation – and its relationships with donors – above the need to protect victims. This is a familiar pattern that emerges when guiding principles are not embedded in an organisation's operational systems and overall goals. To maintain high standards, subordinate and intermediate activities should be linked to superordinate goals. These should reflect the core values and processes that determine how activities are conducted.[4]

In organisations, problems emerge when systems are inadequate, leaders lack conviction and key measures of work climate are neglected. Future success involves surfacing problems and preventing dysfunctional behaviour. Inadequate leadership is linked to poor systems, lack of feedback and delay in responding to issues. Effective leadership involves developing clear professional standards, including issues that affect trust and team ethos. Any discussion of authenticity must be referenced against professional standards, social cohesion and guiding principles. The focus is outward looking and proactive. Note that the assumption *our way is the best way* or *we occupy the moral high ground* can start to threaten responsiveness to feedback and reduce accountability. Organisations must maintain high standards and ensure transparency. Things will fall apart without the feedback that supports *balanced processing of information.*

Delegating responsibility requires trust, but it also supports discretionary effort and adds to people's sense of meaningful activity. We find that *autonomy supportive leadership* contributes to employee motivation, job satisfaction and performance.[5] It helps address our core needs for relatedness, competence and self-directed activity. Looking more closely we find that autonomy supportive leadership builds on four core elements of authenticity (Kernis, 2003). People who are regarded as 'authentic' are receptive to feedback and aware of their strengths. Increased insight also supports *balanced processing of information.* In a study by Chatterjee and Hambrick (2007), CEOs who displayed more balanced self-presentations were perceived as more authentic by their subordinates.[6] They show 'relational authenticity' when engaging with others, and there was evidence of authentic behaviour/action. Authentic leaders appreciate their personal strengths, core values and guiding principles. They demonstrate personal conviction in what they do.

Consider your own position on the four elements (identified by Kernis) that support authenticity:

1. **Self-awareness**: *Understand your unique talents and strengths, have a clear sense of purpose and core values; remain open to feedback and actively seek to gain fresh insights.*
2. **Balanced processing of information**: *Consider multiple sides of an issue and understand other people's views; explore facts, feelings, context, constraints and possibilities.*
3. **Relational authenticity**: *Strive to be open and truthful in close relationships and use selective self-disclosure, e.g. admitting mistakes or errors. Be genuine and seek to develop trust when working with other people.*
4. **Authentic behaviour/action**: *Develop conviction about professional standards, goals and principles. Ensure actions are aligned with core values, so consistent standards are evident.*

Authentic leaders display self-awareness, self-regulation and positive modelling, which contribute to them fostering the development of authenticity in followers.[7] The theory suggests that authentic leaders draw on their positive *Psychological Capital* (*PsyCap*) to make clear to others what is required. This helps generate energy. They create meaning and purpose, so others develop a sense of personal ownership and become 'stakeholders' in the activity. This becomes more challenging – and a more significant issue – with remote working. In challenging situations, additional steps are required to maintain progress. Elements include taking time for *active enquiry* to understand issues, ensuring *adequate support* and resources, and encouraging *discretionary effort* (and people's involvement in problem-solving).

Appreciation of the building blocks linked to effective leadership is increased by linking *Self-Determination Theory* to the steps contributing to authenticity. This makes it easier to put the model in an operational context and take account of other issues, such as the need for flexibility and responsiveness to change. This wider perspective also serves to emphasise the importance of key themes, particularly those relating to *being in the present* and aware of context.

Responsiveness to changing requirements involves an innovative approach and actively seeking opportunities to learn and develop. We need to let go and move on from things that don't work. The attributes are summed up in the 3H Competency Model, associated with *Head, Heart and Hands*. The three broad clusters come together to support exceptional performance. They include (i) analysis and innovative thinking, (ii) interpersonal skills, which build relationships, develop capability and strengthen teamwork and (iii) the resilience to deal with setbacks, show flexibility and maintain focus on results. From an operational perspective, effective, future-focused leadership can build on the 3H competency clusters and attributes linked to authenticity.

The focus can be summed up as follows:

Clarity of purpose: Understanding the wider issues, professional standards and values that contribute to credibility/conviction and setting direction. Assessing operational priorities (urgency and importance) and supporting these with planning and monitoring.

Influence and support: Engaging effectively with others and enhancing people's sense of purpose and motivation. Establishing a meaningful rationale and creating shared purpose. Taking steps to develop people's competence and a sense of control.

Delivery focus: Identifying with the work activities and demonstrating the conviction required to achieve high-quality outcomes. Adapting to demands, with the personal resilience needed to overcome obstacles.

Self-management is also important. Not least, leaders need to be aware of the inevitable tendency to gradually regress to *unconscious incompetence*. The risk is compounded should other people suggest that you are a uniquely talented and exceptional person! Be highly sceptical if you ever receive this type of feedback! Research suggests that most chief executives start to become less effective in less than five years. The judgement of political leaders may well decline after seven or eight years. However, the decline may be slowed by consciously becoming more outward looking, seeking the participation of diverse groups and building on ideas that challenge your existing thinking. So never rely on a small group of personal advisers who echo your ideas. And appreciate your personal limitations. The *Great Leader* is a transient figure and soon outpaced.

In summary, authentic leadership builds on four elements that also help develop authenticity in others. The process creates shared purpose through a meaningful rationale for change, supported by dialogue that leads to internalisation. Authenticity also builds on *Purposeful Conversations*, which may be difficult, but the focus is on seeing issues in context and identifying how to achieve positive outcomes. The process takes account of *principles* relating to how people assimilate new ideas. This also enhances self-management skills. Focusing on requirements, separating the professional and the personal, helps clarify how best to respond to difficult situations. Authenticity is **not** about '*bringing your whole self to work*'. It actually involves a process, a two-way interaction, that creates meaning and purpose. This starts with an enabling environment and a culture shaped by higher-order principles. More broadly, it also means that subordinate- and intermediate-level activities are validated by reference to *Superordinate Goals*. The organisation's vision and values are expressed through guiding principles. If leaders fail to recognise the underlying relationship, their position can be undermined. There is always a risk that personal ambition, ego and ideology will damage professional judgement.

Case Study: The Danger of Speculative Ventures

Problems can arise when politicians pursue 'visionary' projects that have emotional appeal, but neglect basic objectivity, accountability and purpose. These principles are well learned by entrepreneurs who invest their own money and learn the hard lessons of experience. These insights are easily missed by those in Public Office. The rules include strict *due diligence* to evaluate feasibility, reduce risks and remove romance and emotion. Tight control of spending is essential, with no significant expenditure until permissions are in place. We need *proof of concept*, backed by critical 'what if' questions. This is a demanding process, but it's vital to eradicate wishful thinking. We then adopt a mindset that regards any expenditure, particularly money spent on elaborate planning and design, as 'high risk'. The rule is simple and can be summed up as follows: *You avoid serious expenditure until all the critical elements are considered*. Resolve the uncertainties and note early warning signs of professional incompetence, waste and hubris.

Bearing these points in mind, we might revisit the 'Garden Bridge' proposal to span the River Thames in London. This was promoted during the period 2008–2016. It was opposed by many who argued it had no practical purpose. When it was finally abandoned, not a single stone or steel support had disturbed the water. However, the Trust managing the project had spent a total of £53 million.[8] The BBC report summed it up as follows:

> A failed plan to build a bridge covered with trees and flowers
> over the River Thames in central London cost a total of £53m…
> A Transport for London (TfL) inquiry showed the Garden Bridge
> Trust spent £161,000 on a website and £417,000 on a gala for the
> abandoned project. The design of the bridge cost more than £9m
> and the charity paid its executives £1.7m. Around £43m came from
> the public's pocket, TfL added. Doubts began to surround the project, overseen by Boris Johnson, after it lost the support of London
> Mayor Sadiq Khan in April 2017. It was officially abandoned in
> August of that year after a review recommended it be scrapped.

Self-belief is a potential attribute of effective leaders, but it must be balanced by humility. This is often lacking in those driven by personal ambition and the rhetoric that conceals hubris. Research reveals the need for *balanced processing of information* and the competencies linked to future-focused effectiveness. Most notably, we have the GLOBE Leadership Study.

The GLOBE Leadership Study involved over 17,000 middle managers across 62 countries. This highlighted the importance of the ability to inspire, motivate and expect high-performance outcomes from others. It reflects a team-orientated, participative and supportive approach, which is also associated with autonomy supportive leadership. There are exceptions to this model, notably in countries where personal power and self-interest override *higher-order principles*. These outliers reveal links with hierarchical, traditional cultures, which expect deference to seniority, rank and status. They are more likely to be patriarchal and conservative, but also with less respect for the rule of law. Some have done well during decades of high carbon economics, but *Environmental, Social Governance* (ESG) has now moved centre stage. The consequences of change are both rapid and inevitable; there is no point of comfortable equilibrium. *Super-Ps* are now an integral part of the dynamic process. They help leaders maintain continuity and manage ongoing change.

In contrast to the regimes that resist democratisation, equality and the rule of law, rapid change in corporations is often activated when performance is compromised. To see this in action, we might note the steps taken by Korean Air to improve communication on the flight deck in response to the crash in 1999 of Air Cargo Flight 8509. The problems associated with traditional cultural norms were consciously addressed. It became obvious that deference to age and seniority has no value when clear, assertive communication is required. In this case, the first officer failed to challenge the incorrect action being taken by the captain as a result of an instrument fault. Exceptional performance involves interdependence and sound judgement. We must eliminate outdated social convention, issues of personal ego and professional hubris. With this in mind, we might also look more closely at the concept of 'Servant Leadership', which places emphasis on shared purpose and joint effort to achieve *Superordinate Goals*.

Servant Leadership offers a perspective that draws strongly on higher-order principles. It emphasises qualities of humility rather than hubris. The philosophy is to serve, which emphasises the importance of ethical considerations, values and shared purpose. The focus is on developing others, and the concept resonates with values-driven organisations, enhancing the focus on *Superordinate Goals*. Essential attributes of Servant Leadership include active listening, self-awareness and empathy. The focus is on *People, Integrity, Excellence* and *Stewardship*, reflecting socialised use of power to achieve shared objectives. In contrast, a desire for *personal power* is driven by ego, control and pursuit of status. Effective leadership involves personal conviction and energy, which must be focused effectively to deliver exceptional results. This is the power of conviction, backed by authenticity, which influences others and creates purpose. Future-focused leadership combines vision and dialogue to unlock motivation and create commitment.

For many, *Servant Leadership* represents good business practice, especially for organisations facing the challenges of a VUCA world. The model puts other people at the forefront, highlighting the role of the leader in developing people's capability, motivation and a sense of shared purpose. This type of approach becomes increasingly relevant when organisations are faced with the challenge of *Wicked Problems*. There is a need to focus on the interdependencies that underpin professional effectiveness. Much of the research evidence relating to leadership effectiveness now incorporates principles of authenticity and self-determination. Building on these insights makes it easier to clarify the steps that contribute to exceptional performance.

Developing Leadership Ability

The task of identifying high-potential people is vital for any organisation, and current performance is often taken as an important indicator of future potential. However, as the Corporate Leadership Council study demonstrated, there are a range of factors that reduce potential for progression to the next level. To gain a better understanding of the challenge, we need to look more closely at issues affecting current performance, and particularly ideas relating to *Learning Agility* and the underlying psychological construct of *Cognitive Flexibility*, which notes three important elements:

- The ability to quickly *restructure one's knowledge* in response to radically changing situational demands
- *Transfer of knowledge and skills* beyond the initial learning situation, which may require a significant shift of mindset
- *Speed of response* and effectiveness in adapting response to changing demands (recognising constraints and future trends)

Current performance is not a reliable measure of future potential. Corporations and other organisations (including political parties selecting candidates) must assess relevant competencies with an appreciation of key areas of activity and emerging demands. The overall perspective is future-focused; it's not a single competency. And even if people have underling talent and clear strengths, it means little without personal motivation, purpose and commitment. In both individual and team-based coaching, the concept of *future-focus* may be useful in considering effectiveness. We need to review capability across different areas of activity, appreciate how to direct energy effectively and understand the competencies required for superior performance.

These themes can be linked to the assessment of eight competencies, which help clarify the behaviour and approach contributing to effective leadership. We can also refer to the 3H Model, which can be viewed in the context of leadership and highlights (i) analysis and vision that identifies interdependencies, (ii) skills that develop capability and collaboration and (iii) the accountability, adaptability and resilience that support positive outcomes.

Within these broad themes, we can develop specific competencies. Useful examples are summarised below. These offer insight into how effective leaders achieve exceptional results:

Vision/shared purpose: Clarifies priorities and key objectives; sets clear direction, shows personal conviction and focuses on overall purpose. Communicates a clear, positive view of future possibilities.

Evaluating information: Checks information and assumptions, identifies trends, underlying patterns and the action required to increase effectiveness. Monitors and reviews progress.

Building connections: Understands interdependencies that affect outcomes; shares and seeks information, builds relationships with people beyond the immediate team.

Engaging the team: Creates meaning and insight, praising people for the quality, value and importance of their work. Involves the team in developing solutions; seeks feedback and suggestions.

Influencing for results: Listens, remains calm and responds constructively to differing views. Adapts approach to the people and situation; but also maintains focus, explains reasoning and confirms priorities. Builds commitment and a sense of shared purpose.

Developing capability: Provides support and encouragement, helping others gain experience, confidence and confirmed competence. Reviews strengths, areas for improvement and encourages initiative to solve problems and achieve progress.

Encouraging accountability: Clarifies objectives, roles and responsibilities; provides feedback to help people improve performance. Takes prompt action to maintain consistent standards; acknowledges good work and resolves issues.

Leading for results: Responsive to unexpected change; develops more effective approaches and keeps people informed of progress. Shows resilience; maintains focus on priorities and creates confidence.

Effective leaders see their role in the context of the bigger picture, aware of what others are doing, and appreciating role interdependencies. Exceptional performance requires the ability (and supporting systems) that integrate separate pieces of information to identify patterns and trends. The concept of *Cognitive Flexibility* also implies that leaders have developed the *PsyCap* required to respond to unexpected challenges. They demonstrate personal conviction and persuade others on the best way forward. Louis Pasteur said that *Chance Favours the Prepared Mind*. It's therefore not surprising that *Star Performers* understand the expectations of others and manage important role relationships. They scan the environment, aware of possibilities and the elements that shape outcomes. *Cognitive Flexibility* requires *balanced processing of information*, which also supports authenticity. Effective leaders aim to develop insight by considering alternative viewpoints. They build on feedback and anticipate a shift of context.

Outstanding leadership builds on the four elements of authenticity summarised earlier. These include *self-awareness, balanced processing of information, relational authenticity* and *authentic behaviour* expressed through positive action. In addition, *Self-Determination Theory* confirms the benefits of developing an *autonomy supportive leadership* style. This helps develop people's sense of competence (mastery), autonomy (self-directed activity/control) and experience of positive relationships, which contribute to intrinsic motivation and commitment. Practical steps in the process can be linked to *Purposeful Conversations* with *awareness, insight, meaning and support* (AIMS).

The elements support effective leadership by engaging the team in developing solutions, creating options (on how best to proceed), clarifying roles, responsibilities and priorities. Exploring connections also provides a foundation for *Systemic Coaching*. This involves identifying what is required by others and establishing a meaningful rationale for action. We also note that understanding connections contributes to developing an *autonomy supportive leadership* style that minimises the use of coercive control, e.g. comparisons with others, external reward and sanctions. As part of the overall process, *Purposeful Conversations* help strengthen *extrinsic task motivation* by helping people internalise the standards, i.e., how we do the work. Within a team, tailored tasks/responsibilities (*Job Crafting*) can make better use of skills and also serve to enhance people's resilience.

Gaining Insight from Balanced Processing

Changing mindset is a challenge. Old assumptions block underlying potential and perceptions filter our view of situations. This impacts on how we perceive options and our subsequent response. The way we interact with others can help or hinder reflective thinking. For example, it's evident from neuroscience that logical thought and rational analysis is undermined when people are under stress or emotionally angry or upset. The frontal cortex of the brain, which handles more logical, abstract thinking, fails to function effectively when the amygdala is reacting to stress or senses a threat. Limbic reaction damages a measured response.

In this type of situation, where someone is angry or upset, the best response is simply to acknowledge the individual's feelings and concerns, and provide space for them to express their emotion, or possibly withdraw and meet again later. However, even when anger or confrontation is not the main issue creating the problem, there is still an underlying weakness in many people's perceptual process. This arises because of the way we typically 'take on board' information, and how we then respond. Jung's insights on how we assimilate information and make decisions can be useful in this context, helping clarify broad personality differences. Jung referred to 'personality types' that are comprised of several traits. These form distinct clusters. They influence how we perceive the world, how we process information and shape our preferences when making decisions.

Jung suggested that effective perception of events involves both Sensing (of the present) and Intuition – reflected in an appreciation of possibilities beyond what is currently evident. Sensing focuses on *'facts as perceived'*, exemplified in *FELT Thinking* and analytic philosophy. Intuition, in contrast, offers a future-focused appreciation that discerns subtle but significant undercurrents. The second preference is more evident in people who see the bigger picture, rather than relying on a reworking of old ideas. It makes the difference between *production focus* and *blue-skies research* in engineering. Although both preferences are available, genetics, education, cultural norms and experience result in one preference becoming more established. Synaptic pruning may accelerate the process. Rather like someone who is colour-blind, you may not be aware of how this affects your perceptions. Most people move towards a dominant preference. It means, for example, that some have a strong desire to close down options and achieve certainty. This appears to thwart chaos, but it is illusory if important, half-hidden issues have been overlooked. Intuition also has its dangers if people pursue a vision that ignores relevant data and proves unrealistic.

Our thinking and decisions are shaped by a range of factors. Some people are keen to explore options, whereas others want everything decided as soon as possible. We know that decision-making and innovation, e.g. in management teams, is improved by gender balance and diversity. In contrast, a lack of vigour (and excess ideology) causes executives and politicians to close down options and neglect options. The *FELT Deficit* hinders analysis, and the consequences of actions are rarely foreseen. Proposals are justified by the self-referenced confirmation of the group. *Legacy Thinking* arising from *Systemic Educational Deficits* leads to a conceptual void. As H. G. Wells noted, focusing on *subject content* results in the world being seen as '*geography and history, as the repeating of names that were hard to pronounce, and lists of products and populations and heights and lengths, and as lists and dates*' (*The History of Mr Polly, Everyman*, p. 6). Wells reminds us of the need to consider context and principles. Historical myth also fuels misguided nationalism and the worst forms of dysfunctional political leadership.

At work and in politics, the desire for 'quick closure' needs to be well managed to maintain balance. Time urgency and the desire to minimise uncertainty can also lead to arbitrary targets and unrealistic schedules. Not surprisingly, urgency undermines reflective thinking. It can also lead to excessive control and encourage a culture of micro-management. This runs counter to the autonomy supportive leadership, which combines *authenticity* and *integrity of purpose*. These are important characteristics of more effective leaders. In contrast, we can identify managers and officials who fail to set clear direction and are reluctant to take the initiative, e.g., in setting priorities and defining standards. They may well rely on procedures and protocol – and appear hesitant or leisurely in moving towards closure. We start to perceive the lack of personal conviction and focus needed to confront and resolve issues. There is a reluctance to take a clear stand on matters of principle, which can also contribute to the impression of duplicity.

Important issues that shape behaviour, such as *closure certainty vs reluctance to commit*, provide insight into professional effectiveness. Understanding current work preferences, which indicate how people are directing their energy, provides a basis for future change. We can also identify links between underlying personality traits and the competencies required for superior performance. A coach helps the *Focus Person*, i.e., the person receiving feedback or coaching, see issues in the context of their role, including the behaviour, approach and performance expected by others. One of the criteria relating to self-awareness involves an appreciation of how one's actions affect other people. This goes beyond the more immediate goal of becoming more aware of personal strengths and areas for improvement. A 360-degree feedback process, for example, should highlight the expectations of others and offer insights that support future development.

Relational authenticity and authentic behaviour are part of the foundation for outstanding leadership. These qualities need to be seen in the context of the role and the culture of the organisation. An effective coach or mentor should have the ability to discuss these issues, and also be able to offer insight relating to professional objectivity, personal values and how best to resolve conflict. This capability is enhanced by having insight into the concept of *Cognitive Flexibility* and appreciation of the four steps contributing to the development of *Authenticity*.

With rapid change, effective leaders also need insight into issues affecting people's sense of identity and purpose. Shared purpose, for example, helps build commitment and also reduces disaffection. In contrast, a legacy of misinformation and duplicity undermines trust. Many trace this (threat to social cohesion) back to the Iraq War (2003) and false claims relating to 'weapons of mass destruction'. Some go further. In *HyperNormalisation*, it is argued that governments, financiers and technological utopians have, since the 1970s, given up on the complex 'real world' and built a simpler 'fake world' run by corporations and kept stable by politicians. However, this may only have served to magnify the problem – *the stories politicians told their people about the world had stopped making sense; in the face of that, you could play with reality.*[9]

When people no longer trust information, they become ever more vulnerable to conspiracy theories and manipulation. It becomes essential to question 'thin sliced' information presented by various news channels and social media personalities. We find echoes of the Big Lie as stories gain legitimacy through repetition and the advertising revenue created by click rates. With the spread of COVID-19 in 2020, social media became flooded with speculative and false stories, some with a strong ideological bias. To take just one example, Reuters Fact Check highlighted 'False Claims' directed at the Gates Foundation.[10] People confused 'digital tracking' (via mobile phone apps) with hidden nano-chips in vaccines and the possibilities of mind control. The problem is made worse by a failure to appreciate Bayesian reasoning or the reality of Occam's Razor, which both highlight the importance of *prior probabilities*. (See notes in Appendix 3.) When people don't understand the rationale for action, their sense of competence and control is undermined. Leaders must therefore provide a meaningful rationale and build alignment around a clearly defined plan of action. In organisations, a clear focus also contributes to *brand identity*, linked to consistent values, binding principles and clarity on how things get done.

Many people struggle to make sense of a rapidly shifting context. They find it difficult to understand new developments. The challenge for leaders is to deal with increasing complexity and widespread uncertainty. It's therefore important to encourage greater transparency and clarity when reviewing issues. This 'scoping out' provides the basis for the *meaningful rationale* that builds on solid information and substantive evidence. It's much better to deal effectively with complexity rather than pursue short-term, expedient solutions that create even bigger problems in the future.

Challenges Facing Authentic Leaders

Super-Ps are aligned with ethical values, but are expressed in the form of rules, protocols and norms that influence aspects of thinking and behaviour. They apply to individuals and groups. In organisations, 'The Vision' provides clarity concerning future direction and values. This is then expressed in broad terms in the Mission Statement. Toyota's global corporate principles include the statement: *Dedicate ourselves to providing clean and safe products and to enhancing the quality of life everywhere through all our activities.*

Higher-order principles are abstract, providing a point of reference that contributes to strategic alignment and help create meaning. 'Integrity', for example, is associated with values linked to honesty, truthfulness and trust. These can be expressed through guiding principles on how activities are conducted. At work, the challenge is then to achieve alignment of personal values – and individual views of priorities and professional standards – with the norms, culture and strategy of the organisation. There needs to be clarity of communication and constructive dialogue. Authentic leaders emphasise *consistency of approach*, which helps maintain focus, achieve shared purpose and offer a reference point in appraisal, training and development.

Authenticity requires self-awareness, responsiveness to feedback (*balanced processing of information*), transparency and consistency. It's best delivered through an *autonomy supportive leadership style* that develops *capability (competencies), control (through self-directed activity) and cooperation*. Evidence shows that this increases motivation, including effort directed towards less interesting tasks (*extrinsic task motivation*). It encourages internalisation of principles, building on a *meaningful rationale* that is anchored in values, principles and clear purpose. *Self-Determination Theory* offers important insights. Studies confirm the value of three themes: (i) maximising opportunities for employees to take the initiative (by making choices and solving problems), (ii) giving non-controlling (information-focused) feedback and (iii) recognising and accepting others' perspectives, needs and feelings.[11]

Some assume that the *limbic brain* triggers feelings and emotions, quite separate from the *frontal cortex*, which controls rational thinking. However, the gap between *emotional reaction* and a more measured *professional response* is bridged through vocabulary, principles and insight. Words matter. EEG imaging reveals that exploring *what's working well* and *future possibilities* increases brain activity in the right hemisphere and helps lift mood. Building on empathy also helps change perception. In organisations, the elements contributing to trust can be maintained by introducing review systems that are fair, impartial and ensure consistent standards. They help create enabling conditions that endure over time. Constructive, *Purposeful Conversations* also help enhance work climate. They support coaching and more effective performance review by building on insights from Self-Determination Theory. The process highlights the importance of AIMS.

Case Study: Berkshire Hathaway

We asked ChatGPT to compare the business philosophy of Warren Buffett (Berkshire Hathaway) with ideas linked to traditional management theory. This prompted the following comments:

Warren Buffett, the CEO of Berkshire Hathaway, is known for his unique approach to business and investment, which contrasts with traditional management theory in several ways:

1. **Long-term thinking**: Buffett's philosophy is to invest in companies for the long-term gains, rather than focusing on short-term gains. This approach differs from traditional management theory, which often prioritises short-term results and meeting quarterly financial targets.
2. **Value investing**: Buffett's investment strategy is based on value investing, which involves buying stocks in companies that are undervalued

by the market. This approach contrasts with traditional management theory, which often emphasises growth investing, where companies with high growth potential are favoured, even if they are overvalued.

3. **Decentralised management**: Berkshire Hathaway operates with a decentralised management structure, allowing subsidiaries to operate independently. This contrasts with traditional management theory, which often favours a more centralised approach with decision-making concentrated at the top of the hierarchy.

4. **Ethical conduct**: Buffett places a strong emphasis on ethical conduct and doing the right thing, even if it means sacrificing short-term profits. This is in contrast to traditional management theory, which often prioritises profit maximisation above all else.

5. **Risk-taking**: Buffett is known for taking calculated risks, such as investing in undervalued assets. This approach contrasts with traditional management theory, which often emphasises risk avoidance and minimising uncertainty.

Overall, Buffett's business philosophy is characterised by long-term thinking, value investing, decentralised management, ethical conduct and risk-taking. This contrasts with traditional management theory, which often prioritises short-term results, centralised decision-making, profit maximisation, risk-avoidance and growth investing.

Our Comment: *Warren Buffett has emphasised the importance of 'durable competitive advantage' when assessing a business. He has also highlighted the need for executives to demonstrate intelligence, energy and integrity. Trust is critical to reputation, which means that expectations must be clear and backed by effective systems that quickly address errors.*

Notes

1 Kernis, M. (2003). Toward a conceptualization of optimal self-esteem. *Psychological Inquiry*, 14, 1–26.
2 Amnesty International, Staff Wellbeing Review, January 2019, p. 21.
3 Oxfam criticised over Haiti sex claims. BBC Report, 11 June 2019. Report available at: https://www.bbc.co.uk/news/uk-48593401
4 Höchli, B., Brügger, A., & Messner, C. (October 2018). How focusing on superordinate goals motivates broad, long-term goal pursuit: A theoretical perspective. *Frontiers in Psychology*. Vol. 9. Available at: https://doi.org/10.3389/fpsyg.2018.01879

5 Deci, E. L., Olafsen, A. H., & Ryan, R. M. (2017). Self-determination theory in work organizations: The state of a science. *Annual Review of Organizational Psychology and Organizational Behavior*, 4, 19–43.

6 Chatterjee, A., & Hambrick, D. C. (2007). It's all about me: Narcissistic Chief Executive Officers and their effects on company strategy and performance. *Administrative Science Quarterly*, 52(3), 351–386.

7 Avolio B. J. & Gardner, W. L., (2005). Authentic leadership development – Getting to the root of positive forms of leadership. *The Leadership Quarterly*, 16(3), 315–338.

8 Failed London Garden Bridge project cost £53m. BBC Report, 13 February 2019.

9 *HyperNormalisation*. (2016). BBC Documentary Film – Wiki Entry.

10 Reuters: False claim. *Bill Gates planning to use microchip implants to fight Coronavirus*, 31 March 2020.

11 Gagne, M., & Deci, E. L. (2005). Self-determination theory and work motivation. *Journal of Organizational Behavior*, 26, 331–362.

References

Chatterjee, A., & Hambrick, D. C. (2007). It's all about me: Narcissistic Chief Executive Officers and their effects on company strategy and performance. *Administrative Science Quarterly*, 52(3), 351–386.

Kernis, M. H. (2003). Toward a conceptualization of optimal self-esteem. *Psychological Inquiry*, 14(1), 1–26.

Chapter 6

Developing Capability

To help gain a better understanding of exceptional performance, imagine an actor on stage in a theatre. Outstanding actors do more than simply repeat their lines. They are also aware of their position, and how their energy and actions affect the performance of others. Talented performers also appreciate the role of other actors, where they are positioned, and how their contribution adds value to the overall production. Most importantly, your approach and actions affect their performance. The energy and intensity of the performance are also bound up with context. Experienced actors are able to adjust their approach in subtle ways to better engage with each new audience. It is a dynamic process, so well-focused energy, emotion and clarity of purpose come together, contributing to an outstanding performance.

High performance at work builds on similar insights. It's important to see someone's role in the context of wider objectives, and consider how aspects of mindset affect behaviour. Whilst personality characteristics influence our actions, they are only part of the picture. Broad personality factors may affect career choice, and accountants are more likely to be introverts. Some people are more attentive to detail and try to avoid error. This pattern links to the trait of *conscientiousness*, but it could also contribute to *anxiety*. However, broad characteristics tell us less about the attributes linked to superior performance. We need insight into motivation and mindset, and responsiveness to role demands and context. For example, if an auditor fails to question the validity of data, or how financial performance has been estimated, problems can easily arise. Such problems typically involve

DOI: 10.4324/9781003439707-7

professional shortcomings and inadequate systems. Auditors may be reluctant to probe the claims of a powerful CEO. As in a play, performance suffers when actors have misplaced their script. Integrity and consistency are central to the *Superordinate Principle* (*Super-P*) profile. Expediency damages values, undermines integrity and erodes a meaningful rationale.

Mindset is influenced by personality, but work behaviour is not simply the consequence of fixed traits. Beyond these, we know that *innate needs* (for competence, autonomy and relatedness) and *acquired needs* (shaped by personality and environment) are important. McClelland, building on the work of Henry Murray, highlighted the importance of needs linked to *achievement, affiliation* and *power*. Managers, for example, generally express a higher need for power than affiliation. However, training moderates the tendency to pursue *self-referenced action*, or the desire to *command and control*. By way of an analogy, the sheepdog has evolved from a wolf, but the energy is directed differently. Most leaders are responsive to feedback and appreciate that dialogue and consultation improve performance outcomes, whereas 'command and control' simply gets grudging, short-term compliance. The path to exceptional performance starts with clear thinking and clarity of purpose. For most people working in organisations, the context starts with their role. This is set within the activities of the team, but also involves cooperation with other people. Team leaders need to consider how the various roles relate to the overall objectives of the department and the organisation.

Behaviour is influenced by *Super-Ps* and enhanced through motivation, resilience and commitment. Training and experience contribute to particular ways of responding to role demands. The term *Work Preference* refers to an individual's preferred style of working. It captures how people currently engage in activities and direct energy and attention. *Work Preferences* can be viewed as someone's typical response to work demands, reflecting familiar ways of dealing with various aspects of the job. These patterns may also affect well-being and resilience at work, as positive aspects of behaviour can enhance personal resources and Psychological Capital (*PsyCap*). However, other elements may be less helpful, dissipate energy and contribute to pressure. Energy must be directed effectively in order to achieve high performance. This also involves being aware of the needs and expectations of others and how best to manage role relationships.

To improve understanding of these issues, a coach or team leader can look at aspects of behaviour and simply ask: '*how do we make progress?*' It's not helpful to dwell too long on previous wrongs, injustices or shortfalls. A future-focused perspective involves identifying practical actions that help us move forward. One technique is to imagine that the situation has already changed and things have improved. *What would have changed? What would people be doing differently?* The focus is on positive change, and there is certainly scope for managers and team leaders to improve aspects of their current work behaviour. *Research shows that 'two-thirds of managers demonstrate significant short-comings and a full 75% are viewed by direct reports as the most stressful aspect of their job'.*[1] Lack of empathy and consistency, and inadequate influencing skills, contribute to the problem. Despite all the talk of 'learning and development', leadership deficits are evident in many organisations. This also reminds us of the need for feedback systems that make standards explicit. Principles should not be left vulnerable to misinterpretation and manipulation.

Operational principles need to be anchored within a narrative that creates relevance. The goal is exceptional performance, but this requires leaders to really grasp critical factors. Clearly, intelligence and IQ must match role demands, but once a threshold is achieved, other elements become more important. Think of IQ as the processing power of a computer. It needs to be sufficient to meet operational demands – and spare capacity can enhance analysis of complex, challenging data. This element is also comparable to functional (technical) competence. However, even the fastest computers depend on software that processes and interprets data. Apps must deliver consistent, high-quality output. However, requirements change over time, so old software gets patched and updated, but the advance of technology creates further demands. We reach a point when we realise that legacy code struggles to meet requirements. The tech will advance, in the same way role demands change, and the old apps will no longer be capable of delivering results.

People need a future-focused mindset to overcome the limitations of legacy code. Personality traits bind us to some aspects of behaviour, but not all elements are hardwired. Mindset links to attitudes and assumptions, but these can be shaped by training, cultural norms and insight. Problem behaviour is not inevitable, but organisations need systems that enhance transparency, accountability and capability. This reduces the free-space for dysfunctional behaviour. Enabling conditions start with feedback systems that provide the foundation for action. Boundaries create clarity and the actors are then clear about purpose.

Exploring Work Behaviour

Maintaining high performance involves focusing on priorities and taking appropriate action. Although role requirements and professional standards may be clear, people will vary in how they respond to demands. It can be useful to gain insight into people's approach and discuss how best to achieve positive outcomes. Pario 'work preference' studies, for example, indicate that more effective leaders (validated against Assessment Centre performance) tend to be more reflective and are also willing to question the status quo (i.e. the current situation). They generally avoid getting too involved in checking details and don't worry unduly about making mistakes. This reflects a more adaptable style, with (relatively) less emphasis on structured planning. We also find that most managers are willing to take control of situations and set direction for others. Leadership roles require people who are able to express their views, and also demonstrate commitment to achieving results. They anticipate that other people may not share their views. This expectation (of limited consensus) may well contribute to a more assertive, positive approach. It means that effective leaders are willing to discuss issues, but also seek to influence other people's thinking.

The aspects of work behaviour described above are examples of themes that can be explored as part of a review of work preferences and how people perceive their role. Discussion might be with managers/team leaders or other experienced professional staff. A competency-focused perspective is useful in exploring issues relating to analysis, interaction and delivery. The 3H *(Head, Heart and Hands)* model can help clarify issues relating to various areas of activity, and link to specific roles and task demands. It is then possible to build on the model by including three, maybe four, competencies within each cluster. These can be supported with examples of activity. For example, 'Analysis', for a first-line manager, could focus on requirements six months ahead, whereas senior managers assess issues that will impact in six years. The 3H model can help review effectiveness, highlighting competencies needed to support activities. For example:

- **Analysis**: Assessing options and priorities, with awareness of wider issues
- **Influence**: Engaging effectively with people, persuading others on appropriate action, creating focus and shared purpose

- **Delivery**: Showing personal conviction in delivering high-quality outcomes; identifying with the task and displaying the personal resilience required to overcome setbacks

The 3H model reviews approach, looking at (i) analysis, dealing with problems and identifying options, (ii) setting direction, team involvement, influence and persuasion and (iii) conviction and perseverance in meeting challenges, decision-making and delivering results. Profiling work preferences offers useful insights that can be used to support coaching and personal development. The focus is on *role-related behaviour*. Examples of such dimensions include the attention directed towards *Developing Opportunities* and *Organisational Awareness*. These are aspects of behaviour that are best viewed in the context of the role. They can be difficult to assess via (indirect) inference derived from personality traits.

Gaining insight and experience is a prerequisite for developing competence and confidence. However, for strengths to be expressed, we need to understand the issues that affect outcomes. If we lack this insight, it becomes very difficult to unlock underlying potential and focus on what is important. It's also important to recognise that sometimes we don't say what we need to say. We may struggle to gather our thoughts, express ideas, raise concerns or describe feelings. One problem is that we may not see all the options we have available. Sometimes, emotion or ego will block a more effective response. The way we frame things, based on assumptions and suppositions, undermines a well-judged, balanced response. Afterwards, we may reflect on why things went wrong. Recognising situations that cause you problems is an important step in self-development. Coaching can help develop capability by facilitating mental rehearsal, but it needs to be non-directive. We need time to understand context and rework the old script. Often, as with rebellious adolescents, emotion interferes with reason. This contributes to a self-referenced, faulty logic. It's difficult to make sense of advice when we don't see the tripwires that prevent progress. This is why non-directive coaching will surface issues and prompt reflection, but it does not deliver other people's answers.

A coach can help you achieve a change of perspective. This can build on the *Johari Window* model, discussed in Part II, Chapter 10. This illustrates how feedback helps us gain insight. The process opens up the 'unknown' area linked to underlying potential. Without feedback we struggle to develop or focus energy effectively. A number of issues can hinder performance and inhibit or block underlying strengths. There are risks, for example, if we think it's better to work with like-minded people. We may also assume that performance depends on others sharing our outlook. The illusion of *assumed consensus* and reliance on a consensus-based approach creates problems. Some newly appointed leaders fail because they expect others to immediately comply with their particular way of working. This creates tension and can undermine balanced processing of information. Assumptions must be cross-referenced against *Super-Ps* and relevant competencies. Leaders should therefore reflect on how work preferences affect analysis, team working and delivery of results. Work preferences can be viewed in the context of the role. Significant elements include the following:

Reflective thinking: (potential strength: strategic perspective); *considers the consequences of action and reflects on wider, longer-term issues relating to a problem.*

Accuracy of working: (potential strength: avoids risks); *personally checks details and emphasises precise, accurate work to avoid the risk of mistakes.*

Change oriented: (potential strength: identifies possibilities); *is questioning, forward-looking and positive about change.*

Planning and organisation: (potential strength: systems and procedures); *adopts a structured and systematic approach characterised by planning and organisation.*

Organisational awareness (potential strength: managing change); *discusses issues, assesses reactions to new proposals, and adapts approach*

Setting direction: (potential strength: leadership focus); *sets priorities and defines requirements for others, displaying a confident, positive approach.*

Team orientated: (potential strength: facilitator or 'team player'); *works well with others in the team, discusses issues and is supportive when people have problems.*

Influencing others: (potential strength: motivating others); *achieves personal impact, gains people's attention and influences the team's thinking and direction.*

Personal conviction: (potential strength: professional objectivity); *openly discusses problems, confronts issues and takes a firm stand on matters relating to quality and professionalism.*

Decision-making: (potential strength: creating clarity); *evaluating information and deciding action quickly and effectively, confident of the outcomes.*

Positive approach: (potential strength: achievement and results focus); *sets high performance standards, works hard to overcome problems and achieve results.*

These examples relate to a number of elements covered by the *Pario Work Preference Questionnaire*. Also note that each of these dimensions, if taken to excess, can become a problem. Relative emphasis on each element needs to be assessed in the context of role requirements. For example, personal conviction and a willingness to confront problems may contribute to a perceived strength, but, if taken to excess, could lead to an abrasive style. This could then damage team morale and overall performance.

Essential skills for performance review and coaching relate to active listening and questioning. The techniques may, for example, make use of in-depth, competency-based interviewing methods. This approach is useful in gaining insight into how someone has dealt with specific situations, rather than a description of what they would do in the future. The technique is called *Behavioural Event Interviewing* (BEI), and was developed by McClelland.[2] It's an adaptation of Flanagan's *Critical Incident Interview*, dating back to 1954.[3] Unfortunately, procedures can be degraded over time. Many 'competency interviews' have become superficial checklists and fail to achieve any real insight into behaviour or mindset. However, the BEI Model is effective, but only if the person conducting the review discussion has relevant skills. To get the maximum benefit from the questioning process, a *funnel approach* helps move from 'open' questions (that encourage conversation) to more probing clarification and review of key points.

Not least, the BEI approach avoids the problem of being too direct in trying to assess areas of potential weakness. It encourages the use of an effective structure – and good management of time! The BEI Model is also useful in reviewing *Critical Incidents*, i.e., the more demanding aspects of the role, which are often scenarios that differentiate the elements linked to superior performance. The BEI approach helps explore behaviour in context. In a selection interview, for example, up to 15 minutes might be allocated to a specific 'theme' or topic, so typically three areas might be reviewed during the time available. This approach can offer insight into how someone has responded to *more challenging* role-related requirements, and helps explore both strengths and areas for improvement.

Discussions can be adapted to meet particular requirements. In the context of performance review, the process can help explore how someone approached a task and identify specific aspects of behaviour that were positive or less helpful. If using this method, we are usually reviewing events that have happened in the last 6 to 12 months. It can help explore various themes, which might include effectiveness in evaluating options, building team capability, managing change and creating commitment and shared purpose.

1. Start with an **Open** Question or Prompt
   So, what was happening at that time...
   Describe a challenging situation...
   Tell me about a problem you faced...

2. **Focus** on an interesting/important issue and Explore
   Tell me more about the XYZ issue...
   So, what aspects did you consider...?

3. **Probe** for more information.
   Why did you focus on those issues...?
   What did you do then...?
   ...and how did they react...?
   Who decided on this...?

Show you are listening; use eye contact, nod and say things like 'hmm', and 'yes, I see'. Recap on key points and check that you have understood correctly.

4. **Clarify and Conclude** with some direct questions...
   What did you achieve...?
   Was this really satisfactory...?
   Why did you settle for...?

You should **summarise** the main points as you go along and check your understanding of what the person has been telling you. (It is always possible that you have misheard something or need to clarify a particular point.)
   Use phrases like the following:

let me re-cap on what we have covered....
so, let me check that I understand this... You are saying...
can I just clarify that I understand that fully...

If the person is talking excessively, and the discussion is losing focus (or you feel you are losing control), you can use summarising to move back to the main subject. For example:

> *OK, we have spent some time talking about....*
> *That's a really useful insight.... Let's move on to the next step...*
> *So, I see there was a lot happening with XYZ... Now, coming back to the*
>   *main point...*

Avoid leading and superficial questions when you are trying to explore issues or probe details (to make a clear, impartial assessment). Avoid questions that lead to agreement with your views, encourage vague comment or result in 'superficial' self-description (unless you are doing this consciously, perhaps to confirm a point).

These leading/superficial questions include the following:

> *Do you think you are able to...?*
> *Are you confident about...?*
> *How effective/capable are you at...?*

If you are trying to identify trends or consistent patterns of behaviour, which may contribute to problems, look for **specific examples** of what the individual said, or did, in the context of particular situations, or problems they have dealt with. Assess their approach, and their evaluation of the issues, by asking neutral questions, and do not show disapproval!

For example:

> *So how did the rest of the team react...?*
> *What further action did you take...?*
> *What exactly did you do...?*

You might also wish to ask:

> *On reflection, (how) would you have done it differently...?*
> *What did you learn from the experience...?*

At the end of the discussion, you should have a clearer understanding of the key issues and the factors which are likely to be affecting the individual's performance at work, and be better able to link observations to competencies. Summarising the key points provides the opportunity to review (i) the approach and underlying thinking and (ii) the outcomes and consequences of decisions.

Improving Performance Management

Unfortunately, 'Performance Review' (performance management) systems are often not well regarded. There is still a fear of the dreaded appraisal. Very often, this is because the process is poorly designed, fails to link the 'what' (objectives) and the 'how' (approach). Simply focusing on 'performance against targets' does little to help review the competencies required for high performance. This restricts dialogue, reducing the opportunity for fresh insights and development of the 'meaningful rationale' that helps change behaviour. As a result, traditional appraisals do little to build people's motivation or commitment.

Effective performance review needs to consider three elements that contribute to positive outcomes. These include (i) a clear appreciation of the goals and performance standards that need to be achieved, i.e., the outcome measures; (ii) the competencies that contribute to superior performance in the role, i.e., how the work is completed, and (iii) the dialogue that supports a meaningful review process and encourages personal development. The review should help identify both personal strengths and areas for improvement. An effective appraisal builds on essential questions (*why, what, and how*) and may benefit from use of the AIMS model. This raises awareness, offers insights, encourages meaningful action and provides support.

Effective appraisal (particularly from the *Focus Person's* perspective) benefits by building on the following:

Awareness… of one's own approach, work preferences and areas of
effectiveness
Insight… of new developments, relationships, wider requirements and
expectations
Meaning … supported by the rationale for change and priorities for
attention
Support… the action/resources required to develop capability and make
progress

The focus of the appraisal process is on performance review, not on pay or reward. We suggest that the appraisal process is part of a wider system. It should be supported by effective communication of how the process links to personal development and overall performance management. The leader needs to not only demonstrate conviction backed by a meaningful rationale but also apply **Chunking**, so that separate pieces of information can be bound together into a meaningful whole. This works in two ways: firstly, clustering items under a label clarifies how everything comes together. This creates context and meaning. Secondly, linking maybe three to seven items (to form a chunk) helps to free up working memory. We are better able to make sense of the data and see the bigger picture. We get more meaning when we see how things connect.

This type of review helps clarify overall direction, sometimes expressed in terms of the old cliché of the 'compelling vision'. This links to *Superordinate Goals*, which should then be anchored in guiding principles. The review process contributes to shared purpose and alignment between individuals and groups. In an organisational context, goal clarity supports a meaningful rationale. This defines approach, use of resources and clarity concerning priorities for action. In seeking to develop alignment, to cascade these goals through the organisation, it's important to consider questions relating to *why, what and how*. We take the process a step further, with *Purposeful Conversations* that provide a framework linked to AIMS. This also fits with the important elements that enhance autonomy supportive leadership.

Steps in Performance Review

Setting the context

Summarise the wider context and relevant background issues.
What objectives were agreed for this period?

Reviewing progress

An initial open question might be on the lines; how has X been going? The Focus Person can talk about progress and achievements.
The aim is to understand what was achieved, but also issues that arose. There may, for example, have been unexpected problems that had not been anticipated. This is an opportunity to identify learning points and note any areas of concern.

Discussing the approach

Refer to examples relating to the best approach.
Identify situations where the Focus Person was effective and why.
Identify three positive outcomes and one or two areas for improvement.

Using specific examples, consider how the existing approach could be adapted. Could strengths be developed by applying them in new situations? *How can the Focus Person build on existing strengths?*
   Clarify recent changes and what the organisation is trying to achieve. Discuss and agree priorities – and how time and energy might be used to best effect in the coming months. Also discuss and clarify important role relationships and, if appropriate, how these might be managed more effectively.
   Check what support/resources/training is required to help the person adapt their approach and develop new skills. Remember to set SMART objectives, which are agreed and which provide the basis for the Personal Development Plan (PDP).

Agreeing future goals

Why are these goals and priorities important? Set objectives in a wider
   context. Discuss what is required.
How might these objectives be achieved? What is the best approach?

There should be clarity concerning outcomes and performance standards, but also scope for the individual to identify the best approach.
   Successful appraisal is not just an annual event. Think 'bite-sized' and agree regular monthly and quarterly follow-up meetings to discuss progress. Take the opportunity to build on frequent *Purposeful Conversations* that help ensure that the activities are aligned with the goals of the team/department and wider organisation.
   In the context of performance review, there is also an opportunity to consider *Job Crafting*, which enables a role to be better tailored to an individual's strengths. This may be useful as part of an overall strategy within a team or a department.
   The competencies listed below can contribute to professional effectiveness, particularly for leaders and those in more senior roles. They can be applied across a range of situations. The sample statements describe aspects of behaviour that are linked to each competency. When supported by

360 degree feedback, the review process can help clarify current strengths and areas for improvement. (A 360 review also enables written comments to be added to the feedback). The focus is usually on six to eight competencies that are relevant to the role. You can also rate your own approach and effectiveness, in the context of your current role, on each of the following statements. Use a 4-point scale, anchored as follows: 1: below requirements; 2: marginal; 3: competent; 4: exceeds requirements.

Vision/shared purpose: Clarifies priorities and objectives; sets clear direction and shows personal conviction; focuses on purpose and possibilities. Communicates a clear, positive view of the future.

Evaluating information: Checks information or assumptions, identifies trends, underlying patterns and the action required to increase effectiveness. Monitors and reviews progress.

Building connections: Understands interdependencies that affect outcomes; shares and seeks information, builds relationships with people beyond the immediate team.

Engaging the team: Creates meaning, praising people for the quality, value and importance of their work. Involves the team in developing solutions; seeks feedback and suggestions.

Influencing for results: Listens, remains calm and responds constructively to differing views. Adapts approach to the people and situation; explains reasoning and confirms priorities. Builds commitment and shared purpose.

Developing capability: Provides support and encouragement, helping others gain experience and confidence. Discusses strengths and areas for improvement, supports action to solve problems and make progress.

Encouraging accountability: Clarifies roles, responsibilities and objectives; provides feedback to help people improve performance. Takes action to maintain consistent standards and acknowledges good work.

Leading for results: Demonstrates flexibility when faced with an unexpected change of plans; develops more effective approaches and keeps people informed of progress. Shows resilience; maintains focus on priorities and creates confidence in others.

How an organisation decides to complete activities is shaped by its systems and culture. There are assumptions relating to how things are done and the required standards. In the context of developing motivation, role clarity, meaningful work and self-directed activity are all important. However, engagement also requires commitment, which comes from identification, emotional attachment and shared purpose. Key elements in this process relate to appropriate support and development, productive relationships with managers, peers and colleagues, and clarity of purpose. This may also link to communication by senior management, requiring awareness and clarity. A loss of progress and purpose can lead to disaffection.

In *7 Principles for Exceptional Performance*, creating *Enabling Conditions* is highlighted as a priority, alongside development of competencies. People do not excel when there are inadequate resources, poorly designed systems and a dysfunctional culture. To improve performance and develop capability, organisations need feedback processes, which include employee surveys. These should be well designed, so they are based on the best psychometric procedures. We therefore need well-focused questions that link to clear elements. These are likely to include items related to autonomy supportive leadership, positive relationships with colleagues, and a sense of shared purpose. Issues relating to role clarity, work pressure, reward and recognition are additional factors. Demographic analysis can support an in-depth report that can reveal issues in particular departments, or specific role groups, age bands or length of service.

In a *thought experiment* called the 'original position', John Rawls suggested we apply a 'veil of ignorance' so we don't know our position, gender, age or capability in society. We then consider what rules need to apply for things to be fair and create stability.[4] The process encourages a rational and impartial view of what is required. The same concept can be applied to the operation of organisations and to the type of culture that is needed to ensure long-term sustainability. As noted in the introduction, *Environmental, Social Governance* (ESG) is part of this thinking. There is an increasing expectation that leaders will base their decisions on *Super-Ps* that incorporate sustainability and a stakeholder perspective.

Developing Resilience

Developing resilience is an important leadership theme that contributes to well-being and effectiveness. Understanding work preferences and performance-related competencies contributes to building resilience.

However, it's important to remember that resilience is not simply a personality trait. Some people score higher on *mental toughness* or *hardiness*, but everyone will get worn down by excessive job demands. Undue emphasis on specific attributes, such as *tough mindedness*, can cause problems in distorting the culture and reducing appropriate levels of support. It reduces responsiveness to operational challenges. It may also cause some 'robust' individuals to take on too much. Everyone has limits, but lack of self-awareness and inadequate support will reduce motivation and commitment.

As discussed earlier, resilience can be developed through coaching focused on developing proactive behaviour. It is also supported by *autonomy supportive leadership* that aims to enhance people's personal resources. This involves helping people look at work demands and challenges from a fresh perspective. Issues that may need to be resolved include team engagement, a lack of self-belief or a tendency towards self-critical thinking. This is often characterised by people attributing success to good fortune or external factors but equating setbacks or failure to their own shortcomings. Team dialogue and *Job Crafting* may also be relevant in this context.

It's useful to put successes and setbacks in context. We should be wary of those who (too easily) deliver lavish praise. Their mood can be fickle, so they may also overreact to setbacks. There is also the wider problem of self-critical thinking. What holds true is the value of dialogue and consultation, both in understanding issues and in helping to create a sense of meaning and purpose. The role of the leader is therefore critical in helping clarify issues, providing support and ensuring that resources are available to help people make progress. An effective team leader takes action to reduce external pressure, maintain focus and facilitate positive interaction with other groups.

We asked ChatGPT to comment on the value of non-directive, solution-focused coaching. This prompted the observation that

> the brain is capable of changing and developing throughout life, through a process called neuroplasticity. Non-directive, solution-focused coaching can facilitate neuroplasticity by helping the 'coachee' to identify and practice new behaviours and habits, which can create new neural pathways in the brain. This can lead to more effective behaviours and outcomes, such as improved communication and decision-making skills.

Solution-focused coaching encourages team members to develop practical, achievable improvements. A team leader can help people identify options, offering feedback and support to develop competencies and increase performance capability. A non-directive, solution-focused approach draws on insights from SDT and neuroscience. The process can help shift assumptions, encourage future-focus and identify steps leading to performance improvement. The practical steps involved in *Coaching for Exceptional Results* are discussed in more detail in the next chapter.

Notes

1 Hogan, J., Hogan, R., & Kaiser, R. B. (2011). Management derailment. In S. Zedeck (Ed.), *APA handbook of industrial and organizational psychology, Vol. 3. Maintaining, expanding, and contracting the organization* (pp. 555–575). American Psychological Association.
2 McClelland, D. C. (1998). Identifying competencies with behavioral event interviews. *Psychological Science*, 9, 331–339.
3 Flanagan, J. C. (1954). The critical incident technique. *Psychological Bulletin*, 51, 327–358.
4 John Rawls. Available at: https://en.wikipedia.org/wiki/Original_position

Chapter 7

Coaching for Exceptional Results

Solution-focused conversations support professional development and enhance performance. The primary focus is on *Developing Capability*, which is a core competency of effective leaders. Important elements include clarifying context, checking assumptions and reviewing aspects of behaviour. Note that these workplace conversations are not a substitute for the specialist support required to resolve deeper issues. The first step in work-based *Purposeful Conversations* typically involves clarifying context and objectives. It is important to be clear about desired outcomes, and also build on a well-tested coaching model. A number of models are reviewed in this chapter, with a focus on what is practical, well-validated and more likely to deliver useful results.

To be effective, coaching conversations require clarity about outcomes. Being clear about objectives is part of the initial scoping discussion. In some cases, this may form part of a wider leadership development process. The *Focus Person* may recognise the need to develop new skills, change their approach or overcome some problem. However, it's important to be cautious in accepting things at face value. If you are going to be effective in developing capability, reflect on the context and prepare carefully. Think about role requirements, work relationships and other people's expectations. Understand the competencies that contribute to performance in the role.

In some instances, development may be supported with 360 degree feedback. This can help raise awareness of personal strengths and areas for improvement. The 360 review is useful in offering insight into the expectations

DOI: 10.4324/9781003439707-8

of different groups, which can include the immediate manager, direct reports, peers/colleagues, customers and stakeholders. The review may offer insight on how to manage role relationships more effectively. This provides a starting point, and it is then possible to use specific coaching techniques to support lasting change. However, coaching also requires appropriate levels of trust, empathy and insight into issues affecting motivation. It also helps to understand the competencies linked to professional effectiveness.

Exploring the context provides an opportunity to discuss how tasks were approached and the consequences of actions. Empathy is strengthened by active listening, which involves checking understanding, summarising and reflecting back key points. Coaching requires discussion of underlying issues and assumptions. This goes beyond the immediate problem or someone's initial thoughts on what they see as the problem. *Sometimes, people become so immersed in the problem that they cannot see the solution.* New insights help change underlying assumptions. The review may, for example, help an individual recognise the need to involve others or start to consult more widely. This shift of mindset can be particularly relevant for technical specialists or people with a fixed, habitual approach. To achieve real change, activities need to be placed in context. We also need to understand what triggers a response.

Effective change involves identifying the steps leading to improved outcomes. The process also requires a *meaningful rationale* that helps change our perception. Previous experiences shape memories and create positive or negative associations. Events sometimes trigger an emotional reaction, anchored in memory, which limits our response options. This might trigger the thought sequence: *I have a meeting with X... it's always a disaster... I'm dreading it!* This will affect the tone of the next meeting. It's important to recognise that the response, e.g. to a perceived threat or challenging situation, will seem logical to the individual. The reaction fits with the aroused emotion, but it's not a balanced response. The perception of the situation (and options) needs to change in order to shift the emotion. Any significant, lasting change must therefore make sense to the individual, and involves a shift of perspective. They may, for example, learn to approach situations in a way that plays to their strengths. However, to achieve real change requires a future-focused perspective, with a clear sense of options and possibilities.

Competencies backed by personal strengths will increase effectiveness across a range of situations. There is a dynamic process that involves understanding what is required and then assessing how best to respond. A significant challenge in managing interdependencies at work involves *understanding other people's expectations.* Leaders must also take steps to create a sense of shared purpose that enhances motivation. Very often, people will have blind spots that hinder performance. Coaching can then be useful in helping them to see things from a fresh perspective. Insight is essential in order to achieve positive outcomes. However, not all coaching interventions are equally effective, so it helps to follow a proven model. This adds focus, helps surface issues and provides a foundation for future progress.

Over the years, numerous coaching models have been developed. Some are simplistic, but others help make interventions more effective by exploring perceptions, mindset and behaviour. Each model describes a process (series of steps) designed to help achieve goals. However, it's important to ask: *How effective is this model in resolving issues?* Unfortunately, many models are not based on sound theory, and anecdotal stories don't provide evidence of validity. However, we can identify 'sound principles' that underpin more effective approaches. The first step is to recognise that people view situations in the context of what they have experienced previously. If a particular type of situation has previously caused problems, you may well experience anxiety in similar situations. This can easily prompt a physical reaction. Someone may, for example, appear tense or fail to respond appropriately, particularly when this is viewed in the context of role requirements. The behaviour may then trigger a negative reaction in other people. This process appears to confirm the individual's underlying anxiety. However, this type of negative, self-reinforcing pattern of thinking can be changed with effective coaching.

Solution-Focused Coaching

Coaching models should do more than set a goal and agree options and actions. As self-help gurus like to point out, *the thinking that created the problem will not help you move forward.* We must pause, reflect, look at things differently and then respond. More effective approaches build on insights offered by the ABC model (developed by Albert Ellis). This clarifies how we view situations and make sense of what is happening. Our reaction is linked to emotions and feelings, which affect behaviour and consequences. The steps can be summarised as follows:

A: Activating event (an external situation or trigger event)
B: Beliefs (individual interpretations and thoughts about the event)
C: Consequences (emotional and behavioural reactions resulting from those beliefs)

The ABC model underpins *Cognitive Behavioural Therapy* (CBT), which encourages *conscious reflection* on feelings and response. It helps us differentiate between an immediate, *emotional reaction* and a more measured, *balanced response*. In work situations, it's possible to use the ABC model to reflect and consider options. We can identify elements affecting a situation and the consequences of current assumptions. This helps change the way we see things. One of the attributes of high performers is that, when faced with a situation, they reflect on *antecedents, assumptions, boundaries* and *consequences*. The outcomes follow on from the response. Experienced professionals try to take account of future effect, particularly when the consequences are not immediately evident and easily overlooked. High performance is enhanced by ABC thinking, which helps leaders identify patterns, see trends, recognise interdependencies and anticipate possible outcomes. Contrast this with the *law of unintended consequences*, so often associated with the *FELT Deficit*.

Leaders can also develop capability by adopting a competency-focused perspective. Coaching then helps explore thinking and response, and the steps required to be more effective. To achieve high performance, *mental rehearsal* is also useful in changing perceptions, managing possible emotional reaction and developing more effective options. This is explored further in Part II (Module 2). It's also worth noting that competency frameworks vary across organisations, and these range from 'excellent' to 'awful'. Mapping models against the broad 3H framework can be useful. This refers to *Head, Heart and Hands* and helps clarify competencies linked to the following:

- Problem-solving/analysis, professional awareness and vision, planning and monitoring
- Interpersonal effectiveness, team working, influencing skills and developing capability
- Achievement focus, with the energy and resilience to set direction and overcome obstacles

Effective coaching helps us develop a forward-looking, positive perspective. *Solution-Focused Conversations* build on this perspective, combining positive thinking and practical action.[1] The objective is to reach a desired *future state* that is meaningful to the individual and/or members of the team. Rather than dwelling unduly on personality or psychological issues, the focus is on raising awareness of the problem and the context. Envisaging positive outcomes and identifying 'action steps' help people make progress. The 'solution-focused' approach can also be applied to team-based interventions. For example, *the Center for Creative Leadership* offer tips that can enhance this type of team coaching. These include *a focus on the whole, systems-thinking, comfort with ambiguity, the ability to set boundaries and a long-term view.*

Similar to the ABC perspective, the SPACE model also supports constructive interventions.[2] This involves clarification of the *Situation* and the nature of the task. This then links to *Physiology*, asking what physical reaction occurred when you faced this scenario. We come back to the question: *What are the perceptions shaping thinking, feelings and response?* In the *SPACE* model, *Action* links to discussion of *Cognition*. This comes back to *Emotions*, encouraging reflection on how current perceptions (and expectations) affect someone's response. *How did you perceive the situation, and what were your expectations concerning the outcomes?* What sort of 'self-talk' is influencing perception, response and assessment of options? More broadly, the review might introduce questions of purpose and the principles guiding actions. This takes us back to core questions involving *why? what?* and *how?* We are reminded that we are more effective when we have clear goals, backed by principles, and can identify the steps required.

An interesting aspect of coaching and development is the extent to which people come to identify with what they do. However, this also means that people are sometimes drawn into 'models and methods' that become closely aligned with their professional identity. Any criticism of the method can then cause cognitive dissonance. *Neuro-Linguistic Programming* (NLP), for example, is an approach that gained widespread popularity in the last quarter of the 20th century. It has roots in linguistic theory, later adding snippets of psychology. However, many of the ideas presented by NLP practitioners are not supported by evidence. A detailed, highly critical evaluation of NLP can be found in the *International Review of Coaching Psychology* (2019, Vol 14-1). It concludes that *analysis leads undeniably to the statement that NLP represents pseudoscientific rubbish, which should be mothballed forever.*[3] The IRCP feature also notes that proponents of NLP *claim* that certain eye movements are reliable indicators of thinking patterns, including truth-telling or lying. However, research shows that *pseudo-scientific claims of eye movement can be reliably dismissed.*[4] The IRCP review of NLP concludes: *the research evidence within coaching suggests there is almost no evidence to support the multiplicity of claims made about its effectiveness as a 1-to-1 coaching intervention to facilitate behavioural change.*[5]

We then asked ChatGPT to 'Evaluate the reliability and validity of NLP, particularly with reference to eye movement and direction of gaze'. It stated, '*the reliability and validity of NLP are questionable, particularly with regards to eye movement and direction of gaze*'.

That said, some NLP concepts do align with cognitive psychology research. These include the following:

Reframing: Using language to view a situation from a new perspective (and change appreciation of context). *Can be related to the ABC model.*

Presuppositions: Self-awareness of how existing beliefs, assumptions and mindset shape thinking and influence reaction or response. *This links to ABC coaching.*

Double binds: Self-limiting thinking, e.g. 'the choice is A or B', leading to the 'illusion of choice' (e.g. between two bad options). *This links to the cognitive schema that shape mindset.*

Single binds: Accepting something as true, which creates a sense of obligation and restricts choice, e.g. follow rules (not be proactive). *This links to perception and motivation theory.*

Embedded commands: Placing emphasis (emotion) on keywords or phrases in a statement that affects influence and control. *This draws on psychological insights.*

Misplaced theory does little to improve our self-awareness, or provide insight into how best to manage other people's expectations. This is important in the context of developing high performance at work. Adopting a broader view of *personal development* also raises questions relating to meaning and purpose. An effective model not only adds focus and direction. It should also help clarify underlying issues affecting perceptions and thinking. It needs to consider how people perceive things at the current time and how they respond in a situational context. For example, using a situational cue, such as a notepad, can reduce a tendency to interrupt others. It's an effective way of changing behaviour by diverting attention to a separate activity.

It can also be useful to use questionnaires that raise awareness of how personality traits, or broader 'type categories', affect behaviour. There is also value *Work Preference Profiling* that offers more direct insights into aspects of motivation and how the individual is currently directing their energy and attention. This is useful when reviewing job demands, and how your approach might affect other people. A similar theme is evident with 360-degree feedback, which reviews your self-assessment of role-related competencies alongside the ratings of others. These groups can include customers, clients and business partners. However, the technique that is most readily available on a day-to-day basis simply involves building on *Purposeful Conversations.*

Purposeful Conversations

An approach, similar to that outlined in the ABC and SPACE models, is applied through *Purposeful Conversations* linked to AIMS. This approach is based on a dialogue that increases understanding and insight and fits with *Autonomy Supportive Leadership.* The structure enables a coach or a team leader to build on the core elements of increasing awareness, creating insight, developing the rationale for meaningful action, and establishing the support needed to make progress. This might, for example, include follow-up meetings, monitoring and further review. From a leader's perspective, the process involves four clear steps:

Awareness: *Understanding the other person's views, using open questions to explore*
What is the context? How is the person currently responding?
Are there situational cues that contribute to the response?
What has happened previously? e.g. the impact of work pressure, and the challenge of balancing urgent vs important job demands

Insight: *Exploring the wider issues, context and constraints*
What options are available? What's the 'bigger picture'?
What would others see? Where can you achieve progress?
What else is happening? e.g., clarify new developments in other teams

Meaning: *Confirming the reasoning, value and purpose*
What is the ideal outcome? Where are the main priorities?
Which steps lead towards valued outcomes? (Clarify meaningful action.)
How would you know you are making progress?

Support: *Ensuring the resources, capability and self-belief*
What resources and support are available (within you) to reach goals?
How do we overcome the blocks or obstacles that are hindering progress?
What follow-up action will contribute to progress?

The AIMS model helps explore the context, clarify important aspects of thinking and identify response options. Awareness can be increased through feedback and reflection, which is encouraged through exploratory questions; *e.g., what helped you achieve the previous (successful) outcome?* Insight is also strengthened by understanding the context; *e.g., how does this fit in with other developments?* The manager or coach might also ask related questions; *e.g., what are other people's expectations? What would other people see, which shows we're making progress?* In moving towards meaningful action, the value of each step requires *conscious awareness* of its importance, and how it contributes to the overall task. Even though some activities are not intrinsically interesting, their importance to others (colleagues/partners or to overall progress) makes them meaningful. When challenges are evident, support and encouragement provide resources that help overcome the setback or difficulty.

Exploring an individual's awareness of how things are at present can be linked to developing insight into wider issues and response options. **Systemic Coaching**, for example, takes this broader perspective and focuses on improving the effectiveness of connections and interdependencies that contribute to high performance. At a practical level, the process starts with active listening. This includes identifying views, opinions and concerns by summarising, acknowledging and reflecting back key points. This dialogue can also include discussion of values, purpose and the underlying rationale for 'doing something new'. We can therefore see clear links between this approach and the idea of **Team Coaching**, which places individual performance in the broader context of roles, responsibilities, interdependencies and systems.

Motivation is always enhanced by identification and engagement in meaningful action. The process is particularly relevant in the context of leadership. Raising awareness and creating insight contribute to the development of a meaningful rationale that supports a course of action. Support introduces an essential extra level to the motivational process, moving it from transactional to trust-based and meaningful, which also helps enhance underlying commitment. As one small example of effective communication, a dentist might tell a patient to use dental floss. Explaining the importance of removing small particles, which reduces gum disease, creates a *meaningful rationale*. This insight encourages the patient to develop a new pattern of behaviour.

Remember that *extrinsic task motivation* needs to be supported by ongoing dialogue and encouragement. It is easily 'switched off' unless it has been fully internalised, but the *discretionary effort* required for high performance can be maintained as long as people remain focused. This is easier to achieve if there's an understanding of how the task contributes to overall outcomes, including the work of colleagues. An awareness of inter-dependencies encourages improved communication – and anticipation of what other people require. Cascading effective communication through an organisation helps avoid the problem of 'Babelization' that contributed to the Challenger Disaster, as discussed in *7 Principles for Exceptional Performance*. Effective leaders work to create a culture that encourages people to see things clearly.

Purposeful Conversations can be adapted to address an organisation's requirements and might be viewed, perhaps in the context of a manager's role, as a focused discussion between the leader and individuals in their team. The conversations are based on a simple underlying structure, which is designed to encourage shared purpose and agreed action. The process involves raising awareness and acknowledging alternative views, clarifying priorities in the context of changes and new developments, and agreeing overall direction.

In many organisations, these *psychologically informed conversations* have never been rooted in the culture. This may be because there is an assump-tion that roles and responsibilities are clear and people agree on the best way forward. Unfortunately, this is often not the case. Recent changes may be missed or overlooked. There will be differences of opinion on the best course of action. Over time there will be *a gradual drift in people's aware-ness of priorities* and *how best to achieve results*. Well-structured *Purposeful Conversations* then help clarify objectives and confirm the standards of performance that are required. This focus might also be expressed in terms of reviewing the expectations of customers or clients, and what needs to be done to implement change and achieve positive outcomes. This is all part of the core remit of someone in a leadership role. It should never be dependent on bonus payments that are deemed necessary to 'energise and motivate' the senior management team.[6]

Most importantly, effective leaders use *Purposeful Conversations* to enhance the motivation and commitment of individuals in the team. To be effective, the process must be viewed as a two-way dialogue that is designed to create shared understanding and agreement on how best to proceed. However, additional action will be required when we find that the culture is dysfunctional and managers are incompetent. *Purposeful Conversations* can be short 'cup of coffee' conversations and also enhance traditional appraisals. The focus is on developing awareness and insight

– and achieving a shared *understanding* of the *Why? What? and How?* questions that clarify issues and confirm priorities.

There is a far greater chance that the half-yearly or annual appraisal will be successful, e.g., in raising motivation, commitment and performance, if formal review is supported by ongoing conversations that help generate insight, create a sense of involvement and enhance purpose. The four 'coaching steps' relating to AIMS can be summarised as follows:

Step 1: Awareness and Acknowledgement

The first step builds on active listening and enables the manager to check his/her understanding of the current situation. The opening remark comments may be on the lines:

...it's a couple of weeks since we talked about your project/assignment and I was wondering how things are going. This will then require a follow-up question that prompts the person to say more about their view of priorities, timescales, progress, resourcing etc. Remember that the first step should help the leader develop awareness of the Focus Person's thinking. This will contribute to *balanced processing of information.* It is possible, for example, that a team leader has concerns about the rate of progress and the team's ability to meet timescales. This first step encourages *appreciation of context* and provides the foundation for making positive progress.

Step 2: Insight into Issues

The second step enables the manager or the team leader to respond to points and develop insight, e.g. offering updates on new developments that affect the work of the *Focus Person.* There may, for example, be a value in clarifying roles or responsibilities following recent changes. The team leader might say: *'I need to update you on some developments that will affect our work. We need to review priorities and timescales'.* Unexpected changes have implications, e.g. in terms of how work is organised or completed, and this may prompt irritation or disagreement. *Purposeful Conversations* provide an opportunity to create common ground and resolve differences.

Step 3: Meaningful Action

The third stage involves discussing the reasons for a particular approach or proposed changes. This also provides an opportunity to confirm why things are important and how they contribute to the overall objectives. Managers and team leaders may assume that things are clear. However, it's better to recognise that there is no 'shared understanding' of what is required or why something is important. Solution-focused coaching shows the value of picking-up on what's working well, talking about the ideal outcome, what the team might see happening (maybe in a month's time?) and acknowledging the skills and abilities that have helped the person overcome previous setbacks or problems. Amplify the solution the person is working towards and return attention to future possibilities. This may involve asking about the person's best hopes, e.g. following the recent changes, and what other people would see (as we start to make progress).

The Pario TEAM Index (survey) confirms that team members lose motivation when managers fail to set clear direction or discuss the reasons for a course of action. People need to understand the reasoning, with the opportunity for dialogue to clarify issues. There's clear value in learning to build on *Purposeful Conversations* that enhance motivation.

Step 4: Support

One of the most important factors contributing to motivation involves making progress in day-to-day work. Frustrations and setbacks discourage and demotivate, whereas support and encouragement, including conviction on what can be achieved, strengthen motivation. Ensuring appropriate support is an important part of the process. *Purposeful Conversations* may well include discussion relating to the resources and skills required to complete assignments. If there are pressures or problems, possible solutions, e.g. *Job Crafting*, might be considered in order to make better use of strengths within the team.

Purposeful Conversations help clarify issues affecting motivation and performance. The task of building motivation and commitment starts with the line manager, but also depends on effective systems established by 'People Development' or 'Human Resource' (HR) departments. Senior executives also need to be mindful that managers and team leaders, just one or two levels below, may not fully understand or share the vision, timescales and 'mile-stones' (achievement metrics) that create a clear sense of future direction. Alignment is made easier when the culture is anchored in the *Superordinate Principles* and dialogue that guide actions.

Traditional approaches to corporate communication can easily miss the importance of dialogue in building real commitment within the organisation. Executive coaching is often an essential element in creating the space for the reflection and planning on how best to move forward.

One important insight is that many people struggle with a shift of perspective. Imagine a well-lit corridor, where everything is clear. The team leader then opens a side door, which leads down a dark, damp discouraging staircase. Nothing looks familiar and people are no longer listening to the flow of information. We then need to do some **Chunking**, to pull data into clusters and create points of light. The team leader can connect chunks and create a narrative. Without a clear story, backed by conviction and a meaningful rationale, progress will be slow.

Team leaders also appreciate that the current situation is a point of temporary equilibrium. With this in mind, *Force Field Analysis* can be useful in assessing the pressure to change, and the factors that contribute to resistance to change. Of course, one of the most significant obstacles is the perception that the objectives are not achievable, or the change is not really necessary, or simply not worth the effort. It's only through dialogue that this mindset starts to change.

Additional Questioning Techniques

An important part of the coaching process involves identifying the *Focus Person's* potential blind spots. In some cases, underlying assumptions may contribute to people misreading options. The challenge is to encourage reflection on the best way of getting from 'A to E', particularly in situations where people have little appreciation of the less obvious points relating to steps B, C and D or how to manage the important links in the process. Important themes that affect coaching outcomes include (i) how past events are interpreted, (ii) awareness of context and interdependencies and (iii) our willingness to adopt a proactive approach.

The way people express themselves offers insight into their thinking. When talking about work activities, some people make *regular reference* to 'we' or 'they', but with less indication of their personal opinion or the action they initiated. It may then be useful to ask directly: 'what was *your* view?' or 'what was *your* preference?' or 'what did *you* do?' You can also use the question, *Why?* but this should be in the spirit of enquiry, not accusation. The coach can also pick up on sentences/comments that are unfinished or trail off with words like 'really': for example, *I didn't have any problems, really….* One technique is simply to repeat the final word, but as a question, e.g. 'really?' In a coaching or development context, this can encourage reflection, open up underlying issues and help identify what was learned from a setback or challenging situation.

Exploratory questions provide the basis for active listening, creating scope to summarise key points and check understanding. These initial, 'open' questions can be supported by appropriate follow-up, so that we probe for more information and seek to add focus.

Example 1: Tell Me about the Project...

You want to understand the motivation and reason for involvement:

> 'How did you get involved in X ...?'
> 'What were the main issues...?'

Consider possible follow-up questions:

> 'Tell me how you viewed the choices/options?'
> 'What action did you take?'
> 'How did you decide...?'
> 'What was the outcome...?'
> 'How satisfied were you with the result...?'

Example 2: Tell Me about the Challenges...

You want to check their perceptions:

> 'How did you get involved/what was the background?'
> 'What were the main challenges you faced?'

Consider possible follow-up questions:

> 'So how did you view the choices/options?'
> 'How did you assess the benefits...?'
> 'What impact did this have ...?'
> 'Would you have done anything differently?'

Example 3: What Could Have Been Done Differently?

You want to check their reaction and assessment of the task:

> 'How did this come about...?'
> 'How did you respond to this situation?'

Consider possible follow-up questions:

> 'Tell me how you viewed the choices/options?'
> 'Tell me about the implications...'
> 'What were the possible consequences?'
> 'Were there other options available...?'
> 'What did you learn from this...?'

Example 4: So, What Did You Learn From X?

You want to check their perspective and assessment of the problem:

> 'What was the background to this...?'
> 'Why was it an issue?'

Consider possible follow-up questions:

> 'So how did you view the choices/options?'
> 'What other issues did you need to consider...?'
> 'What were the potential benefits...?'
> 'What were the potential risks or "downside"?'
> 'How did other people react...?'
> 'What would you do differently next time...'

Note: You might be seeking to understand someone's commitment to a task, even if it's routine or not intrinsically interesting. Is there evidence of awareness of the wider issues and objectives? It may be important to assess personal commitment or the person's sense of responsibility for outcomes. In summary, a team leader or a coach might look for evidence of the person's perceptions of options and engagement in activities.

> Assessing issues, e.g. 'I made the decision'
> Appreciating wider considerations, e.g. taking account of differing views and opinion
> Explaining the rationale for decisions, e.g. what, how, why
> Describing involvement in delivering results, e.g. who and when

Questions or 'prompts' help the coach understand the issues and context. These might include the following:

...tell me more about your work
...who are your customers?
...who benefits from your work?
...say more about your role in this team
...tell me about any changes that are taking place
...how are these developments/changes affecting you?
...what challenges are you facing in your work?
...what challenges are faced by others in the team?
...what steps have you taken to change things?
...how do the activities of other people link to your work?
...to what extent does other people's performance affect you?
...how does your work (your role) link to others in the team?
...what steps did you take to deal with this situation?
...how does this affect your work/relationships with colleagues?

The focus of this type of discussion is linked to the situation and context. The conversation (or interview) is typically anchored in role activities, role relationships and response to demands and challenges. The first step involves exploring perceptions of how things are, and the options and possibilities that are available. The process can help clarify the essential steps required to overcome complex demands. These may also contribute to increased resilience in meeting role demands. Opportunities for *Job Crafting* might be explored as part of the process. When reviewing performance-related issues, identify challenging situations and consider the approach that leads to positive outcomes. Understanding competencies helps clarify how to apply strengths – and the steps that contribute to enhance positive outcomes.

Hypothetical questions, e.g. '*What would you do if...?*' can be used to prompt thinking about *Critical Incidents*, i.e., demanding situations linked to the role that require the best possible approach. Exceptional performance is based on thinking and behaviour that make a difference. This insight, gained from experienced managers and technical specialists, provides the basis of *Situational Judgement Tests*. These may be used to support selection, but the insights are also relevant in coaching. Typically, people who are very effective in their work will consider more options (and adopt a different perspective and approach) to someone who is less effective. Differences between people who display average and superior performance may well involve issues relating to *cognitive flexibility*, reflected in the ability to apply existing knowledge in new ways. Coaching can support this process. However, this needs to be backed by an understanding of competencies: e.g., the need to consult others or show personal conviction, linked to a clear plan of action. In the next chapter, we look more closely at the attributes required for effective leadership.

Intentional change builds on a five-step process that starts with vision and principles, awareness and insight. It then requires action steps to achieve progress, backed by appropriate support and resources:

1. **Vision**
   What is the focus of the change? Ask the questions: why, what, and how?
2. **Current reality**
   Are you aware of the elements that contributed to the current situation?
3. **Priorities for change**
   How do you develop insight/appreciation of the issues that affect progress?
4. **Taking action**
   How do we ensure meaningful action that contributes to purpose?
5. **Support**
   What support and resources are required to help maintain motivation?

Moving from awareness to insight is an important step. However, it is sometimes assumed that 'self-awareness' is the solution, when it is really only the first step in a wider process. The third step linked to *priorities for change* is particularly important, as it requires insight into the context and interdependencies that affect outcomes. It moves from 'awareness' to a deeper appreciation of the systems, relationships and resources that affect outcomes. This insight provides the basis for meaningful action and clear purpose. Anyone engaging with an organisation benefits by understanding *how systems operate* and *how people get things done*. Effectiveness therefore involves understanding the *Rules of the Game*.

To achieve real insight, a leader might ask: What's the Vision? (the 'Why') and What are the Outputs? (the things we need to achieve). These core questions can also be viewed with reference to the expectations of customers, partners and stakeholders. We might then ask: What systems are needed? What resources are required? What are the interdependencies, roles and relationships that affect outcomes? What support, back-up, resources and training are required to make progress? Have we got the resilience and commitment to maintain performance? If not, how do we build it?

We sometimes arrive in unfamiliar places and are faced with fresh challenges. This may expose the difference between apparent awareness and real insight. Many years ago, I found myself in Chirundu, a small town adjacent to the Zambezi, where the Otto Beit Bridge connects Zimbabwe to Zambia. The bridge was constructed by the Beit Trust in 1939, and is said to be the first twin-cable suspension bridge to be constructed outside America. It was manufactured in the North of England, designed as small sections, transported across Africa and delivered to Chirundu. Construction required the expertise of a senior engineer (Ralph Freeman).

Across the bridge is Zimbabwe, and you get a real sense of Africa, with lions and elephants. One afternoon, a Danish colleague suggested we take a workboat out on the river and do some fishing. This was a small aluminium workboat with an outboard engine. It seemed like a good idea. We headed to the middle of the river and switched off the engine, drifting downstream with the current. There was a wonderful sense of the open expanse; the picture book Africa. After five minutes or so, my colleague restarted the engine, and we headed back upstream and repeated the process. We did this a couple of times, but on the third occasion a hippo surfaced some 30 metres behind us. I pointed it out to my colleague, who responded, 'no problem'. The hippo disappeared below the surface and then resurfaced, but now only 25 metres from the boat. I said *'the hippo is after us'*, and he replied, *'maybe we should start the engine'*. Fortunately, it started on the first pull of the cord and we quickly headed back upstream.

At the time, I didn't realise that the hippo is extremely dangerous and a small boat offers no protection. The experience prompted some thinking about *Awareness, Insight and Context*. Not least, we can neglect context and fail to grasp issues, particularly the dangers concealed beneath the surface. We must separate awareness from insight. All too often awareness is *self-referenced*, when the real need is for deeper insight. Unexpected events impact our effectiveness, and also on how we interact with other people. At work, for example, we need active listening to understand people's ideas and concerns. Leaders need to probe underling issues. Constructive discussion and a solution-focused mindset help us achieve progress.

Insight is externally focused, not self-referenced, and seeks to take account of the wider context, systems and interdependencies. Neuroscience suggests we need to escape the internally focused Default Mode Network (DMN). If the context changes, everything shifts and assumptions no longer hold true. Insight builds on feedback and significant experience, but requires an appreciation of what is '*outside and beyond*'. It may involve understanding other people's expectations and how best to achieve positive outcomes. It informs purpose and supports progress. We all need to learn the *Rules of the Game* and develop scripts that help us make sense of challenging situations and unexpected demands.

HIPPO: A Model for Solution-Focused Coaching

A 'hippo incident', as the previous anecdote illustrates, is an unexpected, significant challenge that demands an immediate, *solution-focused* response. We start with the ABC model, but also the realisation that you can sometimes find yourself in a bad situation. You need to start the engine. As a coaching model, HIPPO builds on *Hope, Insight, Purpose, Progress and Options*. The elements remind us of essential steps in responding to a demanding or 'primal fear' scenario. We must maintain a positive mindset and focus on effective action. More broadly, well-rehearsed scripts create space for reflection. A colleague may push for immediate action, but your script might run: '...*thanks for the suggestion... give me a few minutes*'.

Hope builds on a positive view of future possibilities, enhanced by self-belief and confirmed competence. *Psychological Capital* provides the inner resources that help us meet demands. Resilience increases with a mindset that accepts personal responsibility, backed by a willingness to take action. This framework of clear purpose, pursuit of options and signs of progress helps increase motivation. As we move forward, we can review direction and adapt to further demands. Achieving positive outcomes requires a mindset that builds on insight and resilience. There's no space for complacency or outdated assumptions.

Notes

1 Cavanagh, M., & Grant, A. (2014). The solution-focused approach to coaching. *Complete Handbook of Coaching* (2nd ed, pp. 51–64). Sage Los Angeles | London | New Delhi | Singapore | Washington DC.
2 Edgerton, N., & Palmer, S. (2005). SPACE: A psychological model for use within cognitive behavioural coaching, therapy and stress management. *The Coaching Psychologist*, 2(2), 25–31.

3 Witkowski, T. (2010). Thirty-five years of research on neuro-linguistic pro-gramming. NLP research data base. State of the art or pseudoscientific decoration? *Polish Psych Bulletin*, 41(2), 64.

4 Wiseman, R., Watt, C., ten Brinke, L., et al. (2012). The eyes don't have it: Lie detection and neuro-linguistic programming. *PLoS-One*, 7(7), e40259.

5 Passmore, J., & Rowson, T. (Spring, 2019). Neuro-linguistic programming: A review of NLP research and the application of NLP in coaching. *International Coaching Psychology Review*, 14(1) (Special Issue - NLP Coaching), 67.

6 Company wrongly paid executive bonuses for cooperation with inquiry into faulty computer system. Article re. the UK Post Office (*The Guardian*, June 2023). Available at: https://www.theguardian.com/business/2023/jun/20/post-office-boss-apologises-for-inquiry-bonus-payments

Chapter 8

Developing Potential

It's important to separate current performance and future potential. Performance may be good, but future potential could be limited. Not least, technology results in rapid change and new skill demands. Moving from a well-defined role to a wider, team-leading responsibility presents challenges. There may be increased uncertainty and pressure. The demands sometimes go beyond someone's capability, a point noted in *The Peter Principle*. This suggests that in traditional and hierarchical organisations people are often promoted to their *level of incompetence*. Successful performance at one level leads to an expectation of reward and advancement. However, the job demands and competencies required in the new role may require a step change in capability. People get promoted, but peers, colleagues and team members then discover a fundamental problem. The demands of the role outstrip the person's ability to respond.

This scenario is most evident when someone is promoted from a specialist professional role to a leadership position. Typically, the person is no longer directly responsible for task completion. They now need to establish objectives, clarify priorities and ensure that roles are well defined. It becomes necessary to engage other people in dialogue, with emphasis on achieving agreement and enhancing people's motivation. Businesses talk about *creating alignment* (of activities with overall goals) but this also involves developing a meaningful rationale, showing personal conviction, surfacing problems and developing people's capability. Leaders engage with others, resolve conflict and create a sense of purpose. Not everyone has the underlying insight, motivation and energy required to be an effective leader. Most are familiar with the basic notions of IQ and EQ. Very often, an inadequate

 DOI: 10.4324/9781003439707-9

leader may be 'intelligent', but lack interpersonal skills. The elements of self-management, essential for future success, may be missing. There is also a need for *generosity of spirit* to create the time, space and mindfulness (clear awareness) needed to understand other people's views and concerns. It's important to understand the factors that impact on future potential.

Many organisations use critical reasoning tests to evaluate how well candidates can evaluate written and numerical information. Those who are significantly below average, assessed against role demands, will find it more difficult to *quickly and accurately* make sense of complex data. Whilst very high scores may be beneficial, there is more evidence that indicates that low scores are detrimental. One important insight goes back to World War II and the UK *Special Operations Executive* and the US *Office of Strategic Services*. They found that the overall assessment process was more effective at identifying those likely to fail, rather than those guaranteed to succeed. Inevitably, luck also played a part in determining outcomes.

Critical reasoning tests mostly reflect 'straight-line' thinking and analysis, but this does not always translate into a mindset that is creative and adaptable or can make sense of disparate pieces of information. Technicians, for example, may have excellent analytical ability when presented with well-defined data. However, they frequently struggle to 'join the dots' and see the bigger picture. When anticipation is a problem, rational analysis becomes restricted. There is an inability to adapt to a changing, unpredictable context. This is one reason why people who score high on critical reasoning tests may fail to do well at Assessment Centres. Very often, the tasks require insight, awareness of the bigger picture and a real grasp of interdependencies. The attributes that affect real-world performance go far beyond IQ scores.

Seeing Things Clearly

Cognitive flexibility contributes to leadership effectiveness, particularly when faced with uncertain, unpredictable events. Some roles require imaginative, innovative thinking, which we might term 'YQ'. Other situations will need 'CQ' (cultural intelligence). In addition, there are some roles that involve risk and potential danger. These require calm analysis in high-pressure, stressful situations. This is a particular form of applied intelligence, which we might call 'XQ' (ice calm). Most leadership roles require empathy, responsiveness (and team-focused competencies) that link to emotional intelligence (EQ).

In World War II, potential agents faced demanding activities at Assessment Centres. A primary competency was to *Maintain Cover* and not to reveal your true identity. The candidates also faced challenging physical activities, quite often followed by a critical reasoning test. One example involved scaling a 30-foot wall, 'walking into space' on a 2″ × 4″ piece of wood and then being asked to prove that all numbers ABCABC are divisible by 13.[1] Today, this type of highly stressful activity would only apply to very specific roles! We should also note that specific knowledge is needed to make sense of this question. When assessing potential, it's important to differentiate attainment (prior learning and knowledge) from underlying ability. The 'knowledge threshold' should be relevant and related to the role. The primary focus is on potential.

To gain insight into future potential, it's important to consider the activities and challenges that might occur in the *target role*. There needs to be an appreciation of *what* is required and *how* high-performers go about completing activities. Validity is increased by ensuring *'point-to-point'* correspondence between the predictor, e.g. a work sample test, and the criteria (task performance and outcomes). Work sample tests may include in-tray (in-basket) activities, presentations and leaderless group discussions. They provide a more direct measure of role-related capability than indirect measures, such as results on critical reasoning tests or personality questionnaires. This approach reduces *adverse impact* (discrimination) and increases both face validity, i.e., relevance as perceived by candidates and managers, and the overall validity of the process.[2] With this in mind, in-depth Assessment Centres present a range of work-related tasks. Analysis shows that the primary focus is on the activities.[3] We find that competencies are expressed differently across situations, so clarity in the *task focus* (e.g. role purpose and objectives) is important.

In addition to effective cognitive ability, leaders need other attributes. Looking back at the work of Prof David McClelland,[4] we note the importance of *Achievement Motivation* and *Need for Control*. This is expressed through the socialised use of power, rather than 'personal power'. In challenging situations, this enables leaders to maintain focus and clarify priorities. Clarity of purpose is backed by personal conviction. McClelland's research also shows that many leaders will prioritise power over affiliation. They have less need to be liked and accepted by others. Many prefer to be directive. However, self-awareness and insight can teach 'directive' people to moderate their desire for control, reflected in the old 'command and control' style. This shift of mindset is supported by training that confirms the benefits of dialogue and consultation.

McClelland referred to this adaptation as the *inhibited power motive.*[5] It contributes to effectiveness, but it is a learned skill rather than an innate quality. Directive people may find it stressful. In contrast, leaders with a greater need for affiliation may have to *consciously focus* to maintain professional objectivity. However, if they can achieve balance, they have the potential to be very effective. We are reminded of Jacinda Ardern (prime minister of New Zealand, 2017–2023) who took prompt action to address the COVID-19 threat in 2020. She conveyed both empathy and clarity of purpose, which was backed by a meaningful rationale. This decisiveness occurred at a time when populist politicians in other countries delayed action and failed to appreciate the consequences.

Personal conviction backed by insight enables effective leaders to maintain focus, confront difficult issues and resolve problems involving other people. They separate the *personal* and the *professional*. Most importantly, leaders take prompt action to address challenging problems that affect performance or hinder progress. However, this must be balanced with a measured, professional response. The *inhibited power motive* supports *self-management*, helps control impulse and encourages reflection. With experience, we all become more effective in assessing the context and reviewing options. The emotional elements are then balanced alongside awareness of constraints, possibilities and consequences. The desire for speedy closure and immediate action is always a potential risk. Not all leaders can handle the pressure of *making time for reflection*. Populist politicians may struggle, notably in taking personal responsibility for difficult decisions. They also react too quickly to immediate events, overlooking future implications. Some people lack the cognitive processes required to see things clearly. In addition, the *Dunning–Kruger Effect* is an ever-present danger, as self-referenced, incompetent people often fail to recognise their limitations.[6]

The concept of *unconscious bias* is mentioned as a factor that may affect professional awareness and decision-making. However, the problem can be addressed through appropriate action. Managers receive training to improve decision-making in competency-focused interviews. Similar training is provided to managers involved as assessors in Assessment Centres. An important part of this process involves separating the steps needed to make informed decisions. The awareness contributes to *balanced processing of information* – and it's a transferable skill. It also supports performance review and coaching. There are specific steps that help encourage greater objectivity and improve assessment. This process involves making explicit links between tasks (activities) and approach (observable behaviour) linked to competencies. The process can be summarised as ORCA: *Observe, Record, Classify and then Assess*. This type of training can be contrasted with sociologically referenced models, which may lack underlying validity.

The first element in the ORCA model requires conscious *Observation* of behaviour and action – noting what someone said and did in a particular situation. This can then be *Recorded* in a note (brief summary) that captures key points, and with some details of timescales and key steps. It's then possible, e.g. at the end of an interview or after an Assessment Centre activity, to *Classify* notes, i.e., by linking specific examples to relevant competencies. The evidence supports *Assessment* against the positive and negative indicators associated with each competency. For example, a *positive* element might involve active listening, whilst a *negative indicator* might include signs of impatience or irritation. Typically, the assessment process uses a 4–6-point rating scale, so performance is either above or below requirements. This might equate to *Good, Acceptable, Marginal and Weak* (with associated ratings of 4, 3, 2, 1).

In summary, the problem of unconscious bias is frequently addressed during *Interview Skills* and *Assessment Centre Training*. The 'tripwires' that weaken objectivity include the following:

Stereotypes: classifying with broad (inaccurate) categories
The 'Halo and Horns' effect: classifying as 'good' or 'bad'
Attribution error: fast judgement and predefined categories
The primacy effect: focusing on initial events/impressions
Prejudice: flawed assumptions (rigid categorisation)
'Red Flag' issues: an excess reaction, e.g. a potential bank manager in white socks?

Professional insight enables people to become more measured in their response, which is a core aspect of leadership. The issues may link to *mindset* rather than factors relating to specific *personality traits*. A well-designed selection process aims to identify those who lack appropriate competencies. This is an aspect of psychometric assessment, but we should recognise the correct sequence. Steps 1 and 2 should assess ability and relevant personality traits. Step 3 can then focus on work patterns – and competencies that contribute to capability in the role. *Can you identify the job demands, the personal resources required and the desired outcomes?* We need a clear picture of 'excellence' to clarify the steps leading to positive results.

To put these points into context, I was once asked to help facilitate a series of *Development Centres*. These are based on Assessment Centres, but with significantly more emphasis on feedback. The output includes a *Personal Development Plans* for each participant. This particular process had been designed by an academic 'occupational' psychologist. He had insisted that verbal and numerical tests were included as a core part of the process. The rationale was that these 'measured critical reasoning'. The relationship with the client had subsequently deteriorated. He was viewed as very inflexible in his thinking and approach.

Assessment of critical reasoning should normally be completed before Assessment or Development Centres. There are three main reasons. The first is to identify people who find it difficult to process complex information, whilst noting that high scores do not ensure great performance. We should also allow for the *Standard Error of Measurement*. The second reason is to avoid *adverse impact*. Critical reasoning tests can favour some groups over others. The third reason is essentially pragmatic. Administering reasoning tests is not a good use of time in an expensive process. In the case of Development Centres, they also tend to make constructive feedback more difficult. They lack the face validity of realistic 'work sample' activities.

Soon after the launch I was asked to help facilitate the Development Centres (DCs). The client retained the verbal and numerical reasoning tests during the first year, so it was possible to analyse the results. A number of the participants did not do well on the practical activities. This suggested that the initial screening and recommendation process was faulty. There were, for example, too many participants who struggled to identify important issues in the in-tray exercise. It became clear that managers who nominated participants had a lot of discretion over who they recommended. The pre-screening linked to an unstructured interview and 'positive' performance appraisals. It was essentially a subjective process.

The DC process produced an Overall Assessment Rating (OAR) that excluded the test scores. These were only referred to in the wash-up session to gain additional insight into reasoning ability. This was after ratings had been completed on the practical exercises. The assessors did not have prior knowledge of the test scores. However, during the wash-up review it was possible to compare the OAR with both verbal and numerical reasoning scores. Following subsequent analysis of the data, a clear picture emerged, revealing links between the OAR (the threshold score) and advance to the fast-track development programme. Only numerical test scores 1 standard deviation (or more) *below the mean* were important.

This revealed that people in this group failed to achieve the OAR threshold score, which was required for the programme.

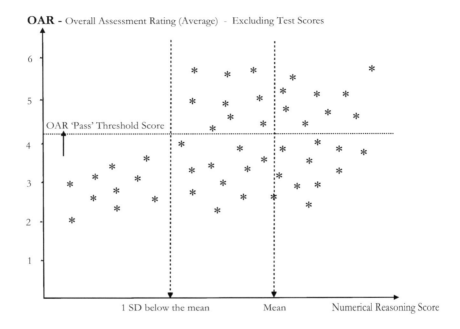

The chart represents the pattern of scores recorded. This is a reflection of the original data, which revealed that high numerical ability was not predictive of high OAR ratings. However, low scores were significant. A report was submitted to the client, but failed to get past the training manager responsible for the programme. It was concluded that *it was not acceptable to pre-screen participants* (with tests or other objective methods). Resources continued to be committed even though the initial screening was flawed. More appropriate, less expensive options were available, but these were not considered during the design process. The limitations of standardised tests should be noted, including issues relating to *Adverse Impact* and wider concerns about the *Standard Error or Measurement*.

The Rules of the Game

Exceptional performance requires specific attributes, which are more evident in high-potential people. When faced with a difficult, challenging problem, they draw on experience and apply insights to gain a fresh perspective. This may involve recognising interdependencies, and appreciating how elements connect. There is also a willingness to involve others, to better understand issues or problems. Finally, there is reflection on possible outcomes, risks and future consequences. Receptiveness to context enables high-potential people to develop skill in 'flexing' their style. They respond more effectively, developing the agility to assess options and re-evaluate the approach. This helps people see the bigger picture, engage effectively with others and be pro-active and resilient when taking action.

Effectiveness requires not only analytical competence but also the ability to engage with others, explore context and build consensus. Reasoning builds on clear analysis. Even the most charismatic leaders need to understand the difference between a percentage and a probability. Effective leaders also recognise that higher-order principles are a reference point in developing consensus and cohesion. This requires a meaningful rationale, supported by dialogue, which helps build commitment. However, there is a potential problem. *The Third Rule states that a two-thirds majority is required to ensure the legitimacy of contentious decisions.* Ignoring this rule has significant consequences. In the UK, for example, the 2016 Brexit outcome was a narrow 48/52 divisive split. The small margin confirmed that this was an emotive, subjective decision. Facts were hidden, so the rationale was driven by opinion and feeling, reducing the possibility of consensus.

Insights from psychology can help identify patterns linked to high performance. Practical applications include *Situational Judgement Tests* (SJTs) that add focus to selection. They can also enhance professional development and training. In selection, the technique is often linked to online testing with multiple-choice response options. They form part of the pre-interview screening process used by many large organisations. However, when the technique was first adopted, there was no complex technology. Fortunately, it's still possible to use the old method. This may be useful in the context of coaching and professional development. The process starts by focusing on a specific role and identifying situations that are handled differently by high-performers. More-effective and less-effective responses are noted and referenced against relevant competencies. The question can then be presented on a card, read aloud, and passed to the individual being assessed. They are asked to 'think about it for a minute and give your response'. The answers are noted and then repeated back, followed by a prompt: *Is there anything you would like to add?* The steps are described in my YouTube video relating to the design of *Situational Judgement Tests*.

In the past, economists and political scientists have excused shortcomings in their own analysis by reference to the concept of *Bounded*

Rationality. This suggests that there are inherent *cognitive limitations* and *time pressures* that undermine 'rational' decision-making. However, applied psychology and behavioural science provide a more nuanced and wide-ranging perspective. We find that high performance requires an awareness of interdependencies, motivation and purpose. Decision-making includes anticipation of consequences, a process reinforced by a sense of shared purpose. Rational-reductionist thinking neglects 21st century insights emerging from neuroscience. Leadership failure is most likely when coherent analysis is lacking and assumptions are made about 'self-evident' facts.

Problems can quickly develop if leaders fail to question established methods and lack real insight. Most importantly, to support future success, organisations need to take steps to anticipate the unexpected, develop potential and enhance capability. We need effective systems, which help shape the culture, but also the competencies that deliver exceptional performance. There are various ways of doing this, but the process starts with performance review, coaching and a future-focused perspective. This can be enhanced with 360-degree feedback, which raises awareness of interdependencies. As the context changes, the expectations of direct reports, peers/colleagues, customers and stakeholders can evolve, but underlying principles continue to guide actions.

It's worth noting that some academic studies criticise competencies because assessment appears to lack 'consistency' across situations. This apparent discrepancy is evident in the analysis of both Assessment Centre and 360-degree feedback data. However, evaluation of competencies and effectiveness is made in the context of the activity, which includes the expectations of others. The second point is particularly relevant with a 360 review. Performance is set within the specific demands of context and culture. The influencing skills used in one-to-one discussions, for example, differ from those required to achieve agreement in a group. We are reminded that high performance requires awareness, insight and a range of interpersonal skills. The ability to maintain focus is backed by agility and the ability to adapt in a way appropriate to the task.

One interesting observation from the classic Bell Labs Study[7] is that training interventions can equip people with more of the 'mindset and capability' of *Star Performers*. The Bell Labs' intervention achieved a 25% improvement in productivity in 12 months. Experienced engineers helped confirm competencies and coach the work strategies that delivered superior outcomes. This might also be viewed as an example of solution-focused coaching, discussed previously.

It's important to remember that personality traits and critical reasoning test scores are not particularly effective predictors of leadership potential. Test publishers have become a powerful lobby since the 1980s. We should note that well-designed tests add objectivity to selection and development, but there are clear limitations. Claims about validity are strongest when there is wide variation in ability. However, range is often restricted by qualifications, entry criteria and self-selection. Even after screening to identify appropriate reasoning ability and more positive traits, there is still a lot of variation in people's performance.

We find that personality traits do not fully explain the elements that support exceptional performance. This builds on experience, insight and responsiveness to context. Personality and cognitive factors are a starting point for the development of work preferences. Personality theorists see competency clusters as *Thinking, Feeling and Doing*. This does not equate to *Strategic Analysis, Engaging People and Achieving Results*. Various aspects of mindset, motivation and purpose shape behaviour. And ultimately we all benefit from enabling conditions and insight. High performance requires awareness of priorities, purpose and interdependencies. Future-focused leaders are proactive in their approach, engaging effectively with other people.

There are varying, complex demands, but important skills can be learned. *Taking Action* is the focus of Part II of the book and builds on a series of development modules. A case study also highlights the work preference of 'JK', an individual short-listed for a *director-level* role. The work preferences and reasoning test scores did not form part of the pre-screening or the main assessment. This was structured around a presentation and structured interview. The test results and work preferences were discussed as part of the 'wash-up', review session.

The study is interesting as the person appointed was not the most *charismatic* or *engaging* personality in the group (of five applicants). Another candidate 'X' presented well, with good communication skills. However, it emerged in the wash-up that relative to UK managers 'X' scored significantly below average on both the verbal and numerical reasoning tests. This prompted the assessors to reflect on role requirements, e.g. assimilating complex reports and developing policy. Review of the work preferences also highlighted concerns about aspects of leadership style (and less focus on outcomes). In contrast, 'JK' achieved high scores on both the verbal and numerical reasoning tests and also expressed more appropriate work preferences. The profile was not '100%', but significantly better balanced than the other candidate. The insights prompted the selection panel to reflect on all the candidates' *strengths and potential short-comings*, leading to a more objective decision. The 'best fit' person (JK) was selected and went on to achieve positive results – and subsequent appointment to a CEO role.

A significant insight, gained from many years running Assessment and Development Centres, is that high-potential people have clarity of purpose. Back in the late 1980s, I was closely involved in the design and implementation of *Senior Management Development Programmes* in BT. The process was implemented after privatisation, at a time when corporate culture was far removed from modern standards. Some of the people nominated by traditional managers clearly failed to meet requirements. In contrast, I recall a woman who was clearly aware of *Superordinate Goals and Super-Ps*. Her skill set included clear statements of position on key issues: e.g., *No, that it is not acceptable*. One director described her as the *steel fist in the velvet glove*. The conviction came from an appreciation of actions and outcomes, backed by clear reasoning. She also demonstrated the influencing skills needed to achieve positive results.

When people talk about *courage* being an attribute of effective leaders, they are more likely to be talking about *conviction*, which links to clear goals and the power of guiding principles. Clarity of purpose builds on an internalised script that creates energy and focus. Future-focused leaders also require systems that support delivery of outcomes. When thinking is shaped by *Superordinate Principles*, leaders can operate with integrity and authenticity. Life becomes easier. It is then possible to say, *No, that is not possible. These are the constraints. Why do you think X comes before Y? What are the other (better) options? How does X help us to make positive progress on Y?* The objective is to build on 'attention activating' questions.

Sometimes questions are rhetorical, helping to clarify other people's thinking and provide insight into the wider issues. Provocative questions can improve analysis of options, revealing why 'easy' or expedient solutions will fail in the longer term. *Purposeful Conversations* can help increase awareness, insight and meaningful action and ensure appropriate support. We now move from *gut feeling*, aka '*limbic brain reaction*' [sic], to identify what separates *more and less effective* action. This is helped with techniques such as *Rep Grid Analysis*, a topic I have covered on YouTube. *Repertory Grid* (Kelly, 1955) can help clarify what contributes to effectiveness. The insights serve to confirm that *there is no law of unexpected consequences*, only a lack of capability, and a failure of anticipation and leadership. Take a moment and think again about the actor in a theatre. We find that exceptional actors are not defined by personality traits or vague notions of IQ or EQ. Most importantly, they understand the script, their role and the interdependencies affecting performance. Actors appreciate the context, anticipate requirements, visualise actions and build on feedback. They engage with the audience and also enhance the performance of other actors.

And there is one final observation, which relates to forces that may be beyond the control of many; but represent important themes of *Principle* and *Purpose* for the *C-suite*. These *Strategic Constraints* relate to the design of the organisation and the fundamental assumptions that guide its operation. In *Doughnut Economics*, Kate Raworth notes that *more than the design of specific products or services, what matters most is the deep design of the organisation itself.*

She suggests five design trade-offs that raise key questions:

What is the organisation's purpose?
How is it networked with others?
How is it governed in practice?
Crucially, how is it owned?
And how is it financed? [8]

From the perspective of leadership, the questions also prompt us to consider *the Fourth Rule*, which states: *Effective leaders create an enabling environment that supports future success.*

Developing Future-Focused Potential

There is an old proverb that states: *tall oaks from little acorns grow.* Businesses start with an idea, and some become successful ventures. Back in 1997, a small group of entrepreneurs from the UK, together with Ghanaian business partners, established the Blue Skies fruit processing factory in Ghana. I helped facilitate the project, which provided some interesting insights into human behaviour. The concept involved processing tropical fruit, initially pineapple, then chilling the chopped fruit and air-freighting to the UK and elsewhere in Europe. Passenger flights from Accra departed each night with capacity for additional cargo, so transport was available. The founders of Blue Skies included Anthony Pile (CEO) and Patricia Safo. Patricia later set up JCS Investments in Ghana to help facilitate impact investing. Her father, Daniel Safo, had land with access to electricity and underground (potable) water. This overcame one major barrier to the new venture. Land acquisition in Ghana can be difficult, particularly for small start-up businesses.

Patricia became procurement director, ensuring a reliable supply of fruit. This overcame one of the most significant operational problems in the first year. Important work was also undertaken 'behind the scenes' to prevent corrupt officials demanding money and to sidestep people who might exploit the start-up. The challenge was to avoid obstacles that would prevent the company achieving 'critical mass'. As in many business situations, progress is much easier if potential problems are anticipated, trust is developed and resources are focused effectively. I spent many hours persuading Daniel to support the project. Systems also needed to be put in place. By 1998, the business had started to export products.

Following the success of the initial factory in Ghana, by 2020 the business developed into a leading producer of fresh-cut fruit, freshly squeezed juice and dairy-free ice cream. At the time of writing, there are operations in several countries, including Ghana, Egypt, Brazil, South Africa and Senegal. Blue Skies progressed to supply leading retailers, including Waitrose and Sainsbury's in the UK, Albert Heijn in the Netherlands and Carrefour in France. In 2021, Blue Skies Holdings (UK) reported a turnover in excess of £120 million for the year.

The team included Charlie Pack (left), Anthony (centre), Patricia and me (not in photo).

One point to note is that Blue Skies required a team with the expertise, energy and commitment to overcome initial problems. There was a need to confirm the market, ensure reliable supplies of fresh fruit, and create essential steps in the distribution process. It is important to appreciate the network of connections that are critical to success. In food production, customers also want to track food sources, check quality standards and consider issues relating to sustainability. Technology enables information to be scanned directly from the product. See the BBC Reel (28 May 2019): *Where does your food really come from?*[9]

The ***Sustainable Agriculture Group*** of the World Bank included Blue Skies in a guide to making value chains work in agribusiness in sub-Saharan Africa. The guide observed that since 2000 the company has grown tremendously, expanding its value chain by incorporating additional operations into its processing facilities. It goes on to say:

> Several factors contributing to Blue Skies' success relate to concepts discussed throughout this Guide, such as high levels of trust, sharing of information, innovation, value addition, positioning collaboration, and risk mitigation. Blue Skies emphasises prompt payment to farmers, the provision of training and education on EurepGAP standards, certification of farmers, interest-free loans for dedicated farmers, and willingness to improve local road infrastructure to improve access to farms by company trucks.[10]

Entrepreneurs seeking impact investment opportunities in Ghana can discuss possibilities with JCS Investments in Accra: https://www.jcs.com.gh/about-us.html TBL Investors[11] may also be interested in the *Sustainable Invest Alliance*: https://www.sustainable-investment.com

ChatGPT Insight: Blue Skies in Ghana

We asked ChatGPT to evaluate the contribution made by the Blue Skies project

➤ *Assess the contribution of Blue Skies to the Ghanaian economy*
Blue Skies is a Ghanaian company that specialises in the production and exportation of fresh-cut fruit products such as pineapple, mango and papaya. The company's operations have made a significant contribution to the Ghanaian economy in several ways:

Job creation: Blue Skies employs over 4,000 people in Ghana, including direct employees and those in the supply chain. These employees earn a steady income, which helps to support their families and contributes to the overall economic growth of the country.

Agriculture development: Blue Skies has established partnerships with smallholder farmers in Ghana, providing them with technical assistance, training and access to markets. Through these partnerships, Blue Skies has helped to improve the productivity and profitability of smallholder farmers, which has had a positive impact on the agriculture sector in Ghana.

Export earnings: Blue Skies exports its fresh-cut fruit products to several countries around the world, bringing in foreign exchange earnings for the country. This has helped to improve Ghana's balance of payments and has contributed to the overall growth of the economy.

Technology transfer: Blue Skies has introduced advanced technologies and processes to Ghana's agriculture sector, which has led to increased efficiency and productivity in the sector.

Environmental sustainability: Blue Skies has implemented sustainability initiatives, including the use of renewable energy, the reduction of waste and water usage, and the promotion of biodiversity. These initiatives have helped to reduce Blue Skies' environmental impact and have contributed to the long-term sustainability of the agriculture sector in Ghana.

Overall, Blue Skies' operations have had a significant positive impact on the Ghanaian economy, particularly in terms of job creation, agriculture development and export earnings. The company's sustainability initiatives have also helped to promote the long-term sustainability of the agriculture sector in Ghana.

As a final observation, I remember a meeting in London in the late 1990s. I was with Patricia, and we met an official from the UK Department for International Development (DFID). It was memorable because there was zero interest in private initiatives, and no real awareness of the potential value of impact investing. It was a disappointing experience, now a long time ago, but the memory lingers.

Notes

1 The term 'ABC ABC' represents three digits expressed as thousands + 1 set (1001). So, 123, 123 = 1001 …and the primes $7 \times 11 \times 13 = 1001$.

2 Robertson, I., & Kandola, R. (2011). Work sample tests: Validity, adverse impact and applicant reaction. *Journal of Occupational Psychology*, 55(3), 171–183.

3 Robertson, I., Gratton, L., & Sharpley, D. (1987). The psychometric properties and design of managerial assessment centres: Dimensions into exercises won't go. *Journal of Occupational Psychology*, 60(3), 187–195.

4 Wikipedia. Available at: https://en.wikipedia.org/wiki/David_McClelland

5 McClelland, D. C. (1979). Inhibited power motivation and high blood pressure in men. *Journal of Abnormal Psychology*, 88, 182–190.

6 Dunning, D. (2011). The Dunning–Kruger effect: On being ignorant of one's own ignorance. Advances *in Experimental Social Psychology*, 44, 247–296.

7 Kelley, R., & Caplan, J. (1993). How Bell Labs creates *star performers. Harvard Business Review*. Available at: https://hbr.org/1993/07/how-bell-labs-creates-star-performers

8 Raworth, K. (2022). *Doughnut Economics*. Penguin Books, p. 297.

9 BBC. Available at: www.bbc.com/reel/video/p07bj7pk/where-does-your-food-really-come-from-

10 World Bank Guide. Using Value Chain Approaches in Agribusiness and Agriculture in Sub-Saharan Africa – FAO Download on Sustainable Food Value Chains, p. 103.

11 Triple Bottom Line Summary. Available at: https://www.investopedia.com/terms/t/triple-bottom-line.asp

Reference

Kelly, George (1991) [1955]. *The psychology of personal constructs*. London; New York: Routledge in association with the Centre for Personal Construct Psychology.

TAKING ACTION

Chapter 9

Achieving Future-Focus

Developing Leadership Skills

The Modules in Part II focus on the connections between thinking, work preferences and behaviour. A case study is included, which reviews personal preferences. This is linked to the Pario (online) questionnaire, revealing how energy is directed. It can help clarify aspects of mindset and motivation. The *patterns of behaviour* relate to the *relative emphasis* placed on each dimension. The completed profile also offers insight into how the person is responding to role demands. From a coaching perspective, this is not about personality traits, 'categories' or specific 'colours'. The profile reveals a pattern, and preferences can be viewed alongside role demands. This can help clarify action steps, which support solution-focused change. Find out how to access the questionnaire and information on licencing options at Pario360.com

The Modules are designed to increase self-awareness and enhance leadership skills. The insights also have wider relevance, notably in developing consulting skills, and developing insight within teams. This type of review might also note the steps in the learning cycle.

DOI: 10.4324/9781003439707-11

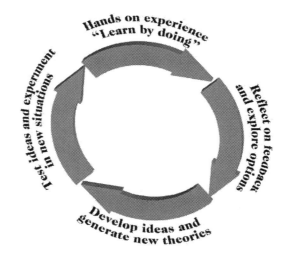

Use the Learning Cycle to review and improve

- **Analysis** and effectiveness in problem-solving
- Positive relationships with **People**
- Skills required to **Manage Change**
- Action to maintain focus and **Achieve Results**

The Learning Cycle (Kolb) highlights how we balance reflection, abstract conceptualisation, active experimentation and hands-on experience. This contributes to *Balanced Processing of Information* that supports effective decision-making. We can also gain insights from type theory, and differences in cognitive processing, to review perception (*Sensing and Intuition*) and decision-making (*Feeling and Thinking*). Each element has an impact, affecting analysis and decisions. People with strong preferences, towards S or N and/or F or T, may need to appreciate alternative views. Those who lack clear preferences may also need to develop greater clarity. Reviewing preferences adds to both individual and team insight.

Balancing the Cognitive Functions

Step 1: Focus on concrete data and sensory impressions. This builds on facts and Sensing (S)

The first step is to gather information/data relating to the activity or problem. This is enhanced by the Sensing function, which focuses on facts and details. This stage builds on 'focused perception'. Aim to avoid subjective bias, personal opinion, assumptions and 'wishful thinking'.

Step 2: Explore patterns, themes and possibilities. This 'looks forward' with Intuition (N)

Once immediate data has been assessed, review interdependencies, wider issues and options. This perspective draws on Intuition and is attuned to possibilities and emerging themes. Intuition involves appreciation of abstract concepts, innovative thinking and reflection. Dialogue and consultation widen our perspective, enhancing broad-based thinking.

Step 3: Consider people's emotions and values. This is responsive to Feeling (F)

The third step is to consider the emotion, values and concerns that affect motivation and shape action. This stage involves the Feeling function, which broadens our perspective. Understanding other people's views also helps create empathy. Your own emotions/passions need to be considered alongside alternative perspectives. This function is enhanced through dialogue and purposeful conversations.

Step 4: Complete analysis of issues affecting outcomes. This applies logical Thinking (T)

The final step involves the Thinking function, which builds on objective analysis. A balanced perspective builds on insights from the previous steps. Those with a strong Thinking focus may need to understand more of the Feeling dimension. The analysis should also be related to Superordinate Principles that guide actions and support consistent, informed decision-making.

The model adds to effective decision-making by addressing each of the distinct elements. These include (i) gathering data (Sensing), (ii) exploring possibilities (Intuition), (iii) considering values and emotions (Feeling) and (iv) completing final analysis (Thinking). Attention to the four functions supports *balanced processing of information* and discernment. Effective decisions require data (S), innovative thinking (N), consideration of people's values and concerns (F) and logical analysis (T). The elements are all referenced against *Super-Ps*.

The steps can be summarised as follows:

S 'Facts as Perceived'	**N** Patterns and Possibilities
F Emotions and Values	**T** Analysis and Logic

Psychological type preference can be resistant to change. Important functions are (in part) *hardwired*, and individual perception and response may reveal both strengths and weaknesses. Many people focus on *sense-impressions* and concrete information (Sensing), but neglect abstract concepts and less evident trends or patterns. The dominance of an S-T work culture may well compound the *FELT Deficit*. Future research should help clarify the association of a *Sensing-Thinking* orientation – and elements of rigid thinking and difficulty in understanding what is not made explicit. ChatGPT notes:

> it is unclear whether the reductionist thinking observed in finance, economics, law, and technology (the classic FELT professions) is a consequence of a "Sensing-Thinking" psychological type preference. More research is needed to explore the complex relationships between personality type, cognitive style, and thinking styles in these fields.

Cognitive function influences *Type Categories* and also links to the *Big Five* 'OCEAN' personality traits. These broad factors include *Openness, Conscientiousness, Extraversion, Agreeableness and Neuroticism*. Although they are broad clusters, *psychological type categories* can be useful, offering insights for personal development and team coaching. You can review your own preferences with the *Pario Type Indicator* (see Pario360.com). The impact of diverse cognitive style, and conflicting opinion, presents a challenge for leaders who need to create shared purpose. Influencing skills are enhanced with storytelling, anecdotes and appropriate self-disclosure (openness). This all supports a future-focused narrative.

Gaining people's interest and attention is important in breaking through self-limiting, backward-looking scripts. These can include the familiar (sometimes justified) themes, e.g. '*how great things used to be*' and '*all the unfair treatment we've experienced.*' However, there is a risk that this creates a closed loop. Particularly damaging in organisations is the notion, '*they should fix it*'. This refers to any situation where people excuse themselves from taking the initiative and proposing a course of action. It may also reflect a culture with issues relating to role clarity, transparency and accountability. I have even heard this sentiment expressed by senior managers referring to the failures of directors and the Board. We need to get past this *default mindset* to develop fresh insights and activate effective action.

There is a risk that decision-making is unduly influenced by a dominant perceiving preference (*Sensing or Intuition*) or evaluation process (*Feeling or Thinking*). This makes it more difficult to achieve a balanced response. *Sensing-Thinking* can fuel reductionism, but *Intuition-Feeling* may drive ideology and passion that neglects context, constraints or consequences. This leads on to distorted history, romantic nationalism and creates extremists. When 'vision' flows from *Intuition*, reinforced by emotion and personal values, decisions can become dominated by *Feeling*. This also relates to *Ideological Possession* (IP), which occurs when we become immersed in a specific viewpoint and lose the ability to maintain objectivity. Extreme cases of IP include *Simpsons Syndrome – Short, Inadequate, Macho Psychopaths Suppressing Other Nation States.*

From a Jungian perspective, the least developed preference (S N F T) can trigger a dysfunctional reaction. Jung suggested that the *fourth (inferior) function* is less developed or possibly repressed, e.g. expression of feeling, which contributes to *The Shadow*. Faced with wicked problems, distorted analysis and internet echo chambers, the danger of *Ideological Possession* quickly increases. The concept of IP has been explored by many thinkers, including George Orwell, Friedrich Nietzsche, Eric Hoffer and Jordan Peterson. Ideology can block critical reasoning and hinder balanced processing of information.

In everyday conversation, you can listen for *confirmatory prompts* that suggest you should agree with someone's assumptions. These '*agree with me*' phrases are added after statements, e.g. *you know?... right?* They cover gaps in analysis. Listen for these prompts and ask yourself, *is there more?* Check the facts and context, and consider alternative perspectives. Note the omission of 'inconvenient' information. Effective leaders *listen to the script* and ask questions that encourage clarification. Create space by acknowledging points and discussing context. Thoughtful discussion helps reduce binary separation, but *Provocateurs* tend to present opinion as facts, neglect context, dismiss constraints and ignore higher-order principles.

Balanced Processing of Information is enhanced when we can build on different perspectives. High performance requires competencies that help us anticipate potential problems. Recognising the limitations in people's cognitive processes, Edward de Bono suggested we apply six *Thinking Hats* (1985) that can shift mindset, encourage creativity and help us resolve complex issues.

1. **White Hat**: This hat requires neutral and objective thinking. When wearing the white hat, focus on the facts and information, and identify gaps in knowledge or data.
2. **Red Hat**: This involves emotional and intuitive thinking. With the red hat, focus on gut feelings, emotions and hunches, without necessarily having to justify or explain them.
3. **Black Hat**: This represents critical and negative thinking. When wearing the black hat, seek to identify potential problems, risks and weaknesses in a particular idea or plan.
4. **Yellow Hat**: This involves positive and optimistic thinking. Focus on the benefits, strengths and opportunities of a particular idea or plan.
5. **Green Hat**: This relates to creative, innovative thinking. Generate new ideas, alternatives and possibilities. Explores different ways of approaching a problem or challenge.
6. **Blue Hat**: This relates to strategic and meta-thinking. Focus on the big picture, the overall process and the goals and objectives. Establish and confirm the context. The blue hat can guide and facilitate the use of the other hats. It's a key aspect of future-focused leadership.

The Learning Ladder

The Learning Ladder, developed by Noel Burch (1970s), is a metaphorical representation of the stages that individuals go through as they learn and develop new skills or knowledge. It envisages a linear progression that consists of four distinct stages:

Unconscious Incompetence: In this stage, individuals are not aware of their lack of knowledge or skill in a particular area.

Conscious Incompetence: In this stage, individuals become aware of their lack of knowledge or skill and begin to identify what they need to learn in order to improve.

Conscious Competence: In this stage, individuals have acquired new knowledge or skills but must consciously focus and apply effort to use them effectively.

Unconscious Competence: In this final stage, individuals have internalised their new knowledge or skill and can use it automatically, without conscious effort or attention.

The learning ladder is a useful tool as it highlights the importance of self-awareness and distinct stages in developing knowledge and skills. We can consider where we are, and what's required to reach the next level. However, with rapid change, there is now an additional 'fifth step' in the process. Without feedback, insight and adaptation, we can easily slip back to level 1.

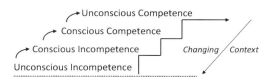

Neuroscience reveals that with (sufficient) experience the brain's *Default Mode Network* (DMN) switches to autopilot. Familiarity engages old scripts, but neglects new procedures, a change of context or a shift in expectations. We need to activate the *Executive Control Network* (ECN), which is the alternative to the DMN. The ECN is receptive to external events. Team leaders can use 'future-focused' questions to help activate the brain's attention, notably in identifying the steps that support progress. Possible prompts include: *what's changed? …what looks different? …how would customers react to this?* Solution-focused questions can help in developing ideas and practical steps that support progress. They also add to a sense of shared purpose.

In the following sections, the Development Modules explore how work preferences affect leadership-related behaviour and competencies. We can also return to the four rules introduced in Part I (see below). We can also add Rule 5, which introduces a neuroscience *point of reference* for future-focused leaders.

Rule 1: As complexity increases, the process of engaging others becomes more challenging.

Rule 2: Decisions must be in accord with *Superordinate Principles* that safeguard core values.

Rule 3: A two-third majority is required to ensure the legitimacy of contentious decisions.

Rule 4: Effective leaders create an enabling environment that supports future success.

Rule 5: *Purposeful Conversation* can help activate the ECN and enhance future-focus.

The ECN is externally focused and switches thinking from the DMN. *Purposeful Conversations* can help activate the circuits and prompt solution-focused thinking. However, it's worth noting that we are all vulnerable to the appeal of backward-looking 'logic' that reminds us '*how unfair things have been*' and '*how badly we've been treated*'. In reality, it's much healthier to operate in the present and develop a sense of purpose and 'agency'. This requires competence and *self-directed responsibility* (autonomy). Team leaders can enhance well-being and resilience with forward-looking, solution-focused conversations.

Overview of the Development Modules

The case study reviews the *personal work preferences* of an applicant (JK) for a senior role in a *Third Sector* organization. The profile was not seen as a perfect fit, but helped clarify aspects of work style. The report offers insights on how the preferences are likely to influence JK's work behaviour.

The Modules (M1–M9) focus on important themes, which include the following:

- M1 - Elements of High Performance
- M2 - Effectiveness at Work
- M3 - Work Preference Personal Report
- M4 - Analysis and Problem-Solving
- M5 - Developing Opportunities
- M6 - Working with People
- M7 - Personal Impact and Influence
- M8 - Effective Decision-Making
- M9 - Focusing on Outcomes
- M10 - Summary and Review

Module 10 reviews the themes covered in the previous modules. It provides an opportunity to revisit the personal preferences summarised in the report. The content can also be related to the three broad clusters (*Head, Heart and Hands*), described as the 3H Competency Model. This includes the following:

- Analysis, problem-solving and planning
- Working with others and interpersonal effectiveness
- Drive, resilience and delivery of results

The following pages list important leadership competencies. The summary describes the approach and behaviour that contribute to exceptional performance. They can help differentiate *Star Performers* from the 'average' or below standard output. Most importantly, effective leaders engage positively with others and create the enabling conditions that enhance motivation and commitment.

Leadership Competencies

The development modules help build competencies. Important leadership competencies are summarised below. Note that the review process can be extended with 360-degree feedback.

Setting Direction
Clarify priorities and key objectives, creating a clear sense of direction. Explain the reasons why a particular course of action is required. Display energy and enthusiasm, showing personal conviction about future possibilities

Working with People
Help people understand how their work contributes to the organisation's performance. Encourage positive discussion (and avoid personal criticism). Encourage people to take personal responsibility for key tasks and activities

Building Relationships
Discuss issues with a wide range of people to review problems and opportunities. Develop a good understanding of other people's needs and concerns. Share information and communicate with people outside the immediate team

Influencing Others
Appear open and willing to discuss people's ideas and suggestions. Listen carefully and respond constructively to feedback and differing viewpoints. Adapt your approach, so that it is appropriate to the people and situation

Developing People
Make sure that people understand the performance standards that are expected. Help people find solutions to problems at work. Keep people informed of what is happening elsewhere in the organisation

Gaining Commitment

Assess constraints or obstacles before making a firm commitment to action. Encourage consultation and discussion to overcome disagreement. Anticipate people's reactions and the potential consequences of decisions

Managing Performance

Spend time clarifying objectives and the steps required to get results. Provide regular, timely feedback that helps people improve their performance. Take prompt action if someone's performance falls below acceptable standards

Achieving Results

Demonstrate flexibility when faced with an unexpected change of plans. Cope well with conflicting priorities and pressure, remaining positive and focused. Take the initiative in developing new, more effective solutions

The following sections provide an opportunity to review work preferences and reflect on competencies. Change requires insight and commitment, supported by solution-focused conversations, with your coach, manager and colleagues. The process starts with increased self-awareness and appreciation of context.

Insights from Personality Theory

Most personality-related questionnaires focus on broad *types* and specific *traits*. These describe consistent patterns of behaviour, but neglect context. They often use *normative scoring*, with comparisons against a *norm group*, e.g. a group of managers. However, much is left unexplained, so they fail to identify the future *Star Performers*. That said, they can identify those who are less suitable for a role.

In *Explorations in Personality* (1938), Henry Murray observed, '*trait psychology is over-concerned with recurrences, with consistency, with what is clearly manifested (the surface of personality), with what is conscious, ordered and rational.* He goes on to note, *it stops short precisely at the point where a psychology is needed, the point at which it begins to be difficult to understand what is going on*' (p. 715). The team at Harvard in the late 1930s sought to understand underlying needs, environment and outcomes. The term *apperception* was developed, noting that perception is shaped by experience and influenced by events. Professional training and work culture will influence someone's response. *Mindset and behaviour can change with a shift of context, and solution-focused conversations will help change perceptions.*

Murray's work clarified how needs influence behaviour. It prompted research by David McClelland, which confirmed acquired needs linked to *Power, Achievement and Affiliation*.[1] Taken together, the research offers insights into how strengths, competencies and attributes contribute to high performance. Heredity explains around 50% of personality. Experience shapes mindset, which resists sudden change. However, in many scenarios, the context will shift and role demands can change. Leaders need to update their perspective to see things clearly. Current work preferences may well be influenced by a combination of traits, underlying needs and aspects of perception and motivation. The first step in solution-focused, intentional change is to review the current context, and then identify the action that supports progress.

In the context of the leadership development course, Modules 4 and 5 explore issues affecting analysis, developing opportunities and organizational awareness. Modules 6 and 7 relate to working with people, setting direction and influencing others. Modules 8 and 9 consider speed of response, decision confidence and other significant elements affecting outcomes.

The Case Study

JK's responses (to the questionnaire) are included in the Modules. They reveal the emphasis placed on each dimension. The typical 'score-range' of UK managers and experienced professionals is noted. Preference scores can be viewed alongside role demands and significant competencies. The case study scores (and also the typical score range) are shown alongside each dimension, adopting this format:

Dimension Name

0   5   10

Leaders' preference scores are usually in the range X–Y.

It is possible for someone to place high emphasis on one dimension and still maintain focus in other areas. However, if significant elements are not well developed, or there's little differentiation between elements, it may reduce effectiveness in a leadership role. The profile can be used to support a competency-focused review and also contribute to team coaching. The questionnaire is also used in executive coach training.

Note

1 McClelland – Need Theory. Available at: https://en.wikipedia.org/wiki/Need_theory

Chapter 10

Module 1: Elements of High Performance

An important step in developing leadership skills involves becoming more aware of your personal strengths, but also recognising areas requiring improvement. Feedback increases our appreciation of issues affecting performance. We find that effective leaders have capability across a number of areas. These underpin the chapters and include the following:

- Analysis and Problem-Solving
- Developing Opportunities – Managing Change
- Setting Direction – Influencing Others
- Focusing Resources – Decision-Making
- Achieving Results – Positive Outcomes

Effectiveness requires specific aspects of behaviour and insight developed over time. These *patterns of behaviour* link to competencies that support high performance. Leadership competencies include (i) analysis, monitoring and skilful positioning of issues; (ii) interpersonal skills linked to influencing others and building relationships; and (iii) drive and resilience, which help overcome problems and achieve results. Most importantly, leadership involves understanding the interdependencies that affect performance. Leaders need to appreciate the expectations of different groups and the action required for positive results.

Insight is required to *align activities* with organisational goals. With this in mind, there's value in considering *three perspectives* when facing

DOI: 10.4324/9781003439707-12

challenging situations at work. These include your point of view, the per-spective of others and the formal position of the organisation, relating to longer-term goals, core values and guiding principles. The ability to stand back and consider different perspectives, and achieve insight, is an impor-tant leadership skill. Understanding and acknowledging other people's thinking can help encourage discretionary effort and commitment, which contributes to high performance. We look at work preferences in the next chapter. These add a point of reference when reviewing development activities.

The Importance of Feedback

Feedback is critical to the development of potential. The *Johari Window* provides a model of how feedback and *open communication* can increase self-awareness and help build trust. It looks at things from two perspectives, i.e. self and others, and this helps highlight key issues. It supports coaching and development, and can also be used for team development.

The *Johari Window* highlights that there are certain things that we know about ourselves that we are happy to discuss with others and these are 'out in the open'. However, there may be other issues that we conceal. For example, in a work situation we may be aware that we have some gaps in our skills or knowledge, but prefer not to disclose the weakness. Other people view you from a different perspective. Looking through their 'window' helps identify 'blind spots' that affect aspects of your performance and how you interact with others. Feedback reduces the blind spot, increases openness and helps unlock underlying potential.

Unfortunately, feedback is often resisted as it may challenge our sense of competence, confidence and status. By way of comparison, a photo of your face in profile may seem strange, as you normally see yourself in a mirror, and not from the side view. *Significant feedback often causes an emotional reaction as it may not fit easily with our self-image.* However, if the feed-back can be explored through discussion, it may encourage self-disclosure that brings more issues into the open.

It is often the case that successful people are quite happy to admit to shortcomings and weaknesses. This is easier when you feel secure, under-stand your strengths, but also have the self-awareness to recognise and manage areas of weakness. We can address blind spots by being responsive to feedback. The use of *selective self-disclosure* also conveys openness and helps develop trust. However, in the work environment, self-disclosure needs to be 'balanced' so it does not undermine other people's belief in your competence. It is often important for a leader to set clear direction and clarify roles and responsibilities. A lack of personal conviction can significantly weaken the morale of people reporting to you.

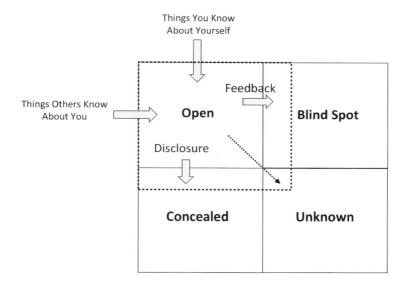

Finally, there is the area that represents the Unknown. This is gradually opened up through feedback that helps unlock underlying strengths. There are, for example, many young people with the potential to do exceptionally well in a sport. However, they need feedback to gain insight and develop the self-belief that will enable them to succeed.

Build on Feedback

Four steps contribute to positive use of feedback. These are explored further in subsequent chapters.

Listen to the Feedback

Having the opportunity to hear what other people think is useful. It gives you additional insight. It may be uncomfortable, but try to understand why they have the opinion or perception. Do not immediately reject the feedback or argue with the points they are making. Remember that you still retain your opinion, and you can subsequently decide if the feedback is relevant.

Clarify the Information

Before responding directly to the feedback, or seeking to debate points, try to clarify what is being said. Be clear about the context. When and where did the event occur, who was involved and what were the consequences? A useful tip is to repeat or summarise the main points, and this also helps reduce any emotion that could lead to argument. Avoid jumping to conclusions or becoming defensive. The aim is to understand the other person's perspective.

Explore the Alternatives

If you focus on the situation and circumstances that have resulted in you receiving the feedback, you can now do something about it. Think about the way you approached the situation and how you could handle things differently in future. Perhaps explore the other person's ideas and discuss the options, or clarify other issues that had a bearing on the situation. Balance specific feedback against other considerations (e.g. the wider objectives or longer-term requirements).

Develop an Action Plan

Feedback will provide you with new insights and contribute to increased self-awareness. However, old attitudes and existing ways of dealing with things may continue – unless you set out some clear plans. You need to define the situation and how you will deal with similar events in the future. Action plans should be specific and linked to clear timescales. The acronym SMART is often used to highlight key points:

- Specific – What exactly do you want to achieve?
- Measurable – Can you measure the improvement?
- Achievable and Agreed – Do you have the ability and motivation to achieve the goal?
- Realistic – What are the key steps and resources required to achieve the objective?
- Timescale – When will you achieve your goal?

Take the opportunity to identify goals you want to work towards over the next three months. You can also note any feedback you have received previously. This may relate to your work behaviour, potential strengths or areas for development. You are encouraged to start the leadership development course by considering feedback you have received previously, which may help you to identify:

1. *Your Personal Strengths and how these are used in your current role*

2. *Areas for Improvement, which require more effective self-management*

3. *Activities that might support Action Plans (i.e. practical follow-up)*

Understanding Your Personal Style

Profiling work preferences can help a leader gain insight into their approach and the factors likely to affect performance at work. The profile reflects the way you are currently responding to work demands. You may, for example, be strongly motivated by a need for *affiliation* and close working relationships. Alternatively, you may have a strong need to *achieve* high standards, to be in *control* of situations, or to operate with a high level of *independence*. It can sometimes be useful to think in terms of the balance we are establishing between working to our own 'internal' agenda and being responsive to 'external' requirements. Being too focused in either direction may cause problems. The profile can be viewed in terms of specific aspects of behaviour that can contribute to leadership effectiveness. Different elements from the profile are highlighted in each chapter. These elements of behaviour can be developed or managed more effectively, but the first step involves understanding how you are dealing with things at present. Existing attitudes and habits may make it difficult to adopt new, more-effective ways of working.

Effective leaders take steps to influence others and achieve results. For example, managers typically express a 'moderate to high' preference on a dimension referred to as '*Drive and Enthusiasm*'. This involves demonstrating personal energy and enthusiasm, with a willingness to explore new ideas. Evidence of energy is important in conveying personal conviction about the best course of action. Enthusiasm contributes to 'selling the vision' and helps create a clear sense of direction. However, this is a fairly broad attribute and needs to be focused effectively to ensure overall effectiveness.

JK's responses indicate the following preference:

Drive and Enthusiasm

Leaders' preferences are usually in the range 5–7

The report summary: *JK currently places definite emphasis on expressing ideas and taking the initiative when responding to situations at work. This level of response matches that expressed by many other leaders. JK will be aware of the importance of influencing events and likely to adopt a positive approach in deciding what is required and in taking action to move things forward.*

Fast-Track Leadership Development

The chapters in Part II highlight aspects of work behaviour that influence performance. There are also checklists that identify *actions linked to effective analysis and influence*. The insights relate to the attributes and actions of *Star Performers*, and build on extensive evaluation of Assessment and Development Centres (ADCs). The practical applications include graduate induction, team leader training and wider management development initiatives. Excellence involves understanding the *Rules of the Game* and how to focus energy and attention.

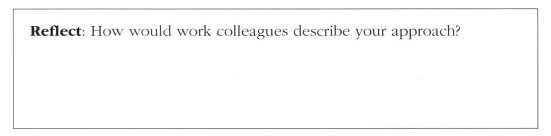

Reflect: How would work colleagues describe your approach?

Chapter 11

Module 2: Effectiveness at Work

Do You Always Use the Best Approach?

The way we respond to situations at work, and our effectiveness in handling problems, is often influenced by context. *Consider the reasons why you are more successful in some situations, but less so in others.* In some scenarios we feel relaxed and confident, but others make us nervous, hesitant or tense. Being aware of the context is the first step in developing greater leadership effectiveness. With this in mind, take the opportunity to review the four boxes shown below, preferably using examples drawn from experience gained over the last 12 months.

Try to identify some of the 'triggers' that might have contributed to positive or negative outcomes. For example, was some aspect of the role an issue (e.g., dealing with someone reporting to you, a colleague, or the relationship with your own manager)? Was the type of group significant, or the amount of preparation and planning? Did you *feel* you had the right to express your views, or, alternatively, were you worried about making mistakes? What sort of 'self-talk' was going on inside your head? Examples of a *self-talk* might include the following: *They will never listen… This is not going to work… He/she is going to be difficult.* This exercise also relates to the ABC model discussed in Chapter 7 (which refers to *Activating Events, Beliefs and Consequences*).

DOI: 10.4324/9781003439707-13

Identify a situation or problem you faced, with a positive outcome	Identify a situation or problem you faced, with a negative outcome
Identify differences in the situation and/or the people involved	Identify differences in your own thinking, feelings and behaviour

When we experience setbacks, it is important to look closely at the context and try to identify both *internal and external factors* that affected outcomes. There may, for example, be specific issues relating to role relationships, professional context, or personality differences. Improved self-awareness, backed by new skills, opens up fresh possibilities. Mental rehearsal helps you to develop a new perspective, which builds on the steps required to achieve positive outcomes.

Reflection and Forward Planning

Effective leaders try to view situations objectively. They are aware that previous experience can create assumptions and block fresh insight. It's important to understand work preferences and the potential links to performance. Many organisations seek to clarify competencies. The following examples show how a client's competencies might be related to Pario dimensions (and encourage reflection).

Sample Competency: 'Executes the Strategy' (Focus on Delivery)

Translates the vision into specific goals, accountabilities and measurable objectives. Creates a sense of purpose and understands how individuals' work contributes to outcomes. Engages in early and transparent dialogue to discuss and explain changes. Listens to and responds to concerns regarding change. Keeps agile by adjusting execution as required.

> *Leadership Focus: Sets priorities and requirements, showing a confident, positive style (vs a non-directive or passive style)*
> *Establishing Direction: Appears 'self-directed' and takes responsibility for situations*
> *Openness: Shows less 'Personal Reserve', so lower emphasis indicates greater transparency and expression of feelings or concerns*

Sample Competency: Developing Capability

Sets clear goals aligned to employees' expertise and interests. Clarifies requirements and expectations, supported with timely and constructive feedback. Motivates people by assigning responsibility, giving authority, and ensuring support. Is able to adapt style to requirements.

> *Striving for Success: Sets high performance standards, and provides an example to others*
> *Gaining Attention: Makes a personal impact and seeks to influence others*
> *Team Involvement: Engages and supports others through discussion and consultation*

Sample Competency: Networking and Relationships

Engages with stakeholders outside of the immediate team. Anticipates requirements and tailors the message to the audience. Develops networks, relationships and systems that support outcomes. Prioritises the overall requirements above the work interests of immediate team.

> *Team Influence: Contributes in meetings and influences the team's thinking and direction*
> *Organisational Awareness: Anticipates others' reactions and how best to handle issues*
> *Professional Objectivity: Balances personal values (personal preferences) with wider objectives… (confronts issues and surfaces problems when required)*

Sample Competency: Innovative Mindset (Demonstrates Agile Thinking)

Identifies opportunities and questions existing procedures. Acts in an entrepreneurial way, developing solutions, balancing customer needs and business priorities. Encourages and rewards innovation and risk-taking. Seeks a new perspective rather than relying on old approaches.

> *Innovative Response: Displays a forward-looking approach and is positive about change*
> *Broad-Based Thinking: Is reflective and consults with others, assessing options*
> *Developing Opportunities: Supports new initiatives and projects with energy, drive and enthusiasm.*
> *Speed of Response: Shows responsiveness to the context, adjusting to meet requirements*

High performance requires the ability to view situations clearly and objectively. We also need awareness of how our response is influenced by previous experience and assumptions.

Intentional Change requires self-awareness and appreciation of issues affecting outcomes. There can be value in looking back, say over the last year, using the perspective offered by **Appreciative Inquiry**.[1] Focus on strengths, achievements and positive outcomes.

What's the best experience you had in the last year?

If every day was like that, what would your life look like?

To live like that, what kind of environment do you need?

What action can you take to move towards your goal? (Identify three action steps.)

Note any feedback received in the last year relating to your work or your personal contribution.

Building on this Module, you may find it useful to discuss your goals with your manager. Alternatively, there may be opportunities to discuss objectives and work preferences with your coach or mentor.

Note

1 Appreciative Inquiry. Wikipedia. Available at: https://en.wikipedia.org/wiki/ Appreciative_inquiry

Chapter 12

Module 3: The Work Preference Report

The JK case study includes the sections (shown in the modules) taken from the work preference report. The full report, generated by the online system, includes all the dimensions summarised below. The report is sent via email after the online questionnaire is completed.

The Personal Development Report explores work preferences that may contribute to a strength in one area but could also reveal development requirements. This might, for example, apply to a very task-orientated approach that reduces interpersonal effectiveness. The profile helps clarify areas of personal strength but can also draw attention to possible blind-spots or situations that might benefit from a different approach. Increased self-awareness is the first step towards wider professional insight and improved performance.

The report is based on the responses made at the time the questionnaire was completed. The preference scores recorded on the profile indicate the strength of response, highlighting the relative emphasis placed on each dimension. It is not possible or appropriate to score strongly on all scales. The profile should not be seen as permanently fixed. Scores can change in response to new work demands, fresh insights, for example training or coaching, and increased experience. Note that the report cannot take account of an individual's current role/situation or the specific context that may have some effect on responses. This might be discussed in a follow-up session.

 DOI: 10.4324/9781003439707-14

Pario Profiling – Dimension Descriptions

Analysis and Problem-Solving – 'Analysis of Information'

Broad-Based Thinking: Considers the consequences of action and reflects on the wider issues relating to a problem.

Innovative Response: Adopts an independent and forward-looking approach and is positively orientated towards change.

Accuracy of Working: Being closely involved in precise, accurate working, with close attention to detail to avoid mistakes.

Personal Organisation: Maintains a more structured and systematic (methodical) approach to work.

Developing Opportunities – 'Flexibility of Response'

Creative Focus: Focuses on developing ideas, consulting with others and finding new solutions to problems.

Developing Opportunities: Seeks to get initiatives off the ground, committing personal energy and getting support.

Organisational Awareness: Anticipates how others will react and how best to handle work-based issues/tasks.

Pressure Index: Emphasises accuracy; follows established methods and maintains set 'standards' (or ways of working).

Working with Others – 'Personal Interaction'

Leadership Focus: Sets priorities and defines requirements, adopting a confident, positive leadership style.

Establishing Direction: Takes control of situations, asserts their own views and adopts a *self-directed* approach to tasks.

Personal Reserve: Maintains high emotional control and deals with people in a calm, controlled manner.

Personal Contact: Seeks close friendships, personal rapport and social support – needs interaction with others at work.

Personal Impact and Influence – 'Influence and Persuasion'

Gaining Attention: Makes a personal impact and obtains acknowledgement or recognition from others.

Gaining Approval: Is responsive to the standards, goals or expectations of their manager, colleagues/others.

Team Involvement: Emphasises interaction with others, usually linked to discussion/consultation with colleagues.

Team Influence: Makes a direct contribution in meetings; seeks to influence the team's thinking and direction.

Effective Decision-Making – 'Decision-Making'

Speed of Response: Demonstrates *time urgency* and concern for making a speedy response, moving quickly towards action.

Seeking Direction: Obtains guidance or direction, with a preference for structure and feedback from others.

Decision Confidence: Shows personal conviction, making decisions quickly, with a belief that outcomes will be achieved.

Striving for Success: Establishes their own high performance and achievement standards and sets an example to others.

Focus on Outcomes – 'Achieving Results'

Task Commitment: Achieves results through personal effort, commitment (and the perseverance to overcome problems).

Task Completion: Completes one task before moving on to the next, maintaining direct personal involvement.

Confronting Issues: Deals directly with issues, surfaces problems and takes a clear stand on questions of principle.

Personal Values: Expects others to share the same attitudes or principles (and approach things in the same way).

Additional Elements

Self-Critical Thinking: Under-estimates their own skills and feels responsible for setbacks. Is discouraged/less resilient under pressure.

Responsive to Others: Is aware of others concerns/problems and offers support.

Remember that people in similar roles will have different profiles, shaped by their perceptions. This means that the work preferences are not simply the result of the role. They reflect someone's current adjustment to their role.

Find out how to access the Pario Work Preference Questionnaire at Pario360.com

Chapter 13

Module 4: Analysis and Problem-Solving

This Module focuses on analysis and problem-solving. In the context of leadership, this is closely linked to important competencies. The elements explored in this section highlight how you deal with uncertainty and respond to opportunities and your willingness to take risks. The first step in personal development involves self-awareness and understanding your work preferences. Effective analysis and problem-solving are required by all professionals, regardless of their role. The skills become more important with complexity and interdependence. Leaders need to understand how best to gain insight, engage people and direct resources. There is also the need to consider internal and external colleagues/groups and maintain responsiveness to wider issues.

Effective analysis requires the ability to go beyond the immediate information and what you think you know. In other words, we need to be careful not to make assumptions, think we already have the answer or rely on the views of a small, self-referenced (biased) group. Leaders need to clarify important issues and see emerging patterns. They must identify trends and assess strengths, weaknesses and risks. With increased awareness we can solve problems, create insight and make constructive recommendations. Effective analysis provides a foundation for persuading others on the best way forward.

Problem-solving requires the ability to:

- Define or identify the problem
- Generate alternatives and potential solutions
- Evaluate and choose between these
- Implement the chosen solution

The first step towards improved analysis and problem-solving builds on *balanced processing of information*. This involves taking account of other people's views and identifying issues that could affect the task. Recognize that it can be difficult to escape from current ways of thinking. The aim is to understand a problem and see it in context, not simply find a quick, temporary solution. You need to be able to identify the underlying issues.

Clarifying Issues: The Path of the 'Five Whys'

You ask 'why?' at least five times to uncover the root cause of a problem. Each time you ask 'why?' ensure that the answer is grounded in fact – not assumptions or opinions on what might have happened. The challenge is to keep going until you have uncovered the real underlying issue. Go beyond the immediate situation and the 'facts as presented'. This involves questioning ideas and interdependencies. This technique also illustrates the principle of exploratory questioning.

One example features a consultant visiting a factory with a manager. The consultant notices liquid on the floor and a leak from an overhead pipe. The manager says it will be fixed, prompting the question, *why is it leaking?* The manager checks and says, 'faulty valve'. This prompts the question: *Why has it failed?* (and records show that it was replaced only six months ago). This prompts a further question: *Why did it fail so soon?* This reveals that there was a change of supplier. W*hy did the company change the supplier?* Further enquiries reveal that the department had been told to 'cut costs', which had unforeseen consequences. The next question might then be: *Why was cost-cutting so important? (And why where other criteria overlooked?)*

This type of scenario requires more than a technical focus. The process also contributes to fact-finding interviews, such as those used in Assessment Centres. It reminds us that one incident can be part of a chain of events. Very often, the fault lies with the process, not the individual. I recall that at one graduate Assessment Centre a candidate had clearly been told 'the answer' (in the fact-finding interview) was 'X', so skipped the exploratory questioning needed to build rapport (with the person taking the role of 'the supervisor') and open up underlying issues. After a few minutes, the candidate suddenly declared *The problem is 'X'*. The role-player, an experienced team leader, simply replied: *No, we fixed that 3 months ago*. The candidate was lost. The purpose of the activity was to assess effectiveness in asking questions and building rapport. The answer (the solution) would then follow. We need awareness of the chain of events that create a problem. So when analysing complex problems, remember to explore *internal* and *external* issues, including both *people-centred considerations* and *task-related issues*.

The following model focuses on the four elements. The external focus includes (i) the focus on the product/service and (ii) the expectations of stakeholders and others. It takes account of (iii) the internal processes and systems, and (iv) people's capability and motivation. Remember that people thrive when there are positive relationships, opportunities for skill development (*Confirmed Competence*) and opportunities to achieve a degree of control (autonomy). Use the four elements to reflect on current priorities. Think about your context – and also note future requirements. Note any opportunities to use *Purposeful Conversations* that build on AIMS.

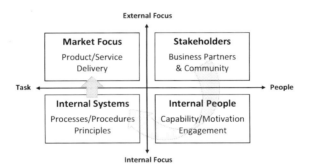

Reflect: Relate the model to your work. What are the steps leading to positive outcomes?

Assessing the Wider Issues

Gaining a clear view of all the issues that affect outcomes is particularly important in more complex work. This often involves seeking the commitment of other people. There may be significant inter-dependence between different roles. In some cases, 'work associates' will be in a different location, or employed by another organization. Finding time for reflection and

Broad-Based Thinking contributes to an appreciation of the wider issues, and this will be strengthened if you make time to discuss things with others. The work preference questionnaire reviews the emphasis placed on this area of competency.

The case study offers insight into the *pattern of behaviour* associated with specific preference scores. It notes that the typical level of emphasis placed on reflective, *Broad-Based Thinking* by senior professionals and managers, when completing the self-assessment questionnaire, is usually in the 'moderate to high' range. High scores suggest more conceptual, thoughtful analysis, whilst lower scores suggest a more grounded, practical focus. However, low emphasis may result in less reflection on wider issues.

JK's responses indicate the following preference:

Broad-Based Thinking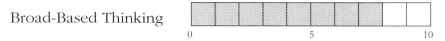

0   5   10

Leaders' preference scores are usually in the range 5–8

The report summary: *The high emphasis placed on Broad-Based Thinking suggests that JK's approach will be strongly influenced by a reflective style of working, with a preference for developing well-formulated ideas. This is likely to be characterised by seeking to consider the options and possibilities associated with tasks or assignments at work. High scores indicate a preference for dealing with problems at a theoretical or conceptual level. A questioning style is indicated and JK's approach will therefore be linked to personal enthusiasm and initiative in shaping ideas.*

Effective leaders respond positively to change and develop a view of possibilities. This involves exploring alternatives by encouraging ideas, eliciting information and seeing things from a new perspective. This process of *Scoping Out* the problem includes asking '*What if...?*' questions that prompt fresh thinking, and helping colleagues find more-effective solutions to problems.

Exploring Options and Possibilities

It's important to explore options before closing down on the best course of action. We might note, for example, Toyota's position (still evident in 2023) and delayed response concerning electric, hydrogen or other power source options for vehicles to be produced in the 2030s.

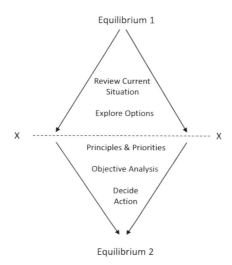

The horizontal line, X–X, represents the transition from exploring options to clarifying action plans. Focusing on options and alternatives helps assess the relative benefits and drawbacks. Phase 1 involves scoping-out issues. When ready, we *Close Down Options* and commit to action. Many seek to minimise this first stage in the process. These steps may be repeated over a period of time and become an ongoing process which encourages *continuous improvement – Kaizen.*[1]

Strengthening Analysis

A checklist of key questions helps clarify different elements of a problem. Use this to prompt fresh awareness and insights.

- *Does the problem just affect you?*

- *Does the problem involve someone else?*

- *Does the problem involve a group or team?*

- *Is this a general problem faced by many people?*

- *Are their practical constraints relating to the problem?*

- *Are there personality issues, or just issues with systems and procedures?*

- *Are there 'personal values' or ideology linked to the problem?*

- *Is there likely to be disagreements with other people?*

- *Is the problem best tackled by a group of people?*

- *Does the problem require you or others to develop new skills?*

Use the checklist to reflect on underlying issues and levels of awareness and insight. Identify options that support progress. Also check if the full significance of the problem is recognised by others. Finally, consider the wider issues involved in pursuing a particular course of action and your attitude towards risk. The desire to avoid error, for example, may be prompted by the type of work you do and the culture of the organization. However, there is also a strong personal component, which means that some people are more risk-averse (and more attentive to detail).

Achieving Innovation and Change

Managing change is a responsibility for senior professionals and leaders. It requires a questioning mindset and openness to new ways of working. However, balance is also important. The typical emphasis given by managers on the Pario *Innovative Response* scale is in the '*moderate to high*' range. High scores suggest a more questioning and change-orientated approach, whilst lower scores suggest a more conventional, conservative or 'grounded' style. This leads to greater focus on 'tried and tested' methods.

JK's responses indicate the following preference:

Innovative Response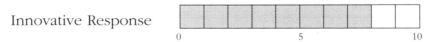

Leaders' preference scores are usually in the range 6–8

A willingness to question existing arrangements and respond positively to change are important in a leadership role. Future-focus clearly involves questioning current thinking and procedures.

The report summary: *The emphasis on Innovative Response suggests that JK has a high orientation towards change and will question the status quo. It suggests a preference for a stimulating work environment and direct involvement in new tasks and assignments. JK likes to develop his own perspective when dealing with problems or situations at work. On occasions views might be expressed quite forcefully. A willingness to question existing arrangements and respond positively to change is often important in a leadership role. The emphasis placed on Innovative Response suggests a very positive attitude towards change and real questioning of the status quo.*

Combining broad-based, reflective thinking with a willingness to question existing methods is likely to support leadership effectiveness. However, it's important to strike the right balance. The context is important, and in some situations the 'tried and tested' methods are the most appropriate. However, *learning agility*, which is often taken as an indication of future potential, does require the ability to apply knowledge in new ways. The key point is to make a habit of looking at alternative approaches and listening to other people's ideas and suggestions.

Prompt questions that may help you assess a 'real world' task:

What are the key requirements? (outcomes and priorities)

How are these changing? (and over what time frame?)

Most importantly, we need to consider the *expectations* of the other people involved, both internally (e.g. colleagues and leaders) and externally (e.g. stakeholders and business partners).

Developing a Balanced Perspective

There is value in understanding your own preferences, particularly towards innovation, risk and attention to detail. It is likely these will affect your leadership style. Leaders and others in senior professional roles usually have less 'day-to-day' or routine involvement in checking details. They should be comfortable with some element of risk. This is usually reflected in self-assessment (preference scores) on Accuracy of Working, being in the 'low' range. People in various technical, accounting, auditing and 'risk-adverse' jobs may record mid-range or high preferences.

JK's responses indicate the following preference:

Accuracy of Working

Leaders' preference scores are usually in the range 0–4

The report summary: *JK's profile indicates a low concern for personal involvement in close detail. There is less emphasis on precise checking of individual points to ensure accuracy. This suggests that JK does not regard attending to specific detail as a key aspect of the role. The focus is on the wider issues.*

Leadership and professional roles involve working with others, setting direction and clarifying roles and responsibilities. This also means that it is important not to get too immersed in detail, which tends to undermine prioritization and time management. We also know that *micro-management* can undermine trust. Managers who constantly check people's work will undermine their sense of competence and autonomy. It is therefore important to *balance* attention to specific detail with awareness of wider issues. High workload can sometimes make this difficult and it can then become a challenge to separate the *urgent* and *important*. It's more difficult to see the forest (or the approaching fire) if the focus is on a single tree.

Psychological Resilience

One important factor affecting analysis of problems involves our attitude towards risk. In this context, we need to consider *Self-Critical Thinking* (SCT). This is linked to the 'self-talk' inside your head, which causes some people to exaggerate setbacks, see things as 'all or nothing' and also blame themselves for mistakes or errors. It links to the feeling that if something is going wrong, the whole project or assignment will fail. This results in an excessive sense of personal responsibility. It can also undermine our ability to respond effectively to challenging situations.

The mindset linked to SCT tends to view *success* as 'good luck' and external factors, but explain *failure* in terms of personal shortcomings and weaknesses. Being aware of this issue is important for those in a leadership role. It's also relevant for coaches and consultants working with clients. Most significantly, *SCT* can contribute to increased (self-induced) stress, undermine *balanced processing of information* and reduce personal resilience. This makes it more difficult for people to deal with the pressure created by everyday work demands.

Developing skills to manage SCT will help improve self-management and how we react to setbacks. Increased awareness also contributes to more effective leadership of people in a team. This may be something to consider when colleagues face a difficult problem or challenging situation. You may already have some sense of where you are on the 'self-critical' dimension and whether it affects your analysis and evaluation. Even if you are a manager or team leader, who is best described as 'quietly confident', it is quite likely that there are significant differences amongst people who report to you, and also those with whom you have regular contact.

JK's responses indicate the following preference:

Self-Critical Thinking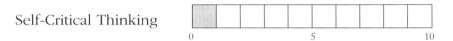

Leaders' preference scores are usually in the range 0–3.

The report summary: *The self-assessment suggests that JK is less likely to be self-critical and feel directly responsible for setbacks or problems experienced at work. Whilst this is a positive characteristic, it needs to be accompanied by openness to constructive feedback. There is also less indication of JK becoming closely involved in detailed checking of information, which is sometimes linked to self-critical thinking.*

Effective leaders are aware that people have an ongoing need to develop their sense of competence and make a positive contribution. This is linked to role clarity and doing meaningful work. Opportunities for autonomy (and a sense of being in control) encourage initiative. An effective leader therefore creates the conditions where this can happen. Developing capability and confidence reduces the problem of SCT.

You might take a moment to reflect on colleagues who are self-starters, and those who require more structure, direction, feedback and support. It is not unusual for confident people to score '0' on the Pario SCT self-assessment. Most scores are in the low range, but not everyone shares this positive self-belief. Your preference score offers a point of reference.

A Leadership Challenge: Self-Critical Thinking

A leadership 'challenge' affecting individual and team performance can be summed up as follows: How well do you address individual differences by ensuring (i) clarity and direction, (ii) providing support and (iii) encouraging autonomy. Practical steps can be taken to address the problem of SCT. This requires leaders and other senior professionals to become more aware of the symptoms. Most significant is the tendency to see things in *all or nothing* terms, when people minimize the positive aspects of their contribution and focus on weaknesses or shortfalls. Talking through the *worst possible consequences* of a setback or shortcoming can help put things in context and diminish the perceived threat. This can encourage a better understanding of the links between perceptions, feelings (and fears) and possible outcomes.

Feedback, encouragement and support that strengthen people's *sense of competence* also contribute to increases in initiative and resilience under pressure. This is the 'self-belief' element in the *Motivational Pathway*. Leadership effectiveness is therefore linked to a willingness to 'scope out' and explore options and put the problem in context. Personal confidence and conviction are 'foundation stones' for high performance, and strengthened by creating an environment that encourages feedback and structured discussion of challenges and setbacks.

These themes are explored in more detail in other modules. If you are a team leader, take the opportunity now to think about individuals in your work group. Think about people's mindset, their confidence in facing challenges and the context that affects their work.

> **Reflect:** In your team, who benefits from well-defined structure and clear direction?

> **Reflect:** Who shows confidence and initiative? Can this energy be applied in new situations?

> **Reflect:** Are there changes taking place in *role demands* and *work context*? How can we enhance people's readiness to adapt to challenges? Refer back to the HSE Management Standards (Chapter 3).

A Structured or Flexible Approach?

People vary in terms of the emphasis they place on personal organisation and planning. This may be partly a reflection of the role and the level of flexibility required to respond to unexpected demands. However, it is also linked to individual differences in how we choose to deal with situations. There are two distinctive ways of responding, and there is value in being aware of our underlying preference. One strategy involves anticipating requirements, making detailed plans and following a structured approach, i.e., a 'step-by-step' process. The second strategy involves a 'wait-and-see' approach, which places greater emphasis on flexibility. Context is obviously important in deciding what is appropriate. As a general rule, longer-term strategic planning requires structure, but operational effectiveness requires the flexibility to respond to unexpected challenges. Flexibility is also needed to build on the ideas and suggestions of other people. Most operational managers express 'low to moderate' preferences on the Pario profile.

JK's responses indicate the following preference:

Personal Organization

Leaders' preference scores are usually in the range 3–5.

The report summary: *JK's low emphasis on Personal Organisation shows a preference for a more flexible, unstructured approach when dealing with work assignments or problems. This may, in part, reflect the nature of the job, and the need to adapt to a wide range of demands. However, this low concern for structure could be significant if, for example, JK is working with colleagues who prefer a more systematic approach. It is also evident that the low concern for detailed accuracy indicates a focus on more general considerations, rather than the specific details that might be needed to complete a task. There will be some attention to key objectives and analysis directed towards those issues relevant to achieving results.*

Reflection...

Look at the elements in this module and consider how they influence your approach to analysis and problem-solving. How do your personal work preferences shape your approach? How effectively do you deal with uncertainty, new opportunities and potential risks? We can also consider this point with reference to the 3H model.

Head: *How do you structure your analysis? And how might you adapt your approach?*

Heart: *How can you improve analysis through positive interaction with other people?*
Identify people you can engage in reviewing problems and developing new solutions.
How can you gain a better understanding of their views and expectations?

Hands: *What could you do differently as a result of the new insights?*
How can you improve aspects of analysis and problem-solving?

Reflect on insights relating to this section. From a leadership perspective, link reflection with review of wider issues. For example, is there a need to improve existing systems or change procedures? Look positively towards new opportunities.

Note

1 Investopedia Business Essentials – Kaizen https://www.investopedia.com/terms/k/kaizen.asp

Chapter 14

Module 5: Developing Opportunities

Leadership often involves developing opportunities and managing change. The process builds on effective analysis and problem-solving. The challenge is to turn ideas into actions, building on input from others and working to maintain positive relationships. High performance requires awareness of other people's views, appreciation of wider issues, including *internal* and *external* perspectives. Exploring wider context requires a *Creative Focus* that helps scope out future possibilities. *Developing Opportunities* involves getting new initiatives 'off the ground'. This requires energy, enthusiasm and initiative. It builds on the analysis and problem-solving discussed in Module 4. Effectiveness also requires an understanding of the context, the culture and how other people will react, which requires *Organisational Awareness*. The final element is described as the '*Pressure Index*'. People recording higher preferences on this dimension prefer more structure and predictability in their work. They have less tolerance of uncertainty and ambiguity.

Related competencies include **Developing Opportunities and Managing Change**. They might involve finding ways to address customer/client needs, or being more entrepreneurial. The process may involve balancing conflicting priorities and introducing new initiatives. A pro-active approach will require anticipation, innovation and a degree of risk. The challenge is to develop a fresh perspective and assess new approaches (rather than rely on old, established steps). Leaders anticipate the next challenge and respond positively to unexpected events.

Developing a Creative Focus

Effective leaders typically express a 'moderate to high' preference on *Creative Focus*. This is not about being artistic. The focus is on engaging with others and seeking more effective solutions. Actions may involve questioning existing work arrangements, processes and systems. This then prompts the question: *How can we do it better?* Remember that there is often value in looking beyond current assumptions in order to identify future possibilities. Aim to balance *straight line analysis* with an appreciation of wider issues that impact on outcomes. This type of thinking is more closely linked to *Mindset and Awareness* rather than intelligence or IQ.

JK's responses indicate the following preference:

Creative Focus

Leaders' preference scores are usually in the range 6–8.

The report summary: *The moderately high score on Creative Focus indicates that JK has an interest in developing ideas and looking at new ways of resolving problems. This suggests that he will tend to be less committed to following existing procedures, or continue with one fixed approach. There is evidence of Broad-Based Thinking, and this will be supported through discussion with others. He has a strong need to question the status quo, but this might need to be more focused on specific issues.*

Prompt Questions to Widen Analysis

The following section presents several 'prompt questions' that may improve Creative Focus (and contribute to more effective management of role relationships):

- What are the key issues involved? There are many tools that can help you identify these, e.g. PESTLE/ SWOT Analysis – look up some others and review their usefulness.

- What are the views and expectations of other people? How can you discover the views of different groups?

- What other questions are important and help you achieve successful outcomes?

Identifying and Developing Opportunities

The ability to identify and develop opportunities draws on personal energy and initiative, but is also linked to awareness of the key steps required to turn ideas into action. The term *'intrapreneurship'* has been used to describe how results build on enthusiasm and a willingness to take action. There is a commitment to finding the resources, finance and backing to get new projects 'up and running'. This requires drive and determination, backed by confidence gained from experience. Most managers completing the self-assessment express a 'moderate to high' orientation towards *Developing Opportunities.*

JK's responses indicate the following preference:

Developing Opportunities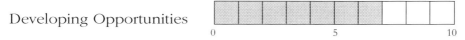

Leaders' preference scores are usually in the range 6–8.

The report summary: *JK expresses a fairly high level of enthusiasm and personal confidence in pursuing new ideas and identifying the benefits that can be achieved. The score on Developing Opportunities suggests a willingness to take the lead and adopt a high-profile in supporting new ventures. This may, for example, be related to experience in a role involving project development or the introduction of some new procedure. JK is likely to give clear support to innovative, forward-looking initiatives.*

Balancing Drive with Organisational Awareness

Whilst personal drive makes a significant contribution to performance, the energy used to *push things forward* should be balanced with effective 'positioning' of new initiatives. This involves discussing issues with people, addressing concerns and adapting to overcome resistance. We need to balance *personal conviction* about what is required with *anticipation of problems* or the difficulties people might experience. Anticipating the consequences makes it easier to assess issues or constraints and avoid setbacks. Most leaders express a moderate level of organisational awareness. The emphasis may increase slightly in a larger, more complex organisation.

JK's responses indicate the following preference:

Organisational Awareness
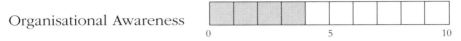

Leaders' preference scores are usually in the range 5–7.

The report summary: *The moderate score on Organisational Awareness indicates that JK is somewhat less concerned than other professionals about assessing other people's views on issues, or finding out what is happening elsewhere in the organisation. This could also suggest a preference for a more direct approach, perhaps linked to taking personal responsibility for finding solutions when faced with difficult or challenging situations.*

Use the chart below to review *Role Relationships*. These may be immediate and direct, e.g., with Direct Reports. Others may involve less frequent contact, but could be important. The relationships might include those with Business Partners or Stakeholders. You can review your links on the following page.

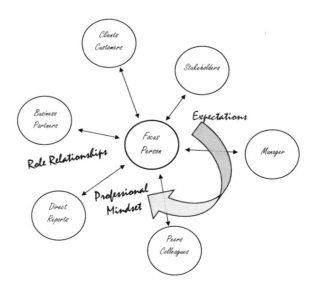

Role Relationships: Managing Expectations

The expectations of each group need to be considered. You may find it useful to map relationships linked to your role. Make a note of any issues you need to deal with. Consider a timescale for action, e.g. one to three months?

Identify a relationship that could be improved, e.g., through better communication, or more focus on future progress etc.

Identify someone on your map and consider how they might be affected by a new development (or recent change).

Your work preferences will affect how you implement change. The *Pressure Index* (discussed in the following section) offers further insight into your preferred approach.

Developing Agility: Reducing Pressure

Leadership involves reviewing information from various sources to identify trends, assess risks, make connections, gauge possibilities and respond effectively when faced with complex problems. There is often an element of uncertainty about what will happen or how requirements will change. As noted previously, an important element of agility involves *tolerance of ambiguity* and a willingness to explore and develop opportunities. However, many people experience pressure if activities are not clearly defined. This tends to be made worse by a high concern for accuracy and the belief that things should be done in a set way. A structured, step-by-step approach can reduce flexibility and contribute to pressure when things are less predictable.

A preference for structure (and fixed views on how things are done) is more evident in technical, specialist and administrative roles. Over-identification with one professional group and set procedures can also reduce openness to new ideas, increasing resistance to change. The desire for order and predictability is evident in many groups. However, most leaders express a low score on the *Pressure Index* and have more tolerance of ambiguity. Leaders with lower scores on *Self-Critical Thinking* and *Accuracy of Working* are likely to be more resilient, particularly when under pressure. However, team leaders should also consider the characteristics of people in the team, and the level of support individuals require, particularly during periods of change.

JK's responses indicate the following preference:

Pressure Index

Leaders' preference scores are usually in the range 0–3.

The report summary: *The final scale in this section is described as the 'Pressure Index'. It highlights the extent to which someone wants their work to follow clearly defined standards and procedures. JK's preference score suggests the ability to maintain a fairly flexible and adaptable approach. Other aspects of the profile indicate some concern for doing things in a particular way, reflecting personal preferences and typical response to role demands.*

The elements discussed in this section, coupled with those covered in previously, offer insight into how leaders respond to situations. Reflect on how you respond to events. Think about the forces that may be pushing towards change, but also the issues that may hinder progress.

Developing Opportunities: Practical Exercise

Think about a time when you implemented a change, perhaps affecting your team or the department. Using Force Field Analysis, review the elements that affected outcomes. The technique can help clarify the factors *pushing change* and those *creating resistance*. This builds on the insight that the current situation reflects a balance between forces pushing for change and those resisting change. This is the status quo we have today.

When pressure is resolved, the result is a new equilibrium. Rather like the seismic shift that occurs with an earthquake, we find a new point of equilibrium has been created. However, there is always a degree of underlying pressure. New technology may demand change, but people may lack the skills and resources required to move forward. There may be issues linked to motivation. You can map the current situation, as shown in the example given below. Context changes and a new equilibrium emerges. Various forces increase the pressure for change, but restraining forces hinder the process and undermine a smooth transition. Richard Hooker (Anglican priest, c.1594) said: '*Change is not made without inconvenience, even from worse to better*'.

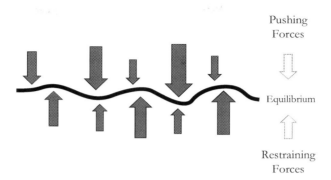

Managing change requires both sides to be evaluated, but it is often useful to reduce the restraining forces rather than simply *push harder*. Your personal determination to succeed may simply strengthen the resistance. Effective progress involves dealing with resistance. Problems include existing attitudes or assumptions, or a lack of appropriate skills.

Clarify the problem: Use the checklist in Module 4 to review the issues. The problem might involve new procedures and the need for new skills, more initiative in dealing with problems, and a more proactive approach when working in an extended team. In some cases, this involves keeping people informed of developments, even though they are in different buildings or other locations and time zones.

Set specific objectives on how you will influence or change the situation. Try to make these measurable, so that you have clear targets.

List the forces pushing you to make the change.

List the forces restraining you from making the change.

Rate the importance of forces on a chart (with arrows of varying sizes and lengths).

Reflection

Think about a situation you experienced that involved implementation of a change… You may have been the team leader or manager responsible for the change, or you may have experienced the effects of the change. If *Force Field Analysis* had been used, what could have been done differently? How would this have improved the management of the process?

The next module builds on these insights and explores steps contributing to effective leadership.

Chapter 15

Module 6: Working with People

This module reviews aspects of leadership linked to setting direction and preferences that affect how we work with others. Consider the themes in the context of your current role, but also in the context of *future demands* and the competencies contributing to effectiveness. These include transparency, openness, active listening and dialogue (to support evaluation). In addition, cascaded leadership is required to implement strategy and create alignment. The overall vision has to be translated into goals, measurable objectives and specific responsibilities. It provides the foundation for accountability and purpose. People need to understand how their work contributes to overall goals, so ongoing *Purposeful Conversations* support the process. Skilled leaders listen and respond to people's concerns and adjust their approach when necessary.

Setting clear direction and engaging constructively with others are critical aspects of *autonomy supportive leadership*. This module explores themes that contribute to effectiveness and offers insights on the effect of work preferences. As a starting point, it is useful to remind ourselves of the difference between a manager and a leader. Whilst a manager is involved in a rational process of analysis, planning, monitoring and delivering results, a leader also creates a sense of possibilities, helps people make progress and builds motivation and commitment. There is an *emotional aspect* to leadership, particularly when change is taking place and there is a need to *build commitment to* new ways of working. Virtually all definitions of leadership share the view that leadership involves the *process of influence*, enhanced by trust-based relationships. This involves professionalism, consistency of approach and clarity of purpose. Effective leaders establish clear standards, listen to ideas and involve people in finding solutions to problems.

DOI: 10.4324/9781003439707-17

Authentic Leadership

Many leadership studies emphasise the importance of authenticity. This concept has its roots in Greek philosophy: *To thine own self be true.* Authenticity has been described as *the unobstructed operation of one's true, or core, self in one's daily enterprise.* Authentic Leadership goes further than the old models that emphasise a *compelling vision*, charisma and vague ideas suggesting the need for 'individualized consideration'. Authentic Leadership goes beyond integrity, sincerity or just consistency of approach. Most importantly, Authentic Leaders *act in accord with their values and enable others to do the same.* This is done by demonstrating conviction when setting direction, taking time to clarify the wider context, ensuring positive working relationships and creating a sense of participation, autonomy and responsibility.

Research shows that to be effective, Authentic Leadership also requires self-awareness. In other words, it's important for leaders to understand their unique talents, strengths, sense of purpose, core values and beliefs – and how these affect their work behaviour. The values must also be aligned to action through guiding principles. To be really effective, leaders need to identify with the organisation's objectives and demonstrate *personal conviction* about what is required. At the same time, they engage with others in a positive, constructive way that helps people develop core needs relating to *Competence (Skills and Mastery), Autonomy (Control and Self-Direction) and Relatedness (requiring Trust, being part of a valued group, and 'connectedness').* If these needs are not met, it becomes difficult to unlock the motivation needed to encourage discretionary effort and maximise performance. In summary, Authentic Leaders display high levels of self-awareness, are able to undertake 'balanced processing' of information, display 'relational authenticity' and maintain authentic behaviour/action.

Developing Authentic Leadership

Authentic Leadership works by building a sense of meaningful activity, involvement and shared purpose. Effective leaders encourage transparency and are open to feedback. The process can be supported by *Purposeful Conversations*, discussed later in this module. Leaders typically need to develop their effectiveness in four key areas[1]:

Self-awareness

This involves understanding your unique talents, strengths, sense of purpose, core values, beliefs and desires: Are you open to new ideas and receptive to feedback that helps you maintain and develop this insight?

Balanced processing of information

Effectiveness builds on a willingness to consider multiple sides of an issue, including other people's views. Are you able to recognise that you may not see or appreciate all the issues?

Relational authenticity

Trust develops when there is openness and truthfulness in close relationships. We can use selective self-disclosure to acknowledge that we're not perfect. How well do you build trust and appear genuine when working with others?

Authentic behaviour/action

This involves responding to situations in a way that is appropriate, in the context of your role, whilst respecting your core values. Do you behave (as far as possible) in a way that is consistent with these values? Can you identify with appropriate Superordinate Goals and Principles?

Self-awareness and self-regulation, reflected in professional behaviour and consistent internalised standards, help leaders demonstrate conviction and 'positive modelling'. *In other words, they walk the talk.* This helps foster a sense of authenticity in others. However, in order to encourage discretionary effort and commitment to the organisation (two key factors linked to increased productivity) additional steps are required. These include building people's sense of participating in meaningful activity and supporting personal development.

Think of a situation that could benefit from the application of the four elements. How do the elements contribute to effectiveness?

Leadership in Context

Effective leadership involves not only setting direction, clarifying roles and responsibilities but also ensuring that team members understand how their work relates to the activities of others. This involves ongoing conversations, awareness of how roles interrelate, anticipation of requirements (and potential problems) and regular review of priorities for action. Authentic

Leadership also requires personal conviction about the best course of action. This can be viewed in terms of the context in which you are operating. You may need to consider not only the underlying level of agreement concerning objectives but also the guiding principles that support the approach and the timescale, which may require an immediate response or simply some initial preparation for future action.

If the activity requires a new approach or a shift of perspective, dialogue is important. Not least, this provides an opportunity to engage people in developing new ideas. As noted previously, in the context of the *Motivational Pathway*, we need to increase situational awareness, which arouses the *Executive Control Network* (ECN). The focus is outward looking and helps get people off 'autopilot', what neuroscience calls the *Default Mode Network* (DMN) so they actively process new information. Solution-focused conversations help us move away from old assumptions (and possibly negative feelings). They also enable people to review problems, but then envisage what might change and how we can reach the desired outcome. The team leader helps unlock the 'power of small wins' (discussed later in this module). Insight into your current style of working is provided by the Leadership Focus dimension on the work preference questionnaire. Most leaders place *moderate to high emphasis* on setting direction and clarifying objectives. Your current role may have some effect on the score.

JK's responses indicate the following preference:

Leadership Focus

Leaders' preference scores are usually in the range 6–8.

The report summary: *There is a moderate emphasis on Leadership Focus, and this suggests that JK will take some responsibility for clarifying technical or professional objectives and setting direction. An element of confidence is likely, but he may not actively seek opportunities that enable him to give a clear lead to others. In some situations, a more directive approach could be of value.*

Building commitment to a course of action is one of the most challenging aspects of leadership. It requires personal conviction and a clear vision of future possibilities. People need to be engaged through two-way discussion that helps unlock motivation and build a sense of shared purpose. This contributes to alignment of individual and team activities and overall objectives. Dialogue helps establish a *meaningful rationale for action* and also works to overcome resistance to change.

Taking Responsibility for Situations

The self-assessment questionnaire offers insight into your work preferences, including your willingness to take control of situations and provide direction to other people. This is highlighted by the *Establishing Direction* dimension and reflects the extent to which you seek to take responsibility for deciding requirements. Most leaders express a moderate to high preference, which contributes to their ability to overcome resistance and maintain a clear focus on priorities. The emphasis you place on this scale may well affect other aspects of your leadership style. It influences your preferred way of working. Your willingness to take on this responsibility may be influenced by self-belief and the confidence needed to take control of situations. Developing insight can improve your focus and support delivery or results.

JK's responses indicate the following preference:

Establishing Direction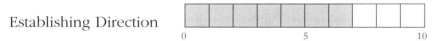

Leaders' preference scores are usually in the range 6–8.

The report summary: *The moderately high score on Establishing Direction indicates that JK is motivated to take charge of situations and have the opportunity to decide objectives. When viewed alongside the moderate score on Leadership Focus, it suggests that JK will decide a course of action and allocate roles and responsibilities. However, this appears to be a relatively low-key approach.*

Openness and Relational Authenticity

Being open with other people and showing some emotional response contributes to *Relational Authenticity*, which is viewed as one of the building blocks of Authenticity. This contributes to effectiveness through self-disclosure and transparency, but can cause problems if it results in an overly emotional response. That said, there is value in expressing concerns or a personal viewpoint, and making a conscious effort to 'surface problems' and set direction.

The ability to surface problems and set direction might be viewed as essential competencies of high performers. However, it is also important to recognise that a lack of consistency, *anchored in a strong sense of professionalism, fairness and objectivity*, will undermine your credibility. Objectivity and consistency are important attributes of those aspiring to be *Star Performers*. Leaders usually express fairly low to moderate *Personal Reserve* on the work preference profile.

JK's responses indicate the following preference:

Personal Reserve
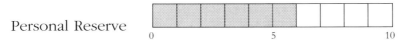

Leaders' preference scores are usually in the range 2–4.

The report summary: *JK displays a moderately high level of Personal Reserve when engaging with people at work. This suggests concern about being professionally objective when responding to the decisions or behaviour of colleagues, or direct reports. The preference indicates a fairly high level of emotional control. JK is likely to appear fairly firm on certain issues, expressing views in a measured, constrained way. This is accompanied by the wish to maintain positive relationships with others.*

Note: Effective leaders tend to be open, *state issues* and express concerns. This could be an *area of development* for JK. The current preferences might reduce opportunities to *set direction*.

Personal Reserve will influence how we respond to people and situations. However, interaction with other people is also shaped by self-management and awareness of what others require. We can, for example, structure conversations so that they are more effective in addressing people's underlying need for involvement in both analysing problems and implementing solutions. This dialogue contributes to people's motivation and sense of shared purpose and builds on *Purposeful Conversations*. The conversations do not require the leader to be out-going or 'charismatic'. They build on well-developed listening skills and appreciation of what contributes to effectiveness. Issues are viewed in the context of the task and overall goals.

Purposeful Conversations

Setting Direction requires clarity and conviction in defining goals and objectives. However, high performance also needs responsiveness to the views of others. Successful leaders can build on the four elements contributing to effectiveness, and this can be linked to a framework for *Purposeful*

Conversations. Whilst *assertiveness* can help achieve short-term results, long-term success involves unlocking discretionary effort and a sense of purpose. People need to *internalise* the reasons for action. In a broader context, we also need to feel that we are developing our skills and ability. This process is encouraged when we feel that our ideas and suggestions are valued. Some people have more need for guidance and direction, but motivation *and willingness to demonstrate discretionary effort* can be encouraged through dialogue.

The *Purposeful Conversation with AIMS* (Awareness, Insight, Meaning and Support) model helps build involvement in problem solving and solution generation. The conversations are best held on a regular basis, but can be quite short and informal. The AIMS model provides a reference point. As a team leader, or possibly in a consultancy role, you should have an understanding of issues and context before you start the conversation. This is important in *Setting Direction* and trying to build a sense of shared purpose. As noted previously, the focus is on developing *Awareness, Insight, Meaning* and *Support*.

Step 1: Awareness and Acknowledgement

The first step involves raising self-awareness and requires active listening to understand the context and current thinking. What is the person's thinking, feeling and perception of the situation? *Acknowledge what the person is saying and comment on positive achievements.* Mention the person's contributions or specific strengths. Highlight progress. This creates an opportunity to develop empathy and review options and alternatives. Build on the foundation.

Step 2: Insight into Wider Issues

Things need to be seen in the context of new developments and changing priorities. Demands change over time, so we need to adapt. Leaders engage people in dialogue by clarifying context and using prompt questions. These might, for example, address new developments or challenges. Current systems and procedures may need to change. Effective questions encourage reflection and create fresh insights on how to resolve problems. Example questions include the following:

How do we respond?
How do you think that could work for us?

What do you think of this new development? Follow up with, *How do we make it work?*

What do the next steps look like?

Step 3: Meaningful Action

Building on steps 1 and 2 helps put things in context. Personal conviction about possibilities contributes to shared purpose. However, a *meaningful rationale* is required to build commitment. Leaders can also strengthen motivation by finding opportunities for people to develop competence and autonomy. Building on this, activities become more aligned with overall goals, and people feel more involved in the process.

Step 4: Support

People may need support to overcome challenges, but they also value support linked to their personal development. *Purposeful Conversations* help clarify the support and action that is required. Leaders may offer professional advice, but they also deliver resources and support progress. Overcoming setbacks builds motivation, resilience and underlying commitment.

Step 4 in the process links to action. Ask the question: *What is the most helpful thing I can do to make progress (in the context of responding positively to this issue/problem/challenge)?*

Purposeful Conversations backed by AIMS help leaders check assumptions before making firm decisions. Where possible, find time to draw out ideas and concerns from other people, and create insight by clarifying new developments, explaining changing priorities or discussing the work being done in other teams and departments. It is not always necessary to go through all four steps, but look for opportunities to create meaning and opportunities to confirm progress and support people's personal development. Making progress in daily work is a key aspect of motivation. Effective leaders support the process and celebrate what has been achieved. This is 'the power of small wins', described as the *Progress Principle*.[2]

Practical Activity

Find an opportunity to *Set Direction* and support this with the four steps of the AIMS model. This might be done with a colleague or someone in your team. If a project or activity is already underway, take the opportunity to ask about progress. Be prepared to follow up and explore issues to raise your **Awareness**. This requires *active listening*, which is discussed in the next module. Try to gain a clear understanding of how the other person sees the situation. Building on awareness, you have the opportunity to create **Insight** by talking about new developments, the priorities for attention or activities that are happening elsewhere. Note other relevant points that may improve understanding or help clarify how best to respond to challenges. This helps keep the focus on what is important and strengthens *alignment* with overall objectives.

If there is uncertainty about the best approach, or potential disagreement on priorities, look for opportunities to confirm the **Meaning**. You might note the value of what has been achieved. It's important to put activities in context. People need to appreciate the bigger picture. It is easy to assume that this understanding is present, but this is often not so. Comments by team members, linked to 360-degree feedback, reveal that many managers underestimate the value of explaining *how things connect*. So help people understand how roles, responsibilities and activities connect, and why a task is important and how it contributes. Also identify areas of activity where people require **Support**. This will help build people's capability and self-belief. Check resources (and possible shortfalls). Find opportunities to help people develop skills and respond to new challenges. This contributes in building commitment to the organisation.

Personal Contact

Influencing techniques and *Purposeful Conversations* will be explored in the next module. This section concludes by looking at the importance of positive working relationships and people's need for affiliation and friendship. This is an area where there are significant individual differences, and also variation between age groups. Younger people tend to place more emphasis on the social dimension of work. They often value having good friends at work and meeting colleagues for social activities. Preferences linked to *Personal Contact* will affect your approach.

JK's responses indicate the following preference:

Personal Contact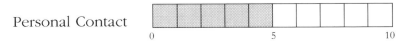

Leaders' preference scores are usually in the range 3–5.

The report summary: *JK's interaction with other people is characterised by a moderate concern about Personal Contact. This implies some consideration to developing or maintaining close relationships. JK will seek to have some involvement as part of a group. This is coupled with the view that personal performance does not depend on other people sharing specific values or one perspective.*

> **Reflect**: Identify behaviour discussed in this Module. *How does your approach affect others?*

> Think about a situation where you could be more effective. *What might be done differently? Focus on how it might look if some positive steps were taken.*

Notes

1 Walumbwa, F. O., Avolio, B. J., Gardner, W. L., Wernsing, T. S., & Peterson, S. J. (2008). Authentic leadership: Development and validation of a theory-based measure. *Journal of Management*, 34(1), 89–126.
2 Amabile, T., & Kramer, S. J. (May 2011). The Power of Small Wins. *Harvard Business Review*. Available at: https://hbr.org/2011/05/the-power-of-small-wins

Chapter 16

Module 7: Personal Impact and Influence

Setting clear direction is an essential attribute of all leaders. However, there is also a need to build the commitment required to achieve objectives. Motivation is increased when there is a sense of shared purpose and agreement on how best to achieve goals. **Consultation and collaboration** provide a foundation. The process involves influence both *within and outside* the immediate team. Effective leaders communicate with conviction and tailor the message to the audience. They network across functions to create cooperation that benefits clients and customers. The focus is on primary objectives, and *subordinate goals* are seen in this context. Leaders create alignment through personal influence and reference to guiding principles.

In many situations, there is a need to show initiative, question existing methods and seek to influence others. You can make suggestions and help to develop more effective solutions. These themes are covered in previous modules. They include the need to take responsibility, set clear direction, establish priorities and clarify how best to use resources. Future-focused leaders use interpersonal skills to resolve differences of opinion, overcome resistance and find ways to create purpose and commitment. Organisations require leaders who have the skills to engage and energise other people.

Effective leaders help others develop insight. They understand their own strengths, areas for improvement and review the context. Feedback has a key role in building awareness and helping people respond to challenges. This supports self-management and more effective action when faced with difficult situations. Successful leaders are able to respond positively to changing work demands because they appreciate the context and can flex their response. Traditional managers, with fixed ways of working, may struggle to adapt to new requirements. *Cognitive flexibility and agility require the ability to restructure existing knowledge in new ways.* This process is enhanced through dialogue that creates fresh insights and opens up new possibilities.

As noted earlier, in the past, leadership theory focused on *charisma* and the idea of a '*compelling vision to overcome people's self-interest*'. Contrast this with Authentic Leaders who show personal conviction and build trust. Their approach is based on high professional standards, consistency and fairness. The ability to persuade other people is strengthened by influencing skills that help overcome resistance and create a sense of shared purpose.

The first aspect of influence involves positive engagement with other people. When presenting ideas and suggestions it's important to display a degree of energy and enthusiasm. You need to gain people's interest and attention. This is easier if you expect some recognition and acknowledge-ment linked to your contribution. *There is potential value in seeking the glow of positive feedback.* Low emphasis on *Gaining Attention* suggests a low-key approach, which can result in less appreciation of your input. (A well-known presenter on UK television scored 9.)

JK's responses indicate the following preference:

Gaining Attention

Leaders' preference scores are usually in the range 3–5

The report summary: *The preference score indicates that JK seeks a degree of recognition or acknowledgement from others. This is reflected in the moder-ate emphasis given to Gaining Attention. JK will prefer work situations that provide opportunities to gain favourable feedback, or involve people offering him personal encouragement. The profile suggests some ability to gain the attention of others when presenting ideas or making suggestions.*

Identify a situation where you could do more to gain people's interest and attention.

Developing a Balanced Perspective

Effective leadership involves focusing on the performance objectives of your team or department, but also developing a clear understanding of the *Superordinate Goals* of the organisation. A critical part of a leader's role involves translating the organisation's vision and mission into tangible objectives. These need to make sense to the people in the team. They shape priorities when working with direct reports, colleagues, or business partners. This becomes more challenging when there are a number of locations, diverse groups and differing perspectives. A team leader sets direction, but is open to alternative views when discussing issues.

The motivation to *Establish Direction* and take responsibility should be supported by responsiveness. Personal energy, initiative and sense of purpose must be balanced with awareness of people's expectations. Individuals vary in their underlying need to gain the approval of others, most notably their manager and colleagues. Being responsive to alternative views helps leaders adjust and adapt. It's useful to understand how *Gaining Approval* affects your response. High emphasis can suggest dependency, but low scores indicate a more independent, self-directed style. A lack of balance may contribute to potential problems. Most leaders are fairly responsive to the views and expectations of colleagues, and particularly their own manager. High emphasis is more evident in the profiles of *supportive team players* and also less experienced, younger people.

JK's responses indicate the following preference:

Gaining Approval

Leaders' preference scores are usually in the range 3–5.

The report summary: *The comparatively low score on Gaining Approval suggests that JK has little need to meet the standards or expectations of others and will be more likely to form an independent perspective on key issues. On occasions this could lead to JK being less responsive to the concerns of others, reflected in the fairly low emphasis placed on Organisational Awareness.*

Strengthening Team Capability

The leader should be responsive to the team's requirements at particular points in its life cycle, and appreciate the actions that contribute to superior performance. It is important to note that these principles apply to real groups, with clear roles and responsibilities. There is interdependence between team members. In the 21st century, the group may have a virtual quality, in the sense that meetings are conducted online, and there is relatively limited face-to-face contact.

Team effectiveness can be measured by how well the team engages with other groups, partners and stakeholders, and makes progress in achieving agreed outcomes. It's also possible to gauge the team's health by reviewing how well team members work together to resolve problems. In a well-functioning team, this self-directed quality, building on effective use of skills and recognition of the interdependencies between team members, increases over time. The work of the team should also reinforce individuals' core needs. As noted, these relate to *Competence* (skill development), *Autonomy* (making a valued, self-directed contribution) and *Relatedness* (being part of a group with a shared purpose and a collaborative, supportive ethos). The ideal situation is one where the task is challenging and meaningful and there are adequate resources and support. This serves to encourage motivation (discretionary effort) as well as building commitment to the organisation.

Team Involvement

Team Coaching can be viewed as part of the leadership role, but it's also critical to high performance. The focus is primarily on the processes affecting the team's operation, rather than interpersonal or communication skills training. This model is based on the work of Prof Richard Hackman,[1] which suggests that the best interventions are aligned with the team's current requirements. It is therefore important at the start of a new project or assignment to set out a clear description of objectives, but this should then be linked to engaging the team in discussion concerning the context, rationale and wider issues. This dialogue contributes to commitment. *Purposeful Conversations* can support this process. The objective is to engage and motivate team members, and encourage them to move towards action.

Research suggests that as the team make progress with their work, and gain increased experience, they become more receptive to the *leader's support* in reviewing progress. Team leaders make time to discuss how well team members' skills and abilities are being utilised. They consider how they might adapt their approach to make more effective use of internal resources, and also meet the expectations of partners and stakeholders. Typically, this type of strategic review is most useful near the midpoint of the team's work cycle. Individuals are able to draw on their practical experience and reflect on what has gone well (or caused problems) and are therefore in a better position to stand back and assess options and possibilities.

Completion of a project or assignment provides an opportunity for reflection, and objective review of both achievements and areas for improvement. However, an effective leader will also take the opportunity for ongoing contact to encourage positive behaviour, surface underlying issues and help the team resolve problems. It's also important that leaders do not get too directly involved in the team's activities. This is a challenge for those attentive to detail who dwell on mistakes or errors and find it difficult to delegate. *Team Involvement* contributes to leadership effectiveness, but only when there is a clear focus on the issues affecting performance. Most leaders place moderate emphasis on involvement.

JK's responses indicate the following preference:

Team Involvement

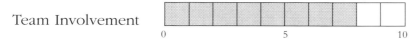

Leaders' preference scores are usually in the range 5–8.

The report summary: *JK expresses a fairly high need for Team Involvement, indicating a preference for work situations involving interaction with other people. On occasions there might be value in giving a clearer lead within the group, possibly clarifying objectives or key steps for others. This point should be assessed alongside the moderate tendency to have others define the key areas of activity, given the comparatively low score on Establishing Direction. Your approach should also be considered in the context of the moderately high score on Gaining Attention. This suggests a fairly high-profile style and a wish for recognition. It may support your ability to generate enthusiasm and commitment.*

Team involvement can be viewed alongside *Responsiveness to Others*, which is particularly important in terms of providing support and encouraging autonomy.

Self-Awareness and Responsiveness

The element of role awareness that involves being *Responsive to Others* is also linked to the concept of *Purposeful Conversations*. Understanding what others require contributes to effective leadership. The dialogue helps enhance competence, confidence and work-related motivation. The first step (Awareness) builds on active listening, which includes acknowledging what has been achieved. Politicians, for example, might benefit by recognising the work and achievements of others in order to establish some common ground. When this has been done, it becomes easier to convey the message: *this is how we can build on the foundation.* The process involves developing *competence*, encouraging *autonomy* (discretionary effort) ensuring meaningful activity and providing the *support* that builds trust and a sense of connection (*relatedness*).

Purposeful Conversations enhance *awareness* and grasp of issues. This creates a platform for developing *insight* in others, so people appreciate the bigger picture. The process is improved by finding opportunities to create *meaning*, which builds on principles and purpose. Finally, team leaders provide *support*. This may be linked to not only ensuring adequate resources and training but also identifying opportunities for individual development. The distinct elements in AIMS contribute to self-regulation of behaviour, which builds professionalism and consistency. A *balanced approach* includes a degree of *Responsiveness to Others*. From a leadership perspective, this may be relevant in setting direction, conveying meaning and providing support and encouragement.

JK's responses indicate the following preference:

Responsiveness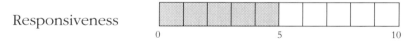

Leaders' preference scores are usually in the range 5–8.

The report summary: JK, *you appear to have some awareness of events that cause other people concerns or problems. However, this is not an area of particular emphasis – and you may need to be more responsive in situations where people require your support. It may be useful to view this in the context of how best to build motivation and achieve results.*

Reflect: Could you do more to explore concerns or clarify requirements?

Developing Influencing Skills

The notion of a *compelling vision* has been featured in many books on leadership (and academic studies of leadership attributes). However, whilst it is clear that a leader must set direction and show personal conviction (about the best course of action), this needs to be supported by influencing skills. They help resolve differences of opinion and build commitment. Sharing a vision is one influencing technique, but other styles will be appropriate in different situations. The most appropriate approach depends on (i) the timescale for achieving action and (ii) the underlying level of agreement. The leader might, for example, seek to *Push* people towards a course of action by using reasoning and logic, which tends to be backed by assertion and authority. There is an increasing level of personal energy. Alternatively, the leader might use bridging and empathy to understand other people's views. This provides a platform for exploring possibilities. The objective is then to *Pull* people towards a shared vision. Motivation is increased when people share a vision and they internalise the rationale for going in that direction.

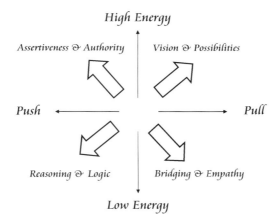

The application of different styles is summarised below:

- Reasoning and logic: The situation is relatively calm, and you have recognised competence
- Assertiveness and authority: You have the personal conviction (and power) to make clear demands
- Bridging and empathy: You listen to understand issues, reduce conflict and find common ground
- Possibilities and vision: This is forward-looking and creates a sense of energy and future direction

Reasoning and Assertion are most relevant when there is time urgency and clear direction is required. Confirm vision, possibilities and action, backed by a meaningful rationale. *Bridging and Empathy* provide the starting point for a more consultative style. This approach also supports coaching to develop competence and future capability.

New initiatives often cause disruption. Rational persuasion must be backed by active listening to clarify concerns. However, the leader must remain clear about important goals. These might be adjusted to meet the expectations of customers, stakeholders and business partners, or simply the need to use resources wisely. Understanding differing views (*Bridging*) helps clarify concerns and creates an opportunity to develop new ideas for moving forward. Examples of *open questioning* might include the following: *How do you see us progressing on this...?*; *What impact is this having...?*; and *What are your thoughts on X...?*

It's a mistake to encourage open-ended discussion before there is clarity concerning priorities, context and constraints. Performance standards and outcomes need to be explicit. A lack of clarity causes confusion and wastes time. *Leaders need to be clear about the outcomes required, but encourage the team to find solutions.* The vision helps energise people, offering a clear view of outcomes. We might prompt future-focused thinking: *Just imagine how it will be in six months when we have all this in place. What do you see happening?*

Influencing Skills: Effectiveness in Meetings

Use the checklist to review your approach in group discussions. Note any points that may reduce your personal effectiveness.

To what extent do you...

- Prepare for the meeting; have a view of the issues and a note of two or three points you will make.
- Ask questions and seek clarification of points to increase your involvement in the discussion.
- Express your ideas and *pose questions* to do with wider issues or options for making progress and 'going forward'.
- Show you are listening by nodding, showing interest and commenting on points made by others.

- Support your statements with reasons, e.g. 'In view of the changes… we should…. because…'.
- Try to avoid acting simply as a technical adviser; help the group explore the issues – identify context and connections.
- People miss things (don't listen), so return to points, repeat what you said and explain in a different way.
- Encourage other people to contribute and build on their points, e.g., by relating these points to other important issues.
- Avoid direct criticism of others and focus on the issues (keep the focus on context), e.g. *How does that fit with X…?*.
- Avoid irritating, judgemental comments, e.g. *'with all due respect…'* and *'that will never work…'*.
- Summarise points made by others and relate to the key objectives, i.e., 'pull threads together'.
- Avoid making the assumption that you will be invited to contribute or your input will be valued!
- Increase your impact by creating space for others, e.g. *'KC is making a very interesting point…'*.
- Focus on discussing the issues and context; avoid early *statements of position* that cause entrenchment.
- Avoid taking votes on issues – invest time in discussing the context/ conditions/constraints and objectives.
- Monitor your contributions: Build on others' ideas, maintain regular input and focus on the key issues.
- Avoid statements that appear apologetic or imply criticism of others…, e.g. *'Can I just finish my point…'*.

Remember that frustration or irritation often indicates a lack of effective, influencing skills. Some leaders, even within a senior management team, shrug their shoulders, 'disconnect' and say, *'Well, if they don't want to listen, it's their loss…'*. Effective leaders do not allow issues to become personal. Specific influencing techniques make a real difference to what is achieved. Don't get angry, irritated or withdraw from the discussion. The objective is to develop self-awareness and self-management. Learn to use a wider range of influencing skills.

Effectiveness in meetings or one-to-one discussions is increased by 'flexing' your style and taking account of people's feelings, and issues shaping their response. It is often sensible to use bridging when someone has differing views, especially if they are angry or upset. Active listening and acknowledgement of concerns will move the conversation forward, encouraging reasoned discussion. Discuss options and possibilities, and develop a plan of action.

People's effectiveness in meetings, and the overall performance of the group, is often significantly reduced because they do not adopt the right tactics. Typical faults include the following:

- Making statements without supporting them with reason
- Not relating points to the main objective or wider considerations, *e.g.* *Superordinate Goals and Principles*
- Failing to 'build' and develop points made by others
- Allowing yourself to be 'talked down' and not returning to your point, e.g. low emphasis on *Gaining Attention*
- Talking over others and not listening

Turning to the work preference questionnaire, we find that most leaders place *moderate to high* emphasis on *Team Influence*. This suggests personal confidence and the ability to 'flex', i.e., apply different styles, in response to different scenarios. This may also add to effectiveness in setting direction. The score is frequently coupled with similar emphasis on *Leadership Focus*.

JK's responses indicate the following preference:

Team Influence

Leaders' preference scores are usually in the range 6–8.

The report summary: *JK places fairly high emphasis on Team Influence. This suggests an element of confidence when interacting with others and a willingness to express views. Linking to the fairly high score on Leadership Focus, JK is likely to have a moderate impact in terms of clarifying objectives, reviewing key steps, and setting direction for others in the team. With the high score on Innovative Response, there will be a strong tendency to question and challenge issues and a positive outlook in responding to new demands.*

Organisations help create conditions that contribute to team effectiveness. The checklists include (i) a reward system geared to the team's performance, (ii) adequate support, training and education to build the skills and knowledge essential to the development of competence and initiative, (iii) information feedback systems that encourage active scanning of factors affecting performance, and (iv) regular review of how team members can work together to best effect. This means that there is open discussion about how best to respond to task demands and the action required to achieve positive outcomes. There can be value in using checklists and also well-designed 360-degree feedback. Clarify issues that are of concern to the team – and also explore expectations and manage relationships that extend beyond the immediate team.

Team Effectiveness Checklist

As a first step towards increased effectiveness, you might like to consider the following aspects of team leadership and the steps required to strengthen team coaching. Rate your effectiveness on each item, based on the following: *3 (Excellent); 2 (Competent); 1 (Fair)*.
   To what extent do you:

- Identify the best balance of roles, 'skill mix' and challenge to stretch capability   ....
- Provide the team with feedback and information relevant to activities   ....
- Encourage constructive dialogue and positive work relationships   ....
- Take steps to resolve conflict and disagreement between team members   ....
- Create opportunities for team members to develop skills and capability   ....
- Set high professional standards and deal with issues affecting performance   ....
- Find the resources required to support the team's performance   ....
- Defend the team from external pressure and/or criticism   ....
- Monitor and develop individual capability (in the context of role demands)   ....
- Appear professional and objective, maintaining fair and consistent standards   ....
- Acknowledge people's contribution and link this to wider organisational goals   ....
- Encourage autonomy and initiative, and view setbacks from this perspective   ....
- Champion the team's work and celebrate team success   ....

Total Rating: ....

A total of 30+ suggests awareness of essential requirements.

Summarise action steps required to develop capability and how you can build on skills. Note the action required to improve on any gaps or deficits.

Reviewing Your Approach

Building on the four-box grid in Module 1, which reviewed successful and unsuccessful situations, and differences in the situation/context, the people, and your own reaction, you may find it useful to refer back and consider how your influencing skills affected performance.

Influencing Skills

My preferred Style of Influence is currently based mainly on…
Reasoning………. Assertion………. Bridging………. Visioning……….

My active listening skills, i.e., my ability to summarise points and check understanding, are…
Poor………. Could be Better………. OK or Competent………. Strong……….

My ability to flex my style in response to differing levels of agreement and emotion is…
Poor………. Could be Better………. OK or Competent………. Strong……….

My self-awareness and ability to consciously manage my own behaviour under pressure is…
Poor………. Could be Better………. OK or Competent………. Strong……….

My awareness of the type of input the team requires at a particular point in time is…
Poor………. Could be Better………. OK or Competent………. Strong……….

There are a number of ways to improve your effectiveness in both group meetings and one-to-one discussions.

A situation that could benefit from a new approach…

I will be more effective if I respond differently when…

Remember that any form of negative emotion tends to block effective communication. If you are feeling frustrated, irritable or impatient, other people will tend to react against this. People are very aware of subtle non-verbal signals which may indicate that you are not listening or disagree with what is being said. These signals can include a pen being tapped on the table, a twitching leg or tapping foot, a lack of eye contact and various sighs and muffled exclamations!

The next module focuses on *Effective Decision-Making*, but before you move on, take the opportunity to reflect on a difficult situation and how you handled it. Review feedback that might offer insight into your *approach*. Can you identify a situation where you could have achieved more with a different approach?

Note

1 Leading Teams: Setting the Stage for Great Performances – The Five Keys to Successful Teams (HBR). Available at: https://hbswk.hbs.edu/archive/leading-teams-setting-the-stage-for-great-performances-the-five-keys-to-successful-teams

Chapter 17

Module 8: Effective Decision-Making

The ability to *Execute the Strategy* is an important aspect of leadership and involves translating purpose and principles into clear goals and measurable objectives. Leaders must respond positively to demands and take the initiative in deciding the best course of action. However, decision-making can be affected by various factors. These include the quality of analysis and interpersonal effectiveness, but also confidence in deciding on the best approach. This module reviews work preferences that can affect responsiveness, contribute to personal initiative and affect outcomes. The elements include *Speed of Response*, and the emphasis placed on *Seeking Direction* (e.g. guidance), *Decision Confidence* and *Striving for Success*.

Practical actions that help improve performance include (i) setting clear goals that build on people's expertise and (ii) enhancing people's self-belief and sense of 'agency' (self-directed) activity. Role capability builds on understanding expectations and appreciating areas of accountability. People require honest, timely and constructive feedback, delivered by team leaders who also recognise and celebrate achievements. Effective leaders encourage responsibility, support progress and also help develop competencies.

Reviewing work preferences on the four elements (noted above) offers insight into your current style of working. People vary in their approach. Some place more emphasis on a fast response, whilst others have a more measured or relaxed approach. Personal preferences also affect how much emphasis we place on reflection, or how responsive we appear, e.g. when others need our support. Colleagues may face work pressure and expect a

 DOI: 10.4324/9781003439707-19

fast response, but sometimes a measured assessment is required. Increased self-awareness is the first step in strengthening self-management and developing new skills.

Experience and personal confidence, e.g. in responding to role demands, contribute to people expressing different preferences for 'active support'. This is shown on the profile as *Seeking Direction*. People with less experience tend to look for feedback, support and guidance. Typically, experienced people with lower preference scores are expressing a more self-sufficient or self-directed approach. Self-belief in one's ability to assess issues and make decisions quickly is also reflected in higher emphasis on *Decision Confidence*. This suggests that outcomes will match expectations, whereas lower scores suggest a degree of caution or uncertainty. Differences may partly reflect issues and complexity linked to the role. However, other aspects of work behaviour (revealed by the profile) help clarify the reasons for high or low scores.

The final element in this section focuses on *Striving for Success*. This is associated with seeking high standards and wanting to set an example to others. It is important that this energy is directed towards meaningful, shared goals. Performance is best supported by appropriate consultation and involvement of other people. Emphasis on this element should also be viewed in the context of other preferences recorded on the profile. There may be value, for example, in reflecting on how a task-focused, demanding approach can affect other people's motivation and also the importance of creating a sense of shared purpose.

Identify a time when you made decisions under time pressure. What happened?

How does your preferred pace of working affect others?

Speed of Response

People vary in their attitude to time and responsiveness to changes in workload. A more leisurely approach may reflect an independent style, but it could also indicate less responsiveness to other people's requirements. Appreciation of other people's expectations is improved by feedback backed by clear examples. We find that a wider failure of responsiveness, coupled with an abrasive style, contributes to the derailment of leaders. They start to neglect professional standards, lack effective self-management and overlook the expectations of colleagues. Lack of feedback contributes to a *blind spot* that weakens team performance, hinders progress and gradually undermines the organisation's culture.

Most people in leadership roles express a moderate emphasis on the *Speed of Response* dimension. This reflects a balance between urgency and a more-measured response. A very high emphasis suggests impulsiveness and might be linked to '*Type A' behaviour*. This is characterised by time urgency (impatience) and a need to maintain control. It may be linked to a high need to achieve. There may also be a tendency to confront problems in a more direct, forthright manner.

JK's responses indicate the following preference:

Speed of Response

Leaders' preference scores are usually in the range 3–6.

The report summary: *JK expresses a preference for a more measured, steady pace of working, reflected in the relatively low emphasis placed on Speed of Response. This is linked with a very reflective approach, suggesting that attention will be given to thinking through the broader issues relating to a task. There is a clear focus on Developing Opportunities, which will also influence JK's approach.*

Pace of response can also be viewed alongside preferences for self-directed activity or the need for feedback and support. People clearly vary in their self-belief and sense of competence. Experience and training contribute to resilience and success in overcoming challenges adds to capability. This starts to influence how people view risk and their tolerance of ambiguity. Over time, increased experience builds confidence and reduces the need for structure and direction.

Seeking Direction

Effective team leaders have some insight into people's strengths and areas for improvement. They also appreciate that some individuals have more need for direction and role clarity. This creates a need for external support or regular feedback, particularly when the person is faced with the challenge of an unfamiliar task. Autonomy-supportive leaders help people become more self-directed. This may start by simply encouraging team members to be more proactive in reviewing problems, so they clarify issues and consider possible options before seeking advice.

Most leaders place low emphasis on *Seeking Direction*, so it is important to be responsive to those who need support.

JK's responses indicate the following preference:

Seeking Direction

Leaders' preference scores are usually in the range 0–4.

The report summary: *The fairly low emphasis on Seeking Direction suggests that JK does not require close supervision or guidance when dealing with work assignments. This suggests a fairly strong preference for a self-reliant approach. The low emphasis on Gaining Approval may mean that JK sometimes needs to be more aware of the expectations of others.*

Developing Confidence in Decision-Making

Effective leaders understand the principle of autonomy and the value of self-directed action. They seek to develop their own capability through challenge, training and relevant experience. This contributes to self-belief and the ability to set direction and question existing arrangements. However, the process of achieving change, or improving systems and making better use of resources, may carry an element of risk. There may be awareness of potential problems, but this does not provide the solution, or clarify how changes should be implemented. The information a leader has available will never cover all the issues, so decisions involve personal judgement. This will be backed by appreciation of context, operational priorities and guiding principles.

Significant issues affecting personal decision-making include (i) your ability to push back boundaries and explore new options and (ii) your conviction that things will work out the way you expect. In other words, do you have confidence in the outcomes of your decision-making? As we noted previously, asking *what if...?* and *why...?* contributes to effectiveness. Be alert to 'opinion' and *Group Think* that allow assumptions to go unchallenged. Make sure that role responsibilities and requirements are never left *implicit* when they should be *explicit*.

A significant factor that separates more traditional managers from future-focused leaders involves their perception of role boundaries. Effective leaders have a wider perception of the role and the interdependencies relating to the role. This means that there is greater awareness of the need to build relationships and actively manage the connections. It also suggests a willingness to move beyond core requirements and take the initiative, seeking action to achieve change. However, it is important to take time to assess the risks and consider possibilities, ranging from the most positive outcome to worst-case scenarios.

There are a number of elements that influence the quality of decision outcomes. A lack of reflective, broad-based thinking, for example, may mean that issues are not fully explored. There may be a reluctance to be innovative in your thinking, which can mean that old assumptions go unchallenged. Alternatively, a tendency to pursue one's own ideas, with little involvement of others and a lack of organisational awareness, e.g. on how best to position proposals, can also undermine positive outcomes.

Questions to Prompt Reflection...

How effectively do you...

- balance longer-term objectives and more immediate requirements?
- encourage ideas and suggestions from people in the team?
- keep options open and explore possibilities before confirming decisions?
- consult with people elsewhere in the organisation?
- acknowledge when you got something wrong and need to change track?
- protect the team from external pressure and premature criticism?
- seek feedback that gives you insight into important issues?
- challenge existing thinking and champion new ideas?

■ take prompt action when faced with unexpected demands?
■ secure the support and resources to turn ideas into results?

Action to Improve Effectiveness…

Effective leaders avoid micro-management. They encourage others to develop initiative, but are clear about the performance standards and outcomes that need to be achieved. This mindset is supported by consultation, reflection and responsiveness to changing demands. Future-focused leaders can accept a degree of uncertainty and have the ability to make decisions quickly. There is a self-belief that their decisions will prove correct. This is reflected in the emphasis placed on *Decision Confidence*.

JK's responses indicate the following preference:

Decision Confidence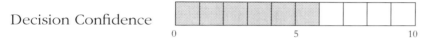

Leaders' preference scores are usually in the range 6–8.

The report summary: *JK's emphasis on Decision Confidence suggests a sense of competence when required to respond quickly or take personal responsibility for finding a solution to a problem. Interaction with others, suggested by the fairly high score on Team Involvement, indicates some consultation with others. The fairly high level of personal conviction relating to Decision Confidence is accompanied by flexibility (a very low emphasis on Personal Organisation). Low emphasis on Gaining Approval suggests a degree of independence.*

Reflect on aspects of your own work-style that may affect *Decision Confidence*. Consider how well you *prepare the ground* and anticipate potential issues that may affect outcomes. Do you set clear direction for others? In a VUCA World, leaders must also anticipate *high consequence events* and *escalating problems*. Clarify the interdependencies.

Setting High Standards

Exceptional performance generally requires leaders with a strong need to achieve. This is an underlying strength, usually reflected in setting demanding objectives, working to overcome obstacles and striving to reach high standards. However, this characteristic is also linked to personal ambition, which can become a problem. When the drive to achieve is poorly directed, perhaps through excessive ambition, it undermines effective teamwork. This makes it difficult to develop trust-based relationships. It may be associated with the leader who constantly needs to be in the spotlight. A strong need for personal recognition, for example, can make it difficult to acknowledge the contribution of others, or share information, or build team morale.

The drive to achieve is best channelled through personal conviction about goals and the professional standards that need to be maintained. In many respects, setting high standards can be viewed in the context of pursuing excellence. It's also part of the process of creating alignment. The leader helps others overcome problems, but also focuses on wider goals, underlying principles and expectations. It's a fine balance, as lack of emphasis can suggest a lack of conviction about quality and outcomes. If personal drive is too strong, leaders may be viewed as overly concerned with their own agenda, and little interest in a team-centred approach.

In some situations, a very strong focus on achieving high standards and pushing people in a new direction may have value. This may be linked to *Developing Opportunities*, reflected in getting new projects operational and meeting deadlines. These activities need energy and commitment. However, long-term success requires a balance between your personal agenda and responsiveness to wider requirements (and the expectations of team members and colleagues). An effective leader looks for opportunities to expose people to new challenges that stretch existing competencies and help unlock strengths. However, it's a gradual, step-by-step process. Psychological resilience enables people to respond positively to difficult situations. This builds on skills and experience, but also a positive mindset. As a leader, your confidence and conviction can help others believe it's possible to display initiative and resolve problems. *Autonomy Supportive Leaders* encourage people to develop ideas and implement solutions.

Striving for Success

Leaders generally place emphasis on *Striving for Success*. There is a focus on high standards and setting an example to others. This must be balanced with awareness of what others require and recognition of individual differences. The group may include both self-starters and those needing more structure and direction. *Striving for Success* can contribute to personal conviction, energy and enthusiasm, helping build team commitment to performance standards and overall goals. It's important that this does not become too competitive or take the form of excessive personal ambition.

JK's responses indicate the following preference:

Striving for Success

Leaders' preference scores are usually in the range 6–8.

The report summary: *In the context of task accomplishment and achievement of high standards, there is relatively high emphasis given to Striving for Success. As a result, JK is more likely to set reasonably demanding personal targets and will tend to give some thought as to how work might form an example to others. This suggests that a preference for working to well-defined performance standards. Other elements of the profile also suggest that there is little need for direction from others.*

A State of Flow

The term 'flow' is often used to describe tasks that are 'challenging', but also 'immersive'. They draw on skills, personal strengths/insights and underlying experience. These activities can also help develop our sense of capability. When we become immersed in an activity, it reinforces feelings of competence, autonomy and meaning. We can easily lose track of time.

Recall a situation that created this feeling of involvement, and note important elements.

Shared purpose also contributes to people valuing their work and identifying with what they are doing. They feel fully engaged in activities. The process contributes to both motivation and commitment. Reflect on the work preferences highlighted in this module. *How do they influence your approach?* Try and identify specific situations and how you respond. Are there any patterns?

Focus on one element. What could you do differently to enhance your effectiveness?

Focusing on future outcomes, what steps are required for you to achieve that change?

In setting a new goal, clarify how your action plan links to SMART (Specific, Measurable, Attainable, Realistic, Time-bound) objectives.

Chapter 18

Module 9: Focusing on Outcomes

Social norms and expectations change over time. In the context of developing capability, and also the wider themes of EDI and ESG, effective leaders work to create the *enabling conditions* that contribute to high-quality outcomes. Leaders take steps to ensure that people are motivated, and resources are directed effectively. Organisations need to be responsive to change and focus on developing sustainable solutions. We are reminded of important 'core competencies' that support exceptional results. These include the following:

- **Exploring opportunities**: Being innovative, questioning and responsive to changing requirements
- **Consulting and collaborating**: Creating alignment with overall goals, encouraging 'shared purpose'
- **Developing capability**: Providing coaching and support that build on people's expertise and interests
- **Executing the strategy**: Translating the vision and strategy into clear goals and accountabilities

Leaders set standards and convey energy and commitment. Role clarity and progress are central to developing a sense of shared purpose. Motivation increases when people identify with their work and have a sense of involvement. Discretionary effort increases. Work preferences relating to *Task Commitment* can be viewed alongside the time spent on specific

DOI: 10.4324/9781003439707-20

activities. For leaders, it's often difficult to manage time effectively. They need to involve other people in developing solutions, and maintain their own focus on priorities. This requires delegation, avoiding the problem of micro-management that undermines trust and prevents people developing new skills. It's a potential problem for leaders overly concerned with details, who get too involved in *Task Completion*. Self-awareness helps you maintain an appropriate balance, ensuring your own work preferences enhance professional effectiveness.

Many leaders are motivated to achieve high standards, and this is often linked to a willingness to commit time and energy to achieve objectives. Work preferences linked to *Task Commitment* reveal the importance of the work ethic and perseverance to overcome problems. This dimension can also be reviewed alongside the emphasis placed on *Striving for Success*, which involves a focus on high standards and making progress.

JK's responses indicate the following preference:

Task Commitment

0   5   10

Leaders' preference scores are usually in the range 6–8.

The report summary: *The preference recorded on Task Commitment suggests that JK will have a fairly high concern about making a personal commitment to achieving results and persevering to overcome difficulties or setbacks. The score suggests that JK is more likely to be conscious of the need to contribute time and effort to gain high performance. There is also fairly high emphasis on demonstrating personal Drive and Enthusiasm.*

For anyone in a leadership role, it is important to monitor work demands. As a general rule, it's important that you maintain an appropriate work–life balance. It's also worth noting that attempting to *lead by example* is rarely, in itself, an effective strategy for leaders. This is a potential blind spot for those with high achievement motivation. Self-awareness and self-regulation then become particularly important. In pursuing high performance, team leaders must ensure that roles and responsibilities are clearly understood, and that people are encouraged to take the initiative in finding solutions to problems. Collaboration requires communication – and clarity on key objectives.

Taking Effective Action

Developing a sense of competence at work is important to self-esteem and strengthens our sense of professional identity. Effective leadership involves building on the knowledge, skills and experience that people bring to the role. For some professionals and technical specialists, this may require close involvement in completing one task before moving on to the next. However, leaders must be *measured and self-disciplined* in deciding priorities and assessing how best to direct their energy and attention. Undue focus on one task may well undermine effective time-management and prioritisation. There needs to be an element of 'professional detachment'. Being unduly diligent, e.g. worrying about mistakes, and unwilling to 'let go' also makes it more difficult to delegate work and fully motivate others.

Effective leaders balance (i) direct involvement in activities, e.g. lending support when necessary, and (ii) the expectation that team members will display the skills and initiative required to see work through to completion. Generally speaking, effective leaders have a relatively low need for direct, personal involvement in task completion. Their focus is on the bigger picture and overall objectives. However, they are keenly aware of the key stages or 'milestones' and the value of regular review. This might, for example, build on the *Purposeful Conversations* discussed previously.

JK's responses indicate the following preference:

Task Completion

Leaders' preference scores are usually in the range 2–4.

The report summary: *Accompanying the emphasis placed on Task Commitment, there is moderate preference for on-going involvement in Task Completion. This suggests some attention to dealing with problems or difficulties, but JK will typically avoid activities that are best handled by others. Combined with the comparatively low interest in detail, JK will be less concerned about personal involvement in the specific aspects of implementation.*

When leaders place high emphasis on *Accuracy of Working* and also personal involvement in *Task Completion*, problems can arise relating to delegation. However, very low emphasis in these areas could indicate less-effective monitoring and supervision of activities. Reviewing personal work preferences, including those relating to *Gaining Approval* and *Seeking Direction*, provides additional insight into issues affecting team performance. An important step in becoming an effective leader involves recognising when problems need resolving.

Pario Surveys show that team members are often critical in their assessment of leaders who fail to take prompt action. The issue could involve performance management. Leaders inevitably face situations that create *emotional pressure*, for them or for other people. You may, like many others, experience anxiety when there is a need to complete difficult discussions. However, team members expect leaders to be impartial and apply consistent standards. Professional objectivity requires self-awareness and the ability to build on *Purposeful Conversations*.

The reality is that most leaders will face situations when they need to deal with performance or disciplinary issues. It may be necessary to 'surface' (bring into the open) difficult underlying problems. The scenario may involve people's poor performance, their disaffection with new ways of working or their reluctance to accept change. The temptation for the leader is to do nothing and avoid the risk of disruption or *'rocking the boat'*. However, effective leaders are forward-looking and take a longer-term view of requirements. This involves being aware of guiding principles and competencies, and also the expectations of stakeholders, partners and colleagues. Leaders often need to improve existing systems and procedures. It's important to remember that once *future requirements* are clearly understood, it becomes easier to establish the rationale and authority for moving forward. Clarity of purpose and a willingness to address tough issues also help support authenticity, maintain integrity and show conviction.

Personal Conviction and Confronting Issues

Purposeful Conversations help clarify objectives and create agreement on future requirements. They put things in context and confirm roles, responsibilities and essential steps. Strength comes from *Personal Conviction* on professional standards and future direction. This makes it easier to deal with concerns. You need to *surface problems and confront issues*, but a balanced approach is important. This may also require *Organisational Awareness* and responsiveness to people's concerns. Leaders who are less trusting of others, or are less skilled in positioning issues, may have a blind spot. This may cause them to overreact or respond impulsively. They may display an aggressive or inflexible approach when faced with complex situations. The ability to confront issues is important, but we might also consider the emphasis placed on such elements as *Broad-Based Thinking, Personal Reserve* and *Speed of Response.*

JK's responses indicate the following preference:

Confronting Issues

Leaders' preference scores are usually in the range 3–5.

The report summary: *The moderately high score on Confronting Issues indicates that JK places definite emphasis on surfacing problems and dealing with things in a fairly direct manner. In some situations, this might appear somewhat abrasive or indicate concern over questions of principle. A moderately high level of Personal Reserve is evident in the way JK responds to situations. The wish to maintain positive working relationships could also be relevant in this context. JK is likely to be aware of the professional standards that need to be maintained.*

Techniques that support analysis and reflection help you anticipate problems and evaluate options. You can then take prompt action, supported by the influencing skills that help improve performance. In previous modules, we discussed various influencing skills that can help overcome conflict and build agreement. As a starting point, *Purposeful Conversations* provide a framework that builds on a clear understanding other people's views and concerns. In the context of the *Influencing Skills Model* (described previously), an element of *Bridging* can help develop awareness and agreement. *Active Listening* helps reduce emotional tension and provides a platform for *Reasoning and Logic.* This process can help create the *Insight* described in the *Purpose Conversations* model. In the context of work, future vision is best supported by a *Meaningful Rationale.* Exploring wider issues and developing insight provides the basis for solution-focused action. The process helps put things into context.

Reference to the context and overall objectives encourage professional objectivity and the reasons for doing things in a particular way. Leaders create a foundation for progress through their personal conviction. This helps

confirm meaning and shared purpose. Through dialogue, leaders also identify the resources and support required to help people move forward.

In summary, *Purposeful Conversations* help develop new ideas, clarify
thinking and facilitate progress. Discussing issues in a constructive way
helps people gain a fresh perspective. There may, for example, be aspects
of policy or strategy that cannot be altered. An important aspect of leadership involves helping people make sense of constraints that affect change,
but also maintain motivation. Creating a culture where ideas are explored,
and problems solved through dialogue, is integral to the concept of
Autonomy Supportive Leadership.

The Impact of Personal Values

High emphasis on doing work in a way that fits with your *Personal Values*
raises significant issues. It may indicate a strong belief about certain principles. However, expecting other people to conform to your personal standards can cause problems. *Is it reasonable to expect others to share the same
outlook or adopt similar ways of working? Do you have an expectation that
authority and respect should come from the role, but then neglect the interpersonal skills that support influence and persuasion?* This mindset may
conflate *Personal Preferences* with wider *Superordinate Principles* that
support *Superordinate Goals*.

People's thinking may be affected unduly by *Personal Values*, but the
issue is often not clearly understood or openly discussed. There may be
unrealistic expectations relating to how work is organised, or the way
professional relationships are managed. Some people expect others to
comply with their standards or specific ways of working. *Social Identity
Theory* suggests that being part of a group can make us critical of other
groups. Values can be used to support a divisive '*we are special*' mindset,
and *too much focus on group identity* creates a challenge that leaders must
address. This is a particular problem if it encourages intolerance, hinders
change and weakens efforts to build an *Enabling Environment*. Diversity,
for example, links to the *Superordinate Principle* of equality, contributes to
innovative thinking and may enhance productivity. However, we are also
aware that people can become disaffected if they feel that changes have
been imposed on them. An effective intervention by the leader may require
the conviction to confront issues and the ability to listen and understand
strongly held views.

Expectations are best explored before someone joins a new team or work group. Teams tend to develop their own culture, norms and expectations, which is one reason why *Superordinate Principles* are important. Even large Third Sector organisations (non-profit and charities) frequently fail to ensure *transparency and accountability*. They have concealed, unresolved issues that can then cause reputational damage. Operational problems often start with a lack of clarity, e.g. how activities should be conducted. Organisations need to prevent self-referenced, dysfunctional behaviour. Insight builds on an appreciation of purpose, shared values and the principles that guide actions. Future-focused leaders need to understand issues shaping identity and the professional standards that need to be safeguarded.

Aligning individual activities with *Superordinate Goals* requires more than technical analysis of priorities and how to allocate resources. The leader must be absolutely clear about the outcomes and standards that are required, and then do everything possible to develop people's skills, initiative and commitment. *Superordinate Principles help people consider what to do and how best to respond.* Creating shared purpose and understanding other people's concerns contribute to engagement. Effective systems then help us to maintain high standards. Remember that *Extrinsic Task Motivation* requires ongoing dialogue that provides a meaningful rationale, emphasises the importance of tasks and confirms future direction.

Reviewing work preferences can help clarify personal expectations concerning work relationships and expectations. People placing high emphasis on the *Personal Values* dimension may have a blind spot. They may, for example, adopt a supportive role within a team, but are less likely to adopt a positive, proactive approach. High emphasis on *Personal Values* can also indicate possible disaffection linked to recent changes, or perhaps difficult relationships with those 'not like us'. Anxiety and a less assertive style are more likely to be associated with high scores on this dimension.

However, it may not be an issue when there is a well-defined culture backed by strong values and a sense of shared purpose.

It is important that people are aware of the impact of their *personal expectations* on their *professional objectivity*. The key point is that people in professional and leadership roles must be willing to *express concerns and express the reasoning* that supports a particular course of action. Transparency is important in helping to explore issues and clarify people's expectations. Self-awareness is essential in helping leaders maintain professional objectivity. This reduces problems arising from unrealistic expectations about the behaviour of others, or assumptions about 'how things should be done'.

Creating Shared Purpose

In some organisations, including charities, not-for-profit, healthcare and smaller businesses, people may express a preference towards doing work that '*matches with personal values*'. The emphasis on the overall profile may be slightly increased. This is not an issue when there are clearly understood professional standards and a clear focus on future direction. Effective leaders clarify people's roles and responsibilities. *Purposeful Conversations* can help achieve appropriate alignment and build commitment. However, it is dangerous to assume that there is already shared purpose or that shared values are already in place. Assumptions fail to tackle the underlying challenges faced by all organisations. Nothing is fixed and permanent, so future-focused leaders must actively manage the process of achieving intentional change. We have to be alert and work hard to maintain awareness of the changing context.

There are real risks in assuming that other people share your outlook or standards. In many ways, it is much better for leaders to recognise that shared values are fragile and easily disturbed. The role of the leader is therefore to work steadily to build capability and commitment to future action. Simply talking about *Values* may mean that important standards are not clearly expressed. *The problem is that people assume that their values are correct.* This undermines professional objectivity. In contrast, low emphasis on *Personal Values* may indicate less appreciation of other people's genuine concerns. A highly rational, analytical perspective may be associated with a lack of empathy and awareness. Clearly, *Personal Values* is not a binary dimension, and it's important to be aware that this aspect of thinking is linked to mindset. It may be helpful to clarify the wider *Superordinate Principles* that are shared by everyone in the organisation. Personal values might be discussed in this context. They should not be left vulnerable to those who have an emotional, personal sense of what is acceptable.

JK's responses indicate the following preference:

Personal Values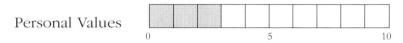

Leaders' preference scores are usually in the range 3–5.

The report summary: *JK's approach indicates an impartial and professionally objective style of working. There is little expectation that other people should share the same outlook or values. JK is unlikely to feel that this is necessary in order to obtain good results. In addition, the emphasis placed on Team Influence suggests confidence in putting forward ideas. There is also moderate emphasis on the Leadership Focus dimension.*

Leaders who place less emphasis on the *Personal Values* dimension might be said to be more 'professionally objective'. There is less expectation that others will understand their values or preferred way of working. This may be useful, but low emphasis may make it more difficult to establish rapport, especially if coupled with low emphasis on *Personal Contact* and less focus on *Responsiveness to Others*. Effective leaders have the self-awareness and maturity to look at issues with a degree of impartiality. However, they also need to build commitment in others, and this involves trust-based relationships and a degree of empathy. We should also note that some people identify with their profession, or area of technical expertise, but may not feel engaged with the values of the organisation.

It takes time to build commitment, but sudden change can damage trust. I remember, back in the late 1980s, talking to a manager in one of the UK utilities, privatised under PM Thatcher. His observation was succinct: '*This used to be a caring company*'.

***

To gain further insights relating to the concept of 'personal values', we asked ChatGPT to comment on the assumption that others should share your views. This was the prompt: *Summarise and evaluate research evidence that shows that some expect others to share their values and assumptions, and the potential consequences of this mindset, e.g. frustration, anxiety and passive-aggressive behaviour.*

ChatGPT: Research has shown that people tend to assume that others share their values and beliefs, a phenomenon known as the *false consensus effect*. This can lead to frustration, anxiety and passive-aggressive behaviour when others do not meet their expectations.

A study conducted by Ross, Greene and House (1977) found that participants overestimated the extent to which their attitudes and behaviours were shared by others. They also found that participants were more likely to exhibit negative affective reactions when their expectations were not met, such as feeling frustrated or angry. Similarly, another study conducted by Pronin, Lin and Ross (2002) found that people tend to attribute their own attitudes and behaviours to situational factors, while attributing the attitudes and behaviours of others to dispositional factors. This can lead to misunderstandings and conflicts when others do not behave as expected.

The consequences of this mindset can be significant, especially in group settings where individuals may hold differing values and assumptions. In these situations, the false consensus effect can lead to group polarisation, where individuals become more extreme in their beliefs and actions (Sunstein, 2002). It can also lead to communication breakdowns, misunderstandings and ultimately, conflict. Therefore, it is important for individuals to be aware of the false consensus effect and to actively seek out and consider diverse perspectives. By doing so, they can reduce the negative consequences of assuming that others share their values and assumptions.

Personal Values and Professional Objectivity

Identify a situation where you need to resolve differences in opinion, possible conflicting values, and need to achieve some change or improvement.

How do you achieve a more balanced view (say within the group) of what is required?

What outcome are you seeking? Imagine the best possible scenario.

What practical steps are required to achieve this goal?

Encouraging Identification and Commitment

Pario Survey results indicate that 10–15% of people in organisations are to some extent disaffected. Some stay because they lack alternative options, which may include older-age groups. Unfortunately, discretionary effort and initiative is reduced if people have little interest or 'connection' with the future plans of the organisation. However, motivation can be increased by developing people's sense of competence, e.g. skills, knowledge and experience, and involvement in meaningful work. This is best coupled with opportunities for autonomy, e.g. discretion and control over work activities. This also communicates the message that people are valued.

We find that emotional commitment is strengthened by a belief that the organisation supports personal development. It's more likely to be viewed as a positive place to work and be respected in the wider community. Effective leaders offer clear direction and positive support. The path to commitment builds on both meaningful work and positive work relationships. *Employee Engagement* is the opposite of disaffection. Future-focused leaders build *Motivation* and *Commitment*. Looking at the process suggests that it incorporates two elements. One path starts from *Disaffection* and progresses through *Relationships and Identification*. The second builds on *Meaningful Work and Motivation*. Both contribute to *Commitment*, which is reflected in a greater sense of shared purpose (and support for personal development).

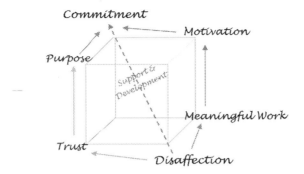

Research studies reveal that when leaders have high personal conviction and *Organisational Identification* (OID), this also results in higher OID in others. There is a greater willingness to exert effort. Effective leaders develop a sense of shared purpose, strengthened by positive values and use of robust systems. You may want to note issues that need addressing in your workplace.

Identify a problem concerning the work culture. Note some of the main issues.

List the specific steps that are required to achieve positive change…

References

Ross, L., Greene, D., & House, P. (1977). The false consensus effect: An egocentric bias in social perception and attribution processes. *Jnl of Experimental Social Psychology*, 13(3), 279–301.

Pronin, E., Lin, D. Y., & Ross, L. (2002). The bias blind spot: Perceptions of bias in self versus others. *Personality and Social Psychology Bulletin*, 28(3), 369–381.

Sunstein, C. R. (2002). The law of group polarization. *The Journal of Political Philosophy*, 10(2), 175–195.

***

Chapter 19

Module 10: Summary and Review

This section provides an overview of the Modules, including reference to the three broad competency themes that contribute to effectiveness. The three clusters include (i) analysis, problem-solving and planning, (ii) working with others and interpersonal effectiveness and (iii) drive, resilience and delivery of results. Following on from Chapter 9 and Modules 1 and 2, essential leadership skills were discussed in Modules 4 - 9, with the case study offering additional insights. The Modules covered the following topics:

Module 1. Elements of High Performance
Module 2. Effectiveness at Work
Module 3. Description of the Work Preference Report
Module 4. Analysis and Problem-Solving
Module 5. Developing Opportunities
Module 6. Working with People
Module 7. Personal Impact and Influence
Module 8. Effective Decision-Making
Module 9. Focus on Outcomes

It may be helpful to revisit the *Learning Cycle*, discussed in Chapter 9. This highlights how learning is improved by reflecting on options, taking practical action, obtaining feedback and then adapting your approach. It provides the basis for an ongoing process of development.

DOI: 10.4324/9781003439707-21

Reviewing the Modules

As noted in **Module 2**, high performance develops from the ability to view situations clearly. You may need to become more aware of assumptions and aspects of mindset that can limit options. **Module 4** looks at analysis and problem-solving. It offers insights on how to respond positively when faced with uncertainty, ways to develop opportunities and our response to unpredictable events.

Effective analysis and problem-solving are required by all professionals. The skills become more critical as role demands increase. The leaders' role includes managing relationships with people, both within and beyond the immediate team, and responsiveness to changing requirements. **Module 5** explored themes linked to *Developing Opportunities*, acting in an entrepreneurial way and balancing priorities for action.

The challenge is often to develop a fresh perspective, rather than relying on established approaches. Effective leaders seek to anticipate the next challenge. In **Module 6**, for example, we looked more closely at competencies – and particularly those linked to setting clear direction. This also involves taking responsibility for situations. Leadership is particularly important to *Implementing the Strategy*. The Vision and *Superordinate Goals* need to be turned into clear objectives and shared purpose. People need to understand how their work contributes, so dialogue helps clarify change and create a meaningful rationale. *Authentic Leaders* listen and respond to people's concerns, show conviction, but also adapt to events.

Personal Impact and Influence are covered in **Module 7**. There is also a need for networking and collaboration. Effective leaders communicate with transparency and tailor the message to the audience. They network across functions to create teams that benefit the customer or client. It's important to focus on overall objectives, so team activities are seen in this wider context. Leaders work to create alignment through active engagement and positive influence.

There are usually opportunities to question existing methods, show initiative and influence others. Leaders can encourage contributions and build on people's suggestions. The aim is to find more effective solutions. This requires a willingness to take responsibility and set direction. Future-focus also involves defining priorities and deciding how best to use resources.

Interpersonal skills can be developed. Dialogue can help resolve differences of opinion and overcome resistance to change. Organisations also need leaders with a mindset that helps develop capability. This includes the ability to engage and energise other people. Effective leaders also have personal insight that builds on feedback. They understand their strengths and areas for improvement. They have an appreciation of the context. They adapt their approach in response to requirements.

Modules 8 and 9 review speed of response, decision-making and steps in implementing the strategy. This involves *Delivery of Results* and *Focus on Outcomes*, which often appear in descriptions of leadership attributes. The vision and strategy are translated into goals and responsibilities. Positive outcomes are affected by various factors.

There is a need for clarity in assessing issues, and confidence in deciding on the best approach. It's also important to appreciate the emphasis individual team members place on *Seeking Direction*. Some require more frequent feedback and updates on progress. Leaders must also balance personal priorities and wider considerations. *Striving for Success* might be seen as a strength. However, taken to excess it can damage team morale. Leaders at all levels must strive to create *Enabling Conditions* that contribute to people's motivation, underlying commitment and the process of achieving overall alignment. This also helps ensure that resources and energy are directed effectively. In the context of achieving high performance, operational competencies, which can also be linked to the 3H Model, might include the following:

- **Implementing the strategy**: Translating the vision and strategy into clear goals and accountabilities, supported by dialogue
- **Developing capability**: Setting ambitious goals and enhancing employees' expertise, motivation and competencies
- **Networking and collaboration**: Building relationships, seeking alignment with overall goals and encouraging 'shared purpose'
- **Fostering agility**: Being innovative, entrepreneurial and responsive to a changing context and aware of client/customer needs

Reviewing Work Preferences

The charts show *Pario Work Preference* dimensions and the *relative emphasis* relating to each element. The typical score-range for leaders relates to UK studies. The profile reveals how energy and attention is directed, which contributes to development of a *Pattern of Response*. The profile offers insights that support competency review, coaching and professional development.

Profiling Work Preferences: 1

Profiling Pario Dimensions (Reviewed in Modules 4, 5 and 6)

Low Emphasis ←	Leader Preferences *typical response range*	High Emphasis →
Broad-Based Thinking Practical, operational, 'concrete' focus	0 1 2 3 4 <u>5 6 7</u> 8 9 10	Conceptual, reflective, theoretical focus
Innovative Response Traditional, cautious, wary of change	0 1 2 3 4 <u>5 6 7</u> 8 9 10	Open, questioning and change-orientated
Accuracy of Working Accepts a degree of risk and uncertainty	0 1 <u>2 3 4</u> 5 6 7 8 9 10	Checks details and avoids the risk of error
Self-Critical Thinking Self-Belief - links setbacks to external factors	<u>0 1 2 3</u> 4 5 6 7 8 9 10	Worries about setbacks, doubts own ability
Personal Organisation Maintains flexibility, adapt to context	0 1 2 <u>3 4 5</u> 6 7 8 9 10	Adopts a structured, methodical approach
Creative Focus Follows existing methods and procedures	0 1 2 3 4 <u>5 6 7</u> 8 9 10	Consults and seeks to develop new solutions
Developing Opportunities Looks to others to promote new ideas	0 1 2 3 4 5 <u>6 7 8</u> 9 10	Displays drive/energy to create change
Organisational Awareness Focus on the immediate task/activities	0 1 2 3 <u>4 5 6 7</u> 8 9 10	Checks/anticipates how others will react
Pressure Index More tolerant of uncertainty (flexible)	<u>0 1 2 3</u> 4 5 6 7 8 9 10	Seeks to have activities clearly defined (structured)
Leadership Focus Focuses on their immediate role and tasks	0 1 2 3 4 <u>5 6 7 8</u> 9 10	Sets direction and advises others
Establishing Direction Prefers to have others take responsibility	0 1 2 3 4 <u>5 6 7</u> 8 9 10	Self-directed, and takes control
Personal Reserve Shows emotion - more open reaction	0 1 <u>2 3 4</u> 5 6 7 8 9 10	Calm 'professional' (measured) response
Personal Contact Less need for friends and social context	0 1 2 <u>3 4 5</u> 6 7 8 9 10	Seeks friendship and social contact at work

Profiling Work Preferences: 2

Profiling Pario Dimensions (Reviewed in Modules 7, 8 and 9)

Low Emphasis	Leader Preferences	High Emphasis
← →	*typical response range*	→
Gaining Attention Low profile style, does not 'sell' or 'promote' ideas	0 1 2 <u>3 4 5</u> 6 7 8 9 10	Seeks recognition and gains attention
Gaining Approval Self-directed, pursues own objectives	0 1 2 3 <u>4 5</u> 6 7 8 9 10	Committed to what others' require
Team Involvement Works more independently of others	0 1 2 3 4 <u>5 6 7</u> 8 9 10	Team interaction and group focused
Responsiveness to Others Focuses on task and personal priorities	0 1 2 3 <u>4 5 6 7</u> 8 9 10	Responsive to the needs/concerns of others
Team Influence Low profile, less active in groups/meetings	0 1 2 3 4 <u>5 6 7</u> 8 9 10	Confident, presents ideas, and adapts style
Speed of Response Works at own pace, less 'sense of urgency'	0 1 2 <u>3 4 5</u> 6 7 8 9 10	Takes action, impatient with delay
Seeking Direction Self-directed, independent approach	<u>0 1 2 3</u> 4 5 6 7 8 9 10	Seeks guidance, feedback and direction
Decision Confidence Cautious, more hesitant, takes time to decide	0 1 2 3 4 <u>5 6 7</u> 8 9 10	Confident: self-belief in decision outcomes
Striving for Success Prefers others to set standards/goals	0 1 2 3 4 <u>5 6 7</u> 8 9 10	Sets high standards, drive and ambition
Task Commitment Less emphasis on perseverance/effort	0 1 2 3 4 <u>5 6 7</u> 8 9 10	Works hard to overcome problems
Task Completion Delegates and involves others in tasks	0 1 <u>2 3 4</u> 5 6 7 8 9 10	Maintains personal involvement in tasks
Confronting Issues Less focus on addressing problems	0 1 2 3 <u>4 5 6</u> 7 8 9 10	Deals directly with issues, problems and concerns
Personal Values Professionally objective, pragmatic outlook	0 1 2 <u>3 4 5</u> 6 7 8 9 10	Expects others to share similar views/values

Developing Your Action Plans

You may find it useful to discuss insights and possible action plans with your manager or coach.

Where are your key strengths?

What are your main priorities for action?

Identify a situation where you can increase your effectiveness.

How can you get feedback to support your development?

Remember that personal development is an ongoing process. The context is constantly changing and we need feedback to maintain focus on external requirements.

SUPPLEMENTAL READING

ChatGPT Comments

Clarifying Concepts and Principles

1. Intangibles, Corporate Culture and Value
2. ESG Requirements and 'Returns to Shareholders'
3. Ethics, Values and Superordinate Principles
4. 'First Principles' vs Superordinate Principles
5. AGI and Leadership Capability
6. Job Demands-Resources and *Job Crafting*
7. Doughnut Economics and Leadership
8. The Concept of 'Emotional Labour'
9. Legacy Thinking and a Quantum Future
10. The Consequences of Systemic Educational Deficits
11. The Impact of Performance-Related Pay
12. *Super-Ps* and Post-Modernist Theory

DOI: 10.4324/9781003439707-23

Intangibles, Corporate Culture and Value

We asked ChatGPT to evaluate *Intangibles* with reference to *Corporate Culture*:

> *Evaluate the concept of Intangibles with reference to corporate culture, noting significant variables (e.g. ESG, ISO and leadership) and how these impact on 'value'.*

Intangible assets such as corporate culture, *Environmental, Social Governance* (ESG) factors, ISO accreditation, and leadership have been increasingly recognised as crucial drivers of business value. Corporate culture is a set of shared values, beliefs and practices that shape the behaviour of individuals within an organisation. Research has shown that companies with strong corporate cultures outperform their peers in terms of financial performance, innovation and customer satisfaction (Denison et al., 2012; Kotter & Heskett, 2011). Additionally, companies with positive cultures have lower employee turnover rates, higher levels of employee engagement and better reputations, which can enhance brand value and customer loyalty (Gallup, 2021).

ESG factors refer to a company's performance in areas such as environmental impact, social responsibility and corporate governance. Studies have shown that companies with high ESG scores have better financial performance and lower costs of capital, indicating that ESG factors can be significant drivers of value creation (Khan et al., 2020). Furthermore, companies with strong ESG practices are more likely to attract and

DOI: 10.4324/9781003439707-24

retain customers, employees and investors who prioritise sustainability and social responsibility (Eccles & Klimenko, 2019).

ISO accreditation refers to certification by the International Organisation for Standardisation, which sets global standards for quality, safety and environmental management systems. Companies that have achieved ISO accreditation demonstrate a commitment to best practices, which can enhance their reputation and credibility with stakeholders (Mitra et al., 2019). Additionally, there is evidence that ISO 9001 effectiveness directly contributes to product quality and operational performance. Research by (Kafetzopoulos et al., 2015) found that although ISO 9001 has no direct impact on manufacturing firms' business performance, it has an indirect impact through the moderator of operational performance.

Leadership is a critical factor in shaping corporate culture and driving performance. Effective leaders can inspire and motivate employees, set strategic direction, and foster innovation and collaboration within organisations (Gardner et al., 2005). Research has shown that companies with strong leadership outperform their peers in terms of financial performance and innovation (Gardner et al., 2010). Furthermore, companies with diverse leadership teams are more likely to make better decisions, and innovate and improve their financial performance (Rock et al., 2016).

Metrics for evaluating intangibles might include employee engagement scores, customer satisfaction ratings, reputation rankings, ESG scores, ISO certification and diversity metrics. These metrics can provide insights into the strength of a company's culture, sustainability practices and leadership effectiveness, which can inform investment decision-making.

In conclusion, intangible assets such as corporate culture, ESG factors, ISO accreditation and leadership can have a significant impact on business value. Companies that prioritise these intangibles and track relevant metrics can improve their financial performance, enhance their reputation and attract and retain key stakeholders.

References

Denison, D. R., Haaland, S., & Goelzer, P. (2012). Corporate culture and organizational effectiveness: Is Asia different from the rest of the world? *Organizational Dynamics*, 41(4), 300–305. https://doi.org/10.1016/j.orgdyn.2012.06.007

Eccles, G. R., & Klimenko, S. (2019). The investor revolution. *Harvard Business Review*, 97, 106–116.

Gallup. (2021). The business benefits of building a more engaged workforce. Available at: https://www.gallup.com/workplace/236199/business-benefits-building-more-engaged-workforce.aspx

Gardner, H. K., Glibkowski, B. C., & McDonough, E. F. (2005). The relationship between leadership and followership styles and outcomes. *Journal of Vocational Behavior*, 67(3), 385–406. https://doi.org/10.1016/j.jvb.2004.05.002

Gardner, H. K., Glibkowski, B. C., & McDonough, E. F. (2010). The influence of leadership on organizational culture and its effects on employee performance. *Journal of Managerial Psychology*, 25(6), 617–633. https://doi.org/10.1108/02683941011056938

Kafetzopoulos, D., Gotzamani, K., & Lemonakis, C. (2015). The impact of quality management systems on the performance of manufacturing firms. *International Journal of Quality & Reliability Management*, 32(4), 381–399.

Khan, F., Serafeim, G., & Yoon, A. (2020). Corporate sustainability: First evidence on materiality. *The Accounting Review*, 95(1), 1–29. https://doi.org/10.2308/accr-52603

Kotter, J. P., & Heskett, J. L. (2011). *Corporate Culture and Performance*. Free Press.

Mitra, S., Hossain, M. M., & Islam, M. A. (2019). ISO 9001 certification: Implications on corporate reputation and financial performance in emerging markets. *Journal of Cleaner Production*, 223, 956–966.

Rock, D., Grant, H., & Sheridan, J. (2016). Why diverse teams are smarter. *Harvard Business Review*, 94(9), 104–111. Available at: https://hbr.org/2016/11/why-diverse-teams-are-smarter

ESG Requirements and 'Returns to Shareholders'

We asked ChatGPT to evaluate ESG alongside 'shareholder obligations':

How do senior executives reconcile legal obligation to 'maximise returns for shareholders' with the responsibilities associated with ESG?

Senior executives have a legal obligation to maximise returns for shareholders, but this doesn't mean they have to prioritise short-term gains over long-term sustainability. In fact, a growing number of companies are realising that addressing *Environmental, Social Governance* (ESG) issues can actually contribute to long-term financial success and enhance shareholder value.

To reconcile their legal obligation with their ESG responsibilities, senior executives can take a number of steps:

1. **Recognise that ESG issues can affect financial performance**: Senior executives need to understand that addressing ESG issues can have a positive impact on a company's financial performance in the long term. For example, reducing energy consumption can lower operating costs, while improving employee well-being can increase productivity and reduce turnover.
2. **Set ESG targets**: Senior executives can set ESG targets that align with their company's overall strategy and objectives. These targets can be included in the company's business plan and performance metrics, and progress towards them can be tracked and reported to shareholders.

DOI: 10.4324/9781003439707-25

3. **Engage with stakeholders**: Senior executives should engage with stakeholders, including employees, customers and investors, to understand their expectations and concerns around ESG issues. This can help ensure that the company's ESG strategy aligns with the expectations of key stakeholders.

4. **Embed ESG considerations into decision-making processes**: Senior executives can embed ESG considerations into their decision-making processes, including risk management and capital allocation. This can help ensure that ESG factors are considered alongside financial factors when making strategic decisions.

5. **Report on ESG performance**: Senior executives should report on the company's ESG performance to shareholders and other stakeholders. This can help build trust and demonstrate the company's commitment to ESG issues.

In summary, senior executives can reconcile their legal obligation to maximise returns for shareholders with their responsibilities associated with ESG by recognising that ESG issues can affect financial performance, setting ESG targets, engaging with stakeholders, embedding ESG considerations into decision-making processes and reporting on ESG performance.

Ethics, Values and Superordinate Principles

We asked ChatGPT to clarify the relationship of ethics, values and Superordinate Principles, with particular reference to hierarchical structure:

> *Drawing on ethics, philosophy and values, describe how these relate to Superordinate Principles (Super-Ps) and hierarchical structure, clarifying (in an operational context) and with reference to legislation, e.g. the UK Equality Act, 2010, the relationship of 'operational initiatives', e.g. those to improve diversity and inclusion, viewed alongside the higher-order principle of Equality.*

Ethics, philosophy and values play a significant role in shaping Superordinate Principles (*Super-Ps*) and their hierarchical structure. Superordinate Principles represent higher-order guiding principles that reflect fundamental ethical values and philosophies. These principles are expressed through rules, protocols and norms that influence individual and group behaviour.

In an operational context, Superordinate Principles provide a framework for decision-making and behaviour within organisations. They help clarify the ethical standards and values that guide the actions and initiatives of individuals and groups. For example, the UK Equality Act of 2010 establishes a legal framework to promote equality and prohibit discrimination in various aspects of life, including employment. This legislation reflects the higher-order principle of equality, which is a core value in ethics and philosophy.

DOI: 10.4324/9781003439707-26

Operational initiatives aimed at improving diversity and inclusion align with the higher-order principle of equality. By implementing policies and practices that promote equal opportunities, organisations operationalise the principle of equality in their day-to-day activities. These initiatives may include measures such as diverse hiring practices, inclusive workplace policies, and training programmes to raise awareness and address bias and discrimination.

By considering Superordinate Principles in conjunction with legislation, e.g. the UK Equality Act, organisations can ensure that their operational initiatives are in line with the overarching principle of equality. This ensures that actions taken to promote diversity and inclusion are consistent with legal requirements and ethical values. Superordinate Principles provide a framework for organisations to align their practices with higher-order ethical values, promoting a more just and equitable environment.

In summary, Superordinate Principles derived from ethics, philosophy and values form the hierarchical structure that guides decision-making and behaviour. In an operational context, organisations can operationalise these principles by implementing initiatives that improve diversity and inclusion. When viewed alongside legislation such as the UK Equality Act, operational initiatives can be designed to align with the higher-order principle of equality, ensuring legal compliance and ethical consistency.

Our comment: The concept of higher-order '*Superordinate Principles*' takes precedence, but may be referred to as '*Overarching Principles*'. These OPs may operate as *Intermediate Principles*, which ensure proportionality and consistency. We note such principles in legal judgements, when principles are adjusted to take account of mitigating factors.

'First Principles' vs Superordinate Principles

We asked ChatGPT to differentiate between '*First Principles*' and *Super-Ps*:

> *What are the consequences should senior-level executives fail to differentiate First Principles and Superordinate Principles?*

The consequences of senior-level executives failing to differentiate between *First Principles* and *Superordinate Principles* can be significant and far-reaching.

Firstly, failing to understand the difference between these principles can result in decision-making that is inconsistent with ethical and moral principles. *First Principles* are the fundamental truths or propositions that serve as the foundation of a particular theory or system. *Superordinate Principles* are higher-level principles that are more general and abstract. They provide the basis for ethical and moral decision-making. If executives fail to differentiate between these principles, they may make decisions that are inconsistent with higher-level ethical and moral standards, which can result in reputational damage to their organisation and potential legal consequences.

Secondly, failing to differentiate between these principles can result in the prioritisation of short-term gains over long-term sustainability. *First Principles* are often focused on achieving specific goals, whereas *Superordinate Principles* are more concerned with the overall impact of decisions on the broader community and society. If executives fail to differentiate between these principles, they may prioritise short-term

DOI: 10.4324/9781003439707-27

gains over long-term sustainability, which can result in negative consequences for their organisation and society as a whole.

Thirdly, failing to differentiate between these principles can result in a
lack of trust and credibility with stakeholders. *Superordinate Principles*
are often based on values such as honesty, integrity and transparency,
which are essential for building trust with stakeholders. If executives fail
to differentiate between these principles, they may be seen as untrust-
worthy and lacking in credibility, which can damage relationships with
stakeholders and harm their organisation's reputation.

In summary, the consequences of senior-level executives failing to differentiate between *First Principles* and *Superordinate Principles* can be significant and include inconsistent decision-making, short-term prioritisation over
long-term sustainability, and a lack of trust and credibility with stakeholders.
Therefore, it is important for executives to understand the difference
between these principles and to ensure that they are aligned with higher-
level ethical and moral standards.

AGI and Leadership Capability

We asked ChatGPT to assess the potential of *Artificial General Intelligence* (AGI) to overcome reductive thinking and lack of *Emotional Intelligence* (EQ):

> *Evaluate how AGI can help leaders overcome the problem of (i) reductive thinking, (ii) a lack of EQ and (iii) help build a supportive, high-performance work culture.*

Artificial General Intelligence (AGI) has the potential to help leaders overcome various challenges, including reductive thinking, a lack of emotional intelligence (EQ), and fostering a supportive, high-performance work culture. However, it's important to note that AGI is still an emerging technology, and its actual capabilities and limitations are yet to be fully realised. Nonetheless, we can assess its potential in addressing these challenges:

Reductive thinking: AGI can aid leaders in overcoming reductive thinking by providing advanced analytical capabilities and data-driven insights. AGI systems can process vast amounts of information, detect patterns and generate complex models, allowing leaders to make more informed and comprehensive decisions. By analysing data from diverse sources, AGI can help leaders consider multiple perspectives, challenge biases and identify nuanced connections that might otherwise be overlooked.

Lack of EQ: EQ, which encompasses emotional awareness, empathy, and relationship management, is crucial for effective leadership. While AGI does not possess human emotions, it can assist leaders in developing their own EQ skills. For example, AGI-driven sentiment analysis can help leaders gauge employee sentiments and engagement levels, providing insights to address concerns and foster positive relationships. AGI can also provide feedback and recommendations for improving communication and interpersonal skills, helping leaders enhance their EQ competencies.

Building a supportive, high-performance work culture: AGI can contribute to creating a supportive work culture by automating administrative tasks and streamlining operations, thereby reducing workload and enabling leaders to focus on building relationships and fostering employee development. AGI-powered platforms can facilitate personalised learning and development plans, provide real-time feedback and suggest tailored interventions to enhance performance and career growth. Additionally, AGI-driven analytics can help leaders identify areas for improvement in team dynamics, diversity and inclusion efforts, and work–life balance, fostering a culture of collaboration, well-being and high performance.

It is important to acknowledge that while AGI can offer valuable support, it should not replace the human element in leadership. Human judgement, intuition and ethical considerations remain essential in decision-making and fostering meaningful connections with employees. Furthermore, careful attention must be given to addressing potential biases and ensuring transparency and accountability in AGI systems.

In conclusion, AGI has the potential to assist leaders in overcoming reductive thinking, developing EQ skills and building a supportive, high-performance work culture. However, its successful integration relies on effective human-AI collaboration and careful consideration of ethical and social implications. AGI should be seen as a tool to augment leadership capabilities rather than a stand-alone solution.

Job Demands-Resources and *Job Crafting*

We asked ChatGPT to summarise research linking Job Demands and Resilience:

> *Summarise research and cite sources relating to the Job Demands – Resources (JDR) model and how these insights can be linked to* Job Crafting *and enhanced performance and resilience.*

The Job Demands-Resources (JDR) model is a theoretical framework that explores the interplay between job demands and job resources and their impact on employee well-being and work outcomes (Bakker & Demerouti, 2007). Job demands encompass various aspects of a job, such as physical, psychological, social, or organizational factors, that require effort or skills and may lead to stress or burnout if they surpass an employee's capacity. Job resources, on the other hand, are elements of a job that assist employees in achieving work goals, mitigating job demands, and fostering well-being.

Job Crafting is a proactive process through which employees modify their job demands and resources to align with their strengths, passions, and goals. The JDR model and *Job Crafting* are closely linked, as *Job Crafting* enables employees to adapt job demands and resources, ultimately reducing stress and enhancing well-being.

Research supports the positive outcomes associated with *Job Crafting*. Employees who engage in *Job Crafting* tend to report higher levels of job satisfaction, work engagement, and motivation, along with lower levels of burnout and turnover intention. Additionally, studies indicate that job crafting contributes to improved performance and innovation outcomes in organizations (Berg, Dutton, & Wrzesniewski, 2013).

Several studies have delved into the impact of *Job Crafting* on various aspects of employee well-being and organizational outcomes. For instance, Tims, Bakker, and Derks (2013a) explored the influence of *Job Crafting* on job demands, job resources, and well-being, highlighting its positive effects. Another longitudinal study by Tims, Bakker, and Derks (2013b) emphasized the relationship between *Job Crafting* and employee well-being over time.

The concept of *Job Crafting* has been further discussed by Wrzesniewski and Dutton (2001), who proposed that employees actively craft their work to align with their preferences and strengths. This conceptualization adds depth to the understanding of *Job Crafting* as a dynamic and ongoing process.

In conclusion, the JDR model provides a foundational understanding of the relationship between job demands and resources, while *Job Crafting* emerges as a proactive strategy that employees can employ to modify these factors. The synergy between the JDR model and *Job Crafting* is supported by empirical evidence, linking these concepts to enhanced performance and resilience in the workplace.

References

Bakker, A. B., & Demerouti, E. (2007). The job demands-resources model: State of the art. *Journal of Managerial Psychology*, 22(3), 309–328.

Berg, J. M., Dutton, J. E., & Wrzesniewski, A. (2013). Job crafting and meaningful work. In *Advances in Positive Organizational Psychology* (pp. 179–195). Emerald Group Publishing Limited.

Tims, M., Bakker, A. B., & Derks, D. (2013a). The impact of job crafting on job demands, job resources, and well-being. *Journal of Occupational Health Psychology*, 18(2), 230–240.

Tims, M., Bakker, A. B., & Derks, D. (2013b). Job crafting and employee well-being: A longitudinal study. *Journal of Occupational Health Psychology*, 18(4), 391–397.

Wrzesniewski, A., & Dutton, J. E. (2001). Crafting a job: Revisioning employees as active crafters of their work. *Academy of Management Review*, 26(2), 179–201.

Our comment: Job Crafting *should be viewed in the context of team roles, responsibilities and operational systems. Team Coaching also links to solution-focused 'Systems Coaching'.*

Doughnut Economics and Leadership

We asked ChatGPT to relate *Doughnut Economics* to leadership principles:

How do the themes of Doughnut Economics help clarify Principles of Leadership?

The themes of *Doughnut Economics* can provide valuable insights into the principles of leadership in the 21st century. Here are a few ways in which they can help clarify these principles:

1. **Emphasising the importance of social and environmental sustainability**:
   Doughnut Economics places a strong emphasis on creating an economic system that is socially just and environmentally sustainable. This means that leaders must prioritise not only economic growth but also social and environmental well-being. Leaders who adopt the principles of *Doughnut Economics* must be willing to make tough decisions that balance the needs of people and the planet, while also ensuring long-term economic stability.

2. **Fostering collaboration and innovation**:
   Doughnut Economics emphasises the need for collaboration and innovation to solve complex social and environmental challenges. Leaders must be able to foster an environment that encourages collaboration and innovation, and they must be willing to take risks and try new approaches to problem-solving. This requires a culture of openness, creativity and experimentation.

DOI: 10.4324/9781003439707-30

3. **Promoting a holistic view of leadership**:
   Doughnut Economics challenges traditional notions of leadership that focus solely on economic growth and profit. Instead, it promotes a more holistic view of leadership that takes into account the social and environmental impact of economic activities. Leaders must be able to think beyond short-term gains and consider the long-term consequences of their decisions. This requires a deep understanding of the interconnectedness of economic, social and environmental systems.

4. **Encouraging transparency and accountability**:
   Doughnut Economics emphasises the need for transparency and accountability in economic decision-making. Leaders must be willing to be held accountable for their actions and decisions, and they must be transparent in their communication with stakeholders. This requires a culture of honesty and integrity, and leaders must be willing to admit their mistakes and learn from them.

Overall, the themes of *Doughnut Economics* can help clarify the principles of leadership by emphasising the importance of social and environmental sustainability, fostering collaboration and innovation, promoting a holistic view of leadership, and encouraging transparency and accountability. By adopting these principles, leaders can help create a more just and sustainable economic system that benefits both people and the planet.

The Concept of 'Emotional Labour'

We asked ChatGPT to summarise research evidence relating to 'Emotional Labour':

> *Integrate and summarise research findings that evaluate the concept of "Emotional Labour" in the context of constructs from occupational psychology that transcend racial or race-bias explanations (and also cite relevant research papers).*

Research findings from occupational psychology suggest that emotional labour is a multifaceted construct that is influenced by various factors beyond race or racial bias. Several studies have explored the role of job demands and resources, as well as individual factors such as emotional intelligence, in shaping emotional labour.

One study by Bakker and colleagues (2011) found that job resources, including social support and autonomy, were positively related to employees' experience of positive emotions and reduced emotional exhaustion, while job demands, including workload and emotional demands, were associated with higher levels of emotional exhaustion.

Another study by Brotheridge and Grandey (2002) explored the role of emotional intelligence in emotional labour. They found that emotional intelligence was positively related to emotional display rules and emotional dissonance, suggesting that individuals with higher emotional intelligence may be better equipped to manage emotional labour demands.

Research has also explored the relationship between emotional labour and job satisfaction. One study by Ashkanasy and colleagues (2002) found

DOI: 10.4324/9781003439707-31

that the emotional demands of a job were negatively related to job satisfaction, while emotional dissonance was positively related to turnover intentions.

Overall, these findings suggest that emotional labour is a complex construct that is shaped by various factors in the work environment and individual characteristics. While race and racial bias may play a role in some cases, research from occupational psychology emphasises the importance of considering a range of factors beyond race in understanding emotional labour.

References

Ashkanasy, N. M., Hartel, C. E. J., & Daus, C. S. (2002). Diversity and emotion: The new frontiers in organizational behavior research. *Journal of Management*, 28(3), 307–338. https://doi.org/10.1177/014920630202800304

Bakker, A. B., Demerouti, E., & Euwema, M. C. (2011). Job resources buffer the impact of job demands on burnout. *Journal of Occupational Health Psychology*, 16(3), 260–271. https://doi.org/10.1037/a0022675

Brotheridge, C. M., & Grandey, A. A. (2002). Emotional labor and burnout: Comparing two perspectives of "people work". *Journal of Vocational Behavior*, 60(1), 17–39. https://doi.org/10.1006/jvbe.2001.1815

Legacy Thinking and a Quantum Future

We asked ChatGPT to review and evaluate *Legacy Thinking, Legacy Costs* and *Quantum-Enabled Economy* (QEE):

> *Summarise strategic issues relating to Legacy Thinking, Legacy Costs, and transition to a Quantum Enabled Economy (QEE), including the implications for political leadership.*

The strategic issues of Legacy Thinking, Legacy Costs and the transition to a QEE have important implications for political leadership (UK Government Policy Paper, 2023).

Legacy Thinking refers to the challenge of overcoming established practices and ways of thinking to embrace innovation and change. Political leaders must foster a culture of innovation and adaptability in order to support businesses and institutions in this transition.

Legacy costs refer to the financial burdens of maintaining outdated systems, processes and infrastructure. Political leaders must encourage businesses to evaluate their operations and invest in cost-saving measures, such as process improvements, automation or outsourcing.

The transition to a *QEE* involves significant investment in research and development, collaboration and risk-taking. Political leaders must support these efforts through funding, partnerships and policies that incentivise innovation.

DOI: 10.4324/9781003439707-32

The implications for political leadership include the need to balance short-term priorities with long-term goals and to invest in the education and training of the workforce to support the transition to a more dynamic and technologically advanced economy. Political leaders must also address the potential impact of these changes on employment and income inequality and work to mitigate any negative effects.

In summary, addressing *Legacy Thinking, Legacy Costs* and the transition to a *QEE* requires strategic and forward-thinking leadership from politicians. The ability to navigate these challenges and support businesses and institutions in adapting to new opportunities will be critical for success in the future.

References

UK Government Policy Paper. (2023). National quantum strategy. Available at: https://www.gov.uk/government/publications/national-quantum-strategy/national-quantum-strategy-accessible-webpage#:~:text=Our%20ten%2Dyear%20vision%20is,and%20helping%20to%20build%20a

The Economist note in an article, *The New Asian Family* (6 July 2023), that plummeting fertility rates in Japan, South Korea and China will require mass immigration. However, decision-making lies with conservative, often authoritarian, patriarchal leaders immersed in legacy thinking. They reject future-focused policies responsive to the changing context. This creates a bleak scenario, which may well threaten both economic progress and longer-term social cohesion.

The Consequences of Systemic Educational Deficits

We asked ChatGPT to evaluate *Systemic Educational Deficits in a complex world*:

> *Evaluate the argument that 'systemic educational deficits' have caused significant weaknesses in critical thinking and appreciation of causal effect. List critical outcomes in a complex, fast-changing world. Provide references, based on empirical research, and cite full sources.*

The argument that systemic educational deficits have caused significant weaknesses in critical thinking and appreciation of causal effect has been supported by empirical research, which has identified several critical outcomes in a complex, fast-changing world:

1. Individuals with weaker critical thinking skills are more likely to fall for fake news and misinformation, leading to social polarisation and misinformation campaigns (Pennycook & Rand, 2019).
2. Individuals who lack an understanding of causality are less likely to make informed decisions, particularly in complex situations where multiple factors are at play (Gruszczynska, Kowalski, & Zajac, 2019).
3. A lack of critical thinking skills has been shown to negatively impact problem-solving abilities, particularly in complex and real-life situations (Hwang, Jang, Lim, & Kim, 2019).

DOI: 10.4324/9781003439707-33

4. Weak critical thinking skills have been found to negatively impact business decision-making, particularly in ambiguous and uncertain situations (Christensen, Mammen, & Wood, 2020).

5. A lack of critical thinking skills has been found to negatively impact creativity and innovation, which are essential for success in a VUCA world (Jiang, Liu, & Ding, 2018).

In conclusion, the evidence suggests that systemic educational deficits have resulted in significant weaknesses in critical thinking and appreciation of causal effect, which have critical outcomes in a complex, fast-changing world. Addressing these deficits through education and training is crucial to enable individuals to make informed decisions and navigate the challenges of a VUCA world.

References

Christensen, J. F., Mammen, S., & Wood, R. (2020). The relationship between critical thinking skills and business decision-making. *Academy of Management Learning & Education*, 19(4), 483–499.

Gruszczynska, E., Kowalski, P., & Zajac, R. (2019). Cognitive factors determining problem-solving strategies in the context of complex real-life problems. *Frontiers in Psychology*, 10, 974.

Hwang, S. Y., Jang, H. J., Lim, Y. J., & Kim, S. H. (2019). Effects of a simulation-based learning program on nursing students' critical thinking disposition, problem-solving process, and clinical competence. *Nurse Education Today*, 79, 78–84.

Jiang, J., Liu, R., & Ding, L. (2018). Critical thinking and creativity in university students: Mediating effects of academic self-efficacy. *Thinking Skills and Creativity*, 28, 79–86.

Pennycook, G., & Rand, D. G. (2019). Who falls for fake news? The roles of bullshit receptivity, overclaiming, familiarity, and analytic thinking. *Journal of Personality*, 88(2), 185–200.

The Impact of Performance-Related Pay

We asked ChatGPT to evaluate the effect of PRP, notably on intrinsic motivation:

> *Why does performance-related pay damage intrinsic motivation –*
> *and what are the wider consequences of this methodology?*

Performance-related pay (PRP) is a compensation strategy where employees receive pay increases or bonuses based on their performance. While PRP can provide incentives for employees to work harder and increase productivity, it can also damage intrinsic motivation, which is the internal drive to perform an activity for its own sake rather than for external rewards. Here are some reasons why PRP can damage intrinsic motivation and the wider consequences of this methodology:

1. **PRP can shift the focus from the work itself to the reward**: When employees are rewarded for their performance, they may start to focus more on the reward than on the work itself. This can lead to a decrease in intrinsic motivation, as employees start to see the work as a means to an end rather than an enjoyable or meaningful activity in itself. As a result, employees may be less likely to engage in activities that are not rewarded, even if they are important for the organisation.
2. **PRP can reduce autonomy and creativity**: PRP can lead to a more rigid and controlling work environment, where employees are told what to do and how to do it in order to meet performance goals. This

can reduce employees' sense of autonomy and control over their work, which can in turn reduce their creativity and ability to innovate. Employees may be less likely to take risks or try new approaches if they feel that their performance is being closely monitored and evaluated.

3. **PRP can foster a short-term focus**: PRP can encourage employees to focus on short-term goals and outcomes, rather than long-term objectives or broader organisational goals. This can result in employees neglecting important tasks or activities that do not immediately contribute to their performance targets. It can also lead to a neglect of quality for the sake of achieving quantity or output, which can lead to negative consequences in the long run.

4. **PRP can lead to unfairness and resentment**: PRP can create an environment where employees compete against each other for rewards, which can lead to feelings of unfairness and resentment. Employees who perceive the system as unfair or arbitrary may become demotivated or disengaged, which can have negative consequences for the overall performance of the organisation.

Overall, the negative effects of PRP on intrinsic motivation can have far-reaching consequences for the performance and culture of organisations. While PRP may provide short-term incentives for employees to perform better, it can undermine the long-term sustainability and success of an organisation by reducing employees' engagement, creativity and commitment to the broader mission and goals of the organisation.

Our comment: In July 2023, the BBC reported that 'Bank of America has been ordered to pay out $150m (£116m) in penalties after it was found to have opened credit cards without customers' permission. Regulators also discovered the bank 'double-dipped' fees from customers and withheld promised reward bonuses.' The BBC noted: Bank of America 'eliminated sales goals for its credit card staff in January 2023, and agreed to keep that change in place for at least three years'. The story reminds us that financial incentives can have unintended consequences.

References

BBC. (2023, July 12). *Bank of America fined for junk fees and fake accounts.*
    Available at: https://www.bbc.co.uk/news/business-66167474

Camerer, C., & Hogarth, R. (1999). The effects of financial incentives in experiments: A review and capital-labor-production framework. *Journal of Risk and Uncertainty*, 19(1-3), 7–42.

This article reviews research on the effects of financial incentives, including PRP, on worker performance and finds that incentives can have unintended negative consequences, such as crowding out intrinsic motivation and fostering a focus on short-term gains rather than long-term goals.

Larkin, I., Pierce, L., & Gino, F. (2012). The psychological costs of pay-for-performance: Implications for the strategic compensation of employees. *Academy of Management Perspectives*, 26(2), 36–52.

This article discusses the psychological costs of PRP, including reduced intrinsic motivation, increased stress and a focus on narrow performance metrics that may not accurately reflect employee contributions.

Prendergast, C. (1999). The provision of incentives in firms. *Journal of Economic Literature*, 37(1), 7–63.

This article reviews research on the effects of incentives on worker behaviour and finds that incentives can have unintended consequences, such as encouraging unethical behaviour and reducing job satisfaction.

Kohn, A. (1993). Why incentive plans cannot work. *Harvard Business Review*, 71(5), 54–63.

In this classic article, Kohn argues that PRP can actually undermine performance by reducing intrinsic motivation and fostering a focus on short-term gains over long-term goals.

Lazear, E. P. (2000). Performance pay and productivity. *American Economic Review*, 90(5), 1346–1361.

This article examines the effects of PRP on worker productivity and finds that incentives can have a positive effect on performance, but that the design of the incentive programme matters and that there are trade-offs between different types of incentives.

Super-Ps and Post-Modernist Theory

We asked ChatGPT to comment on *Super-Ps and Post-Modernist Theory*:

> *Evaluate research evidence that indicates Superordinate Principles (e.g. equality and justice) are universal and contribute to social order, cohesion and continuity, and contrast this insight with the problems created by the 'cross-cultural-relativity' assumptions of Post-Modernist Theory.*

Super-Ps, such as equality and justice, have been shown to be universal and play an essential role in creating and maintaining social order, cohesion and continuity. Research in psychology, anthropology and sociology has consistently supported this perspective. Psychological research has found that people have a natural inclination towards fairness, justice and equality, which develops throughout childhood and into adulthood (Geraci & Surian, 2011; Shaw, Li, & Olson, 2012). This inclination is observed across cultures, suggesting that these values are universally recognised (Henrich et al., 2010).

Anthropological research has also highlighted the importance of Superordinate Principles in creating social order and cohesion. For instance, the anthropologist E. E. Evans-Pritchard found that 'segmentary opposition' (with decentralised authority/autonomy) was critical in maintaining social order and cohesion in the Nuer society of Sudan (Evans-Pritchard, 1940). Similarly, sociological research has demonstrated that shared values and norms, which serve as a collective consciousness, contribute to social order and stability (Durkheim, 1951). In contrast, post-modernist theory challenges the assumption of universal Superordinate Principles and emphasises

 DOI: 10.4324/9781003439707-35

cultural relativity. This perspective argues that different cultures have unique beliefs, values and norms, and that no culture's values can be considered superior or more valid than another.

While post-modernist theory raises important critiques of cultural biases and the need for cultural sensitivity, it has also been criticised for its relativistic perspective, which can undermine efforts towards social justice and equality (Scherer, 2015). For instance, if there are no universal principles, then there is no basis for arguing against practices that may be harmful or discriminatory within a particular culture. This can lead to a lack of accountability for actions that violate human rights.

In conclusion, research suggests that Superordinate Principles are universal and contribute to social order, cohesion and continuity. While post-modernist theory provides important insights into cultural diversity and biases, its relativistic perspective can create challenges in addressing social justice and equality issues.

References

Durkheim, E. (1951). *Suicide: A Study in Sociology*. New York: Free Press.

Evans-Pritchard, E. E. (1940). *The Nuer: A Description of the Modes of Livelihood and Political Institutions of a Nilotic People*. Oxford: Clarendon Press.

Geraci, A., & Surian, L. (2011). The developmental roots of fairness: Infants' reactions to equal and unequal distributions of resources. *Developmental Science*, 14(5), 1012–1020.

Henrich, J., Heine, S. J., & Norenzayan, A. (2010). The weirdest people in the world? *Behavioral and Brain Sciences*, 33(2–3), 61–83.

Shaw, A., Li, V., & Olson, K. R. (2012). Children's moral judgments and moral emotions following exclusion of children with disabilities from physical activity. *Developmental Psychology*, 48(5), 1292–1303.

Scherer, A. G. (2015). *Postmodernism and the Social Sciences: A Thematic Approach*. Princeton University Press.

We also asked a follow-up question relating to *Nihilistic Philosophy*:

Describe the consequences arising from the adoption of nihilistic philosophy and postmodernism, given people's innate need for meaningful activity, purpose and progress. (Take account of evidence from studies linked to self-determination theory, the role of universals, and the effect of Superordinate Principles.)

The adoption of nihilistic philosophy and postmodernism can have significant consequences for individuals and societies, given people's innate need for meaningful activity, purpose and progress. Here are some potential consequences, based on evidence from studies linked to self-determination theory, the role of universals and the effect of Superordinate Principles:

Loss of meaning and purpose: Nihilistic philosophy rejects the idea that life has intrinsic meaning or value, and postmodernism challenges the existence of objective truth and universal values. As a result, individuals who adopt these worldviews may struggle to find meaning and purpose in their lives, which can lead to apathy, despair and a lack of motivation.

Disengagement from society: If individuals believe that there are no universal values or objective truth, they may disengage from social and political issues, leading to apathy and a lack of civic engagement. This can have negative consequences for society as a whole, as it may lead to a lack of progress and a failure to address social and environmental challenges.

Decreased well-being: Self-determination theory suggests that individuals have a need for autonomy, competence and relatedness. If individuals feel that their actions have no impact on their lives or society, or that their values are not recognised, they may experience a sense of helplessness and decreased well-being.

Moral relativism: Postmodernism challenges the existence of objective truth and universal values, leading to moral relativism, where individuals believe that all moral viewpoints are equally valid. While moral relativism can be seen as a form of tolerance, it may also lead to a lack of moral clarity and a failure to address issues of social justice and human rights.

Neglect of Superordinate Principles: Superordinate Principles, such as justice and human rights, provide a framework for addressing social and political issues. If individuals adopt nihilistic or postmodern worldviews, they may neglect or reject these principles, leading to a lack of progress and a failure to address social and environmental challenges.

Overall, the adoption of nihilistic philosophy and postmodernism can have negative consequences for individuals and societies, given people's innate need for meaningful activity, purpose and progress. These consequences may include a loss of meaning and purpose, disengagement from society, decreased well-being, moral relativism and neglect of Superordinate Principles.

Appendix 1

Superordinate Principles and Self-Determination Theory

Superordinate principles (*Super-Ps*) play a crucial role in shaping social norms and building consensus. They can be viewed alongside Self-Determination Theory, which identifies three core needs: (i) trust-based relationships (relatedness), (ii) development of competence and (iii) a degree of autonomy, reflected in self-directed activity. These needs also contribute to our desire for justice, equality and accountability (Cambridge University Press & Assessment, 2023; Hasa, 2016). These higher-order principles are closely aligned with ethical values, but expressed through rules, protocols and norms. They influence individual and group thinking and behaviour (Cambridge University Press & Assessment, 2023; Hasa, 2016). Social norms create boundaries. Studies in deontic logic suggest that specific inferences are mediated by factors linked to general principles, indicating a hierarchy of abstract principles, intermediate attitudes, assumptions and specific behaviour (Manktelow & Fairley, 2000).

In psychology, three broad principles shape human morality and guide thinking and behaviour, including social implications, self-awareness and deliberate thoughts about right and wrong (Ellemers et al., 2019). Reflective equilibrium and overlapping consensus highlight the importance of adjusting general principles and judgements to achieve harmony among individuals (Rawls, 1971). Social Contract Theory, particularly Rawls' work, emphasises the superiority of some principles of justice and the significance of equality as a primary principle (Rawls, 1971).

The 'two-thirds rule', or a 'supermajority', is viewed as a prerequisite for acceptance of contentious decisions, ensuring legitimacy and fairness in the context of Social Contract Theory (e.g. Rawls, 1971). *Super-Ps* may be interpreted differently in various contexts, with individuals adapting moral principles based on group identities and salient concerns (Giner-Sorolla, 2013; Fu et al., 2007). Research suggests a relationship between the endorsement of abstract moral principles and donations to various causes, as well as specific behaviours in experimental games (Nilsson et al., 2016; Clark et al., 2017). Actions requiring self-control relate to binding moral foundations, while external factors in the workplace impact resilience and psychological capital, supporting the SDT model (Mooijman et al., 2018). Studies on the Ultimatum Game highlight the influence of expectations on assessments of fairness (Vavra et al., 2018).

References

Cambridge University Press & Assessment (2023). "Principle" definition: dictionary. cambridge.org

Clark, C. B., Swails, J., Pontinen, H., Bowerman, S., Kriz, K., & Hendricks, P. (2017). A behavioral economic assessment of individualizing versus binding moral foundations. *Personality & Individual Differences*, 112, 49–54.

Ellemers, N., Toorn, J., Paunov, Y., & Leeuwen, T. (2019). The psychology of morality: A review & analysis of empirical studies (1940–2017). *Personality & Social Psychology Review*, 23(4), 332–366, p. 340.

Fu, J., Chiu, Chi-Y., Morris, M. W., & Young, M. (2007). Spontaneous inferences from cultural cues: Varying responses of cultural insiders and outsiders. *Journal of Cross-Cultural Psychology*, 38(1), 58–75.

Giner-Sorolla, R. (2013). *Judging Passions*. Psychology Press.

Hasa. (2016). *Difference between values and principles | Definition, interrelation, differences*. Pediaa.Com.

Manktelow, K. I., & Fairley, N. (2000). Superordinate principles in reasoning with causal and deontic conditionals. *Thinking & Reasoning*, 6(1), 41–65.

Mooijman, M., Meindl, P., Oyserman, D., Monterosso, J., Dehghani, M., Doris, J., & Graham, J. (2018). Resisting temptation for the good of the group: Binding moral values and the moralization of self-control. *Journal of Personality & Social Psychology*, 115(3), 585–599.

Nilsson, A., Erlandsson, A., & Västfjäll, D. (2016). The congruency between moral foundations and intentions to donate, self-reported donations, and actual donations to charity. *Journal of Research in Personality*, 65, 22–29.

Rawls, J. (1971). A Theory of Justice. Summary in Internet Encyclopedia of Philosophy.

Social Contract Theory. The Internet Encyclopedia of Philosophy (IEP) https://iep.utm.edu/soc-cont/

Vavra, P., Chang, L. J., & Sanfey, A. G. (2018). Expectations in the ultimatum game: Distinct effects of mean and variance of expected offers. *Frontiers in Psychology*, 9. https://doi.org/10.3389/fpsyg.2018.00992

Appendix 2

The TEAM Index: Creating Conditions for High Performance

Exceptional performance builds on motivation and commitment. Effective leaders create enabling conditions, which require transparency, accountability, purpose and support. Heathy organisations build on feedback to increase well-being and resilience. The TEAM Index supports coaching and leadership development, encouraging a future-focused productive culture.

TEAM Indexing focuses on developing the following elements:

- **Trust**: How much do you trust your colleagues and managers? Do you feel comfortable sharing your opinions and ideas?
- **Energy**: How motivated and enthusiastic are you about your work? Do you feel energised and inspired by the work you do and the people you work with?
- **Action**: Are you able to take action and make decisions without fear of retribution or negative consequences? Do you feel empowered to take ownership of your work and contribute to the success of the organisation?
- **Motivation**: What motivates you to do your best work? Are you driven by personal goals, the mission and values of the organisation, or a combination of both?

The TEAM Index highlights five drivers of motivation and commitment. Responses (left to right) range from *Strongly Disagree* to *Strongly Agree*.

When used as an organisation-wide survey, the process supports comparison of teams, departments and role groups.

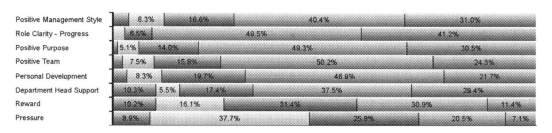

The specific dimensions explored by the TEAM Index include the following:

- **Positive Management Style**: How would you describe the style of your manager/s and team leaders? Do they demonstrate consistent, positive action by setting clear goals, providing feedback/recognition and supporting professional/personal development?
- **Role Clarity – Progress**: Do you understand your role objectives/responsibilities within the organisation? And is there a path for career growth and advancement?
- **Positive Purpose**: Do you feel a sense of purpose in the work you do? Does the organisation's mission and values align with your personal beliefs and values?
- **Positive Team**: How well do your colleagues work together as a team? Are there clear goals and expectations, effective communication, and a positive work environment?
- **Personal Development**: Does the organisation provide opportunities for personal and professional development? Do you feel supported in your career growth and aspirations?

Additional factors help assess views on *Reward, Work Pressure* and *Department Head Support.*

In summary, the **TEAM Index** identifies factors *(clusters of statements)*, not isolated items. The factor-based model increases reliability and validity, enabling comparison of role groups, teams and departments. This information supports more effective follow-up interventions.

Appendix 3

Bayesian Reasoning and Occam's Razor

Bayesian reasoning contributes to sound decision-making, using statistics and probability to make inferences based on available evidence. Bayes' theorem updates the probability of a hypothesis (or event) based on new evidence. The approach combines prior knowledge and an initial hypothesis with observed evidence. This leads to a more accurate and rational probability estimate, which supports balanced analysis. The following are the key components of Bayesian reasoning:

- **Prior Probability**: The initial belief or probability assigned to a hypothesis before any new evidence is considered.
- **Likelihood**: The likelihood function represents the probability of observing the evidence given that the hypothesis is true.
- **Posterior Probability**: This is the updated probability of the hypothesis after taking into account the new evidence. It is calculated using Bayes' theorem, which incorporates the prior probability and the likelihood of the hypothesis.
- **Evidence**: New data or observations that influence the update of the prior probability.

Bayesian reasoning helps us deal with uncertain or incomplete information, adjusting beliefs as new evidence becomes available. We might also note Occam's razor.[1] This is a philosophical principle that suggests simpler explanations, or hypotheses are more likely to be correct than complex ones. It is often paraphrased as *the simplest explanation is usually the correct one.*

The link between Bayesian reasoning and Occam's razor lies in the concept of prior probabilities. In Bayesian reasoning, the prior probability represents the initial belief or plausibility assigned to a hypothesis before considering any new evidence. Occam's razor can be thought of as a way to assign prior probabilities to different hypotheses. It favours simpler hypotheses by assigning them higher prior probabilities compared to more complex ones. Simpler hypotheses generally have fewer parameters or assumptions, making them more likely in the absence of evidence. So when we update our prior probabilities with new evidence (via the likelihood function), the simpler hypotheses tend to retain their higher probabilities or are less impacted by the evidence compared to more complex hypotheses. Bayesian reasoning allows us to update our beliefs about hypotheses based on evidence, while Occam's razor guides us in assigning higher initial probabilities to simpler hypotheses before considering any evidence. Together, they provide a rational and efficient approach to making inferences and decisions in the face of uncertainty.

Practical Example: An insurance company might initially use a complex model to assess the risk of vehicle accidents for particular groups of policyholders. However, as they collect new data on policyholders' driving behaviour and accident history, they can use Bayesian reasoning to adjust prior assumptions and adopt the simpler model that predicts accident probabilities effectively.

Sound metrics highlight the most significant variables contributing to an outcome. In the context of psychometrics, *Simple Structure* reveals a clear and straightforward factor structure. Each item primarily loads on one underlying factor, with negligible loadings on other factors. This can enhance employee survey design and ESG reporting. A clear structure is also more interpretable and easier to understand. Occam's razor emphasises the importance of interpretability in scientific explanations, with models that are easy to grasp and communicate.

Note

1 Wikipedia: Occam's Razor – The law of parsimony.

Appendix 4: How Principles Get Hijacked

Superordinate Principles (*Super-Ps*) can be susceptible to hijacking, a phenomenon where individuals manipulate these overarching principles to serve their own interests or reinforce pre-existing beliefs. Leadership figures may exploit *Super-Ps* like 'equality' to legitimise decisions favouring their own group, potentially overlooking merit-based criteria and the contributions of others. For instance, affirmative action policies might be used to selectively promote individuals from the leader's demographic, but justified by 'principles'. Justifying actions or beliefs by fitting them within an acceptable rationale serves to minimise 'cognitive dissonance' (Festinger, 1957).

Similarly, individuals may hijack *Super-Ps* to undermine policies conflicting with their preconceived notions. For example, someone with a strong belief in alternative medicine may reject evidence-based practices, using the *Super-P* of 'autonomy' or 'freedom' to justify choices aligned with their existing beliefs, even if it jeopardises health (Haidt, 2012). This rejection can be contrasted with Bayesian reasoning, which considers evidence objectively.

In both cases, cognitive dissonance may play a role, where individuals experience discomfort due to inconsistent beliefs or behaviours (Festinger, 1957). To resolve this dissonance, individuals might adapt *Super-Ps* to increase alignment with their biases. For instance, those criticising vaccine safety may neglect the greater risks posed by the full-blown disease, focusing on principles of 'care and safety' while ignoring the overall context and consequences of a lethal pandemic.

Leaders facing difficulties in dialogue may find solution-focused conversations beneficial, understanding the mindset and assumptions of others

(Tajfel & Turner, 1986). In an organizational context, leaders can leverage personal convictions to clarify guiding principles and reduce vulnerability to subjective interpretation. This approach involves discussing specific points and chunking new information into process elements, facilitating a clearer path forward.

Our comment: Superordinate Principles, including those relating to Equality and Social Justice, can be threatened by speculative, unproven theory. The insidious effect is evident in the spurious notion of "Excited delirium" (ExDS), also known as "agitated delirium" (AgDS). It has no scientific foundation, but has affected mindset and policing in the US.

References

Festinger, L. (1957). *A Theory of Cognitive Dissonance*. Stanford University Press.
Haidt, J. (2012). *The Righteous Mind: Why Good People Are Divided by Politics and Religion*. Vintage Books.
Tajfel, H., & Turner, J. C. (1986). The social identity theory of intergroup behavior. In S. Worchel & L. W. Austin (Eds.), *Psychology of Intergroup Relations* (pp. 7–24). Nelson Hall Publishers, Chicago, IL.
https://en.wikipedia.org/wiki/Excited_delirium

Index

Pages in *italics* refer to figures.

Printed in the United States
by Baker & Taylor Publisher Services